Spatial Economics Volume II

Stefano Colombo
Editor

Spatial Economics Volume II

Applications

palgrave
macmillan

Editor
Stefano Colombo
Dept of Economics & Finance
Università Cattolica del Sacro Cuore
Milano, Italy

ISBN 978-3-030-40093-4 ISBN 978-3-030-40094-1 (eBook)
https://doi.org/10.1007/978-3-030-40094-1

This Palgrave Macmillan imprint is published by the registered company Springer Nature Switzerland AG.
The registered company address is: Gewerbestrasse 11, 6330 Cham, Switzerland

Contents

Notes on Contributors

Giuseppe Arbia is Full Professor of Economic Statistics at the Catholic University of the Sacred Heart in Rome. He is founder and Chairman of the Spatial Econometrics Association and Editor-in-Chief of the *Journal of Spatial Econometrics*. He authored 8 books and more than 200 articles published on international journals on topics related to spatial statistics and econometrics.

Roberta Capello is Full Professor in Regional and Urban Economics at the Politecnico of Milan. She is past-President of the Regional Science Association International (RSAI) and President of the Italian Section of RSAI (AISRe), Editor-in-chief of Papers in Regional Science (Wiley Blackwell), author of many scientific papers and a textbook in Regional Economics, published in Italian (Il Mulino, Bologna), English (Routledge, London) and Chinese (Economy and Management Publishing House, Beijing).

Andrea Caragliu is Associate Professor of Regional and Urban Economics at Politecnico di Milano. Since January 2019 he serves as Executive Director of the Regional Science Association International (RSAI). He also acts as Book Review Editor for *Papers in Regional Science*. He holds a Ph.D. in Management, Economics and Industrial Engineering obtained at Politecnico di Milano in 2010. He also holds a Ph.D. in Spatial Economics, obtained at the VU University Amsterdam in 2015. He has published on various international refereed journals.

Gérard Cliquet is emeritus professor of the University of Rennes 1 (France). He was the director (2002–2007) of the CREM (Center for Research in Economics and Management), UMR CNRS 6211. He is the author or co-author of more than 80 articles published in peer-reviewed journals and is author or editor of 21 books, and he supervised 42 PhD dissertations. His research concerns retailing, geomarketing and franchising.

Maria Michela Dickson is Assistant Professor of Economic Statistics at the University of Trento. She is author of several contributions about spatial sampling and spatial statistics of social and economic phenomena.

Zeynep Elburz is Assistant Professor of City and Regional Planning at the Izmir Institute of Technology and teaches Regional Economic Development and Planning. She is a member of the Turkish Regional Science Association.

Emanuele Forlani is Assistant Professor of Economics at the University of Bologna and Research Fellow at Centro Studi Luca d'Agliano.

Roberto Gabriele graduated in statistics and holds a Ph.D. in Economics and Management. He is now associate professor of Applied economics. He is member of the editorial board of *International journal of Computational Economics and Econometrics*. He is member of SIEPI (Società Italiana di Economia e Politica Industriale).

Diego Giuliani is Associate Professor of Economic Statistics at the University of Trento. His research activities focus primarily on the use and development of statistical methods to analyse micro-geographic data.

Salvatore Greco is Full Professor of Financial and Actuarial Mathematics at the University of Catania. He is member of the editorial board of the *European Journal of Operational Research* and associate editor of *Journal of Multi-Criteria Decision Analysis*. He is coordinator of the EURO Working Group on Multiple Criteria Decision Aiding and president-elect of the Multiple Criteria Decision Making Section of INFORMS (Institute for Operations Research and the Management Sciences). He was member of the scientific committee of AMASES (Associazione per la Matematica Applicata alle Scienze Economiche e Sociali) for which he served as vice president. In 2013, he received the Gold Medal of the International Society on Multiple Criteria Decision Making.

Karima Kourtit is at the Jheronimus Academy of Data Science (JADS), at the Eindhoven University of Technology and Tilburg University. She has worked at the Center for the Future of Places (CFP) at KTH Royal Institute of Technology, Stockholm, and Adam Mickiewicz University, Poznan, Poland. She holds two Ph.D.s, in economics and geography (with distinction), and has a profound interest in regional and urban topics. Her research interest focuses on the emerging 'New Urban World'. Her main scientific research is in the field of creative industries, urban development, cultural heritage, digital technology and strategic performance management. Furthermore, she has been an editor of several books and guest editor for many international journals, and has published a wide array of scientific articles, papers, special issues of journals and edited volumes in the field of geography and the spatial sciences. She is also managing director of The Regional Science Academy.

Katiuscia Lavoratori is Research Fellow in Strategy & International Business at Warwick Business School, University of Warwick (UK). Her work has won several awards, including the Best Paper Award at European International Business Academy and Global Strategy Journal Best Paper Award.

Xinmeng Li is a Ph.D. student at Graduate School of Information Sciences, Tohoku University.

Alessandra Michelangeli B.A. (Bocconi University), M.Sc. and Ph.D. in Economics (Bocconi University & Cergy-Pontoise University), is Associate Professor of Economics at Milan-Bicocca University. Her research mainly focuses on Urban & Regional Economics; Public Economics; Multidimensional Well-being & Inequality. She published several academic articles on international economic journals including: *Journal of Economic Theory*, *Applied Economics*, *Journal of Economic Inequality*, *Urban Studies* and *Regional Studies*. She is editor of a book on urban quality of life published by Routledge, and co-author of a book on quality of life in Italian cities published by Bocconi University Press.

Peter Nijkamp is Emeritus Professor in Regional and Urban Economics and in Economic Geography at the VU University Amsterdam. He is currently affiliated with the Adam Mickiewicz University, Poznan (Poland) and the Jheronimus Academy of Data Science (JADS) in 's-Hertogenbosch. He is member of editorial/advisory boards of more than 20 scientific journals. According to the RePec list, he belongs to the top 25 of well-known economists worldwide. He is also a fellow of the Royal Netherlands Academy of Sciences, and past vice-president of this organization. He was awarded the most prestigious scientific prize in the Netherlands, the Spinoza award. His publication list comprises more than 2000 contributions (articles and books), while his H-index is around 90. He has not only been involved in academic research, but also in many practical policy issues in the field of decision-making, regional development, environmental management, governance of culture, transportation and communication, and advanced data analytics.

Giuseppe Pignataro is Assistant Professor of Economics at the Department of Economics, University of Bologna. He is currently teaching Microeconomics at the School of Political Science in Bologna.

Lucia Piscitello is Professor of International Business at the Henley Business School, University of Reading, where she is also co-director of the John H. Dunning Center for International Business, and Professor of International Business at Politecnico di Milano. Her research interests cover the economics and management of MNEs, the international aspects of technological change, the geography of innovation. Her recent studies focus on agglomeration and MNEs' location strategies, globalization of R&D and technology development in the global network of MNEs, digital technologies, global sourcing and reshoring. She is Associate Editor of the *Global Strategy Journal*, and serves on the editorial boards of several journals. She acts as external expert for the Department of Geography & Environment, London School of Economics, UK. She is a Fellow, Past President and Chair of the European International Business Academy (EIBA).

Flavio Santi is Assistant Professor in Economic Statistics at the Department of Economics of the University of Verona. His research interests mainly focus on modelling and estimation problems in spatial econometrics.

Menelaos Tasiou is Associate Professor of Quantitative Methods & Data Analytics at the University of Portsmouth. He is a member of the Centre for Operations Research and Logistics operating at the Business school, and an editorial member of the International Journal of Emerging Markets. His research interests lie in the intersection of Multicriteria Decision Analysis and Financial Engineering.

Gianpiero Torrisi is an Associate Professor in Applied Economics at the University of Catania since 2018. He is also Visiting Fellow in Economics at Portsmouth Business School, University of Portsmouth. Prior to joining the University of Catania, he worked as Senior Lecturer in Economics at the University of Portsmouth where he acted also as Principal Investigator in the H2020 project Perception and Evaluation of Regional and Cohesion policies by Europeans and Identification with the Values of Europe (PERCEIVE) and as a Research Associate at the Centre for Urban and Regional Development Studies (Newcastle University) being involved, between others, in the Spatial Economic Research Centre (London School of Economic)'s project "Devolution, Spatial Economic Policy and Performance" and in the project "Decentralisation and

Public Service Provisions: The Impact of Efficiency Outcomes" financed by "Department of Communities and Local Government".

Dao-Zhi Zeng is a Full Professor of Spatial Economics at Tohoku University. He is Editor-in-chief of *Interdisciplinary Information Sciences* and a member of the editorial boards of *PLOS One* and the *Journal of Systems Science and Complexity*.

List of Figures

List of Tables

Part I

Development and Cities

1

Urban Resilience and Spatial Economics

Zeynep Elburz, Karima Kourtit, and Peter Nijkamp

1.1 The Resilience Concept: Introduction

Resilience, which has its roots in the Latin word *resilire*, meaning 'bouncing back', is not a new concept. The resilience concept was first used in the field of ecology with the pioneering article of Holling (1973), and this concept is still considered to be relevant in many disciplinary fields at different scale levels, both living and non-living, such as an economy, a micro-organism or a child, in order to understand the process

---

Z. Elburz
Faculty of Architecture, Department of City and Regional Planning, IZTECH,İzmir, Turkey
e-mail: zeynepelburz@iyte.edu.tr

K. Kourtit · P. Nijkamp (✉)
JADS (Jheronimus Academy of Data Science),'s-Hertogenbosch, the Netherlands

A. I. Cuza University, Iasi, Romania
e-mail: k.kourtit@jads.nl

S. Colombo (ed.), *Spatial Economics Volume II*,
https://doi.org/10.1007/978-3-030-40094-1_1

of anticipating, adapting and recovering in the face of major threats or shocks (Masten 2014). The exportability of the resilience concept from ecology to other disciplines, such as economics, engineering, sociology, etc., also plays a prominent role in the success and acceptance of the concept (De Montis et al. 2019). In particular, because of global concerns about major threats, such as disasters, economic crises, diseases, and other threats to human development, the notion of resilience has—despite adversity—become popular over the past decades and has attracted a great deal of international interest (Cassidy 2016; Masten 2014; Barasa et al. 2018).

As a contested concept, resilience is defined in many disciplines on the basis of their intrinsic use needs and priorities (Sharifi and Yamagata 2016). According to the theoretical ecologist Holling (1973), resilience is 'a measure of the ability of systems to absorb changes of state variables and still persist'. There are two ways to define resilience in the ecological literature (Holling 1996). The first concentrates on efficiency, constancy and predictability features, and underlines stability near an equilibrium steady state. This is called *engineering resilience* (see, e.g. Pimm 1984) and is defined as the return time to a single equilibrium state. The other concentrates on persistence, change and unpredictability attributes without any emphasis on one equilibrium steady state. It is called *ecological resilience* (after Holling 1973), and is defined as the amount of disturbance that can be absorbed by the system. The major difference between these two approaches is that—while engineering resilience (also termed the 'roly-poly toy principle') focuses on maintaining efficiency—ecological resilience focuses on maintaining the existence of functions (Holling 1996, p. 33; Gunderson 2000). Moreover, Pimm's resilience definition is based on the strength of the perturbation, while Holling's definition is based on the size of the attractor/stability domain (Reggiani et al. 2002). From an empirical point of view, the measurement of engineering resilience which is based on a simple cause–effect dynamics (Barasa et al. 2018) is easier than that of ecological resilience (Reggiani et al. 2002). However, from a conceptual point of view, while engineering resilience is about resistance to change in order to conserve existing structures (Folke 2006), ecological resilience is more about creating the capacity to work with that change (Walker and Salt 2006, p. 9). Besides, bouncing back to one steady state after a disturbance or a shock may not be a desirable attribute for systems, while the ability to adapt is clearly desirable (Klein et al. 2003).

Based on Holling's (1973) definition of resilience, a third interpretation of the resilience notion, which is called *socio-ecological* resilience, has emerged, as a result of the increasing awareness that ecosystems and human societies affect each other and need to be examined jointly (Sterk et al. 2017). Adger (2000) has highlighted the link between social and ecological resilience by defining social resilience as 'the ability of groups or communities to cope with external stresses and disturbances as a result of social, political and environmental change'. Following the shift caused by Adger (2000)'s definition, Berkes et al. (2003) defined social-ecological resilience as 'the amount of change the system can undergo and still retain the same controls on function and structure', and emphasised the capacity for learning and self-organisation. In the social-ecological resilience interpretation, a disturbance can be seen not just as a threat but also as an opportunity to allow continuous development, renewal of the system, and learning to adapt (Folke 2006). Relating linked social-ecological systems to the concept of resilience (Berkes and Folke 1998), social-ecological resilience extends ecological resilience to embrace the human and cultural elements in a city (Sanchez et al. 2018).

However, there are two opposite views on applying the ecological resilience approach to social science phenomena. Davoudi et al. (2012) has advocated the resilience concept as a bridging concept between ecology and the social sciences based on the synergy that results from integrating different disciplines. It might well be possible that the resilience concept could contribute in a meaningful way to planning theory and practice in particular (Davoudi et al. 2012). Reggiani et al. (2002) demonstrated the great potential of the resilience concept, which stems from the ecological sciences, in dynamic socio-economic systems. It should be noted that there are also many critics of resilience and its use in the social sciences. For example, Swanstrom (2008) argued that this approach might result in dead ends. Moreover, noting the increasing use of the resilience notion in many fields, Davoudi et al. (2012) underlined the suspicion in planning disciplines about the potential of the resilience concept which is considered to be just a new hollow concept and buzzword, like sustainability. They questioned the wisdom of applying the resilience concept which emerged from the natural sciences without any political dimension into the planning discipline. Along with that, MacKinnon and Derickson (2012) criticised the resilience concept from a conceptual and political point of view. They questioned the idea that resilience is a concept that is not always applicable to the capitalist system, and argued that promoting resilience in the face of a crisis only serves 'to naturalize the ecologically dominant system of global capitalism'. Clearly, different views on resilience abound in the worldwide literature on adaptive systems.

The literature on resilience is wide ranging and covers many topics, illustrations and applications. There is also a strand of literature that voices serious criticism. There are several caveats in the use of resilience concepts for socio-economic and spatial dynamics. Examples are: the definition of a shock, the question whether a perturbation is endogenous or exogenous, the evolution of resilience as a positive or negative phenomenon for society, the demarcation of the dynamic system under consideration (e.g. local or national), the effect of governance or policy on the stability of a system, the question of the nature of final equilibrium state, the quantitative assessment of a dynamic system's equilibrium point in one summary indicator, etc. (see for a review also Batabyal et al. forthcoming).

In this chapter, we look at the resilience concept from different perspectives with many dimensions, determinants and levels within a new and broader framework for both the natural and the social sciences. Since there is no universal agreement on the definition of the resilience concept, the existence of various types of definitions from various fields and studies leads to a very complex analysis framework. By adopting the view that this heterogeneity in the definitions arises from a lack of the spatial dimension, we focus here on the urban resilience concept in order to define and measure it in an appropriate operational way.

The present study will zoom in on the significance of resilience for urban systems, hence the concept of *urban* resilience. It will summarize the literature and outline some prominent research and policy challenges. The aim of this chapter is thus to present a new framework on urban resilience with an additional dimension called *spatiality*, by taking into account the spatial advantages and disadvantages of existing urban resilience arguments in the literature. The spatiality dimension includes the spatial characteristics of urban areas, such as urban morphology, urban size, transport network patterns, and accessibility. This study is a novel attempt to map out the spatial characteristics of urban areas in the context of urban resilience with an emphasis on spatial units, spatial heterogeneity and spatial correlation issues.

The rest of the chapter is organised as follows. Section 1.2 presents the different definitions of resilience at different scale levels and discusses their similarities and dissimilarities. Section 1.3 provides a review of the various dimensions of urban resilience, while Sect. 1.4 demonstrates urban resilience measurements and indicators. Finally, Sect. 1.5 concludes our study with a discussion and suggestions for how policy makers can enhance resilience.

1.2 Scale Levels of Resilience

There have been many attempts from different fields to define resilience, but there is a lack of consensus about a clear and broad definition of this concept. In the related literature, resilience, which is simply a measure of a system's integrity (Levin et al. 1998), has been addressed at different scale levels, including the individual (households, businesses), community (faith-based groups, refugees), local area (markets, cities, urban areas), country (national economy) and global (international economy) level (Rose 2017). In this section, we focus on the first three levels of resilience: individual (personal) resilience, community (social) resilience, and urban (city/region) resilience, and, in particular, their definitions of resilience (Table 1.1).

Defining resilience is a complex issue, and it depends on whether resilience is being seen as an attribute, as an outcome or as a process (Southwick et al. 2014). Individual resilience, which is the simplest level to examine (Boon et al. 2012), has been seen as a personal trait (e.g. Kobasa 1982) and also as a process in the early psychological studies. Bonanno et

Table 1.1 Resilience definitions from different disciplines

Author, Year	Level of analysis	Field	Character	Definition
Holling (1973)	Ecological system	Ecology	Attribute	The persistence of relationships within a system; a measure of the ability of systems to absorb changes of state variables, driving variables, and parameters, and still persist
Gordon 1978)	Physical system	Physic	Attribute	The ability to store strain energy and deflect elastically under a load without breaking or being deformed
Egeland et al. (1993)	Individual	Psychology	Process	The development of competence despite severe or pervasive adversity
Adger (2000)	Community	Ecology and social sciences	Attribute	The ability of communities to withstand external shocks to their social infrastructure
Godschalk (2003)	City	Social sciences	Attribute	A sustainable network of physical systems and human communities
Allenby and Fink (2005)	Community	Social sciences	Attribute	The capability of a system to maintain its functions and structure in the face of internal and external change and to degrade gracefully when it must
Folke (2006)	Social–ecological system	Ecology	Attribute and process	A self-organizing capacity of a (social) system while undergoing (ecosystem) change so as to maintain the same function and structure
Campanella (2006)	Urban areas	Social sciences	Attribute	The capacity of a city to rebound from destruction
Gillespie et al. (2007)	Individual	Psychology	Process	An ongoing process of struggling that can be learned any time

Ultramari and Rezende (2007)	Urban areas	Social sciences	Attribute	The ability to transform and retransform urban spaces
Hill et al. (2008)	Region	Economy	Attribute	The ability of a region to recover successfully from shocks to its economy
Norris et al. (2008)	Community	Psychology	Process	a process linking a set of adaptive capacities to a positive trajectory of functioning and adaptation after a disturbance
Lang (2010)	Urban areas	Social sciences	Process	The stability of a system when faced with interference
Zhou et al. (2010)	Social–ecological system	Geography	Attribute	The capacity to resist and recover from loss
Thomas et al. (2013)	Social system	Economy	Attribute	The capacity of a health system to deal with economic contraction and reorganise so as to retain essentially the same policies and functions
Lu and Stead (2013)	Urban areas	Social sciences	Process	An ongoing process, a timescale of reshaping, reorganising and developing new adaptive strategies
Coaffee (2013)	Urban areas	Social sciences	Attribute	The capacity to withstand and rebound from disruptive challenges
Walker et al. (2004)	Ecological system	Ecology	Attribute	The capacity of a system to absorb disturbance and reorganise while undergoing change so as to still retain essentially the same function, structure, identity and feedbacks

(continued)

Table 1.1 (continued)

Author, Year	Level of analysis	Field	Character	Definition
Masten (2014)	Individual	Psychology	Attribute	The capacity of a dynamic system to adapt successfully to disturbances that threaten system function, viability or development
Meerow et al. (2016)	Urban areas	Social sciences	Process	The ability of an urban system—and all its constituent socio-ecological and socio-technical networks across temporal and spatial scales—to maintain or rapidly return to desired functions in the face of a disturbance, to adapt to change, and to quickly transform systems that limit current or future adaptive capacity
De Montis et al. (2019)	Ecological system	Ecology	Attribute	The ability of complex systems to be resistant to very critical disturbances, keep their original characteristics, self-organise and adapt, and eventually evolve by achieving further and stronger conditions

al. (2011) took resilience as an outcome and investigated the factors affecting an individual's resilience after a potentially traumatic event. They found that there are multiple independent determinants of resilience such as personality, demography, socio-economic resources, etc. Similarly, Fraser et al. (1999) defined resilience by referring to 'individuals who adapt to extraordinary circumstances, achieving positive and unexpected outcomes in the face of adversity'. They also categorised three aspects of resilience: overcoming the odds, adapting successfully to high risk, and recovering from trauma, which lead to resilience being characterised as 'to learn from success'. Similarly, Walsh (2006) described resilience as 'the capacity to rebound from adversity strengthened and more resourceful'. On the other hand, some researchers have emphasised the importance of a process when they attempt to define resilience. Hegney et al. (2007) recognised that there is no one steady state within personal resilience: actually the level of resilience changes over time. Gillespie et al. (2007) also described resilience as an ongoing process of struggling that can be learned at any time. Also, according to the American Psychological Association (APA), resilience is 'the process of adapting well in the face of adversity, trauma, tragedy, threats or significant sources of stress. It means 'bouncing back' from difficult experiences' (APA 2019). On the process–outcome debate, van Breda (2018) claimed that the outcome definition of resilience only observes the outcomes without explaining them, while the process definition of resilience concentrates on mediating processes that lead to an outcome, and thus he suggested using the process definition of resilience. Van Breda (2018) defined resilience as 'the multilevel processes that systems engage in to obtain better-than-expected outcomes in the face or wake of adversity'. However, the first challenge in defining resilience, which is whether resilience is a process or attribute, is still open not only at the individual level but also at other levels of resilience.

As a second level of resilience, community (social) resilience has many different definitions and, basically it concerns the stability of the population and thus individual resilience (Boon et al. 2012). Adger's (2000) simple social resilience definition has affected subsequent attempts to define it. Cacioppo et al. (2011) defined community resilience as 'the capacity to foster, engage in, and sustain positive relationships and to endure and recover from life stressors and social isolation', while Norris et al. (2008) described it as 'a process linking a set of networked adaptive capacities to a positive trajectory of functioning and adaptation in constituent populations after a disturbance'. Even though communities are composed of individuals, it is not easy to conclude that resilient individuals generate resilient communities due to the complex composition of the relations between the natural, built, social and economic environment in communities (Norris et al. 2008). According to Kimhi (2016), similar to individual resilience, community resilience is also an important predictor of coping with traumatic experiences such as disasters. Zhou et al. (2010) broadly described resilience as the capacity to resist and recover from loss, and they proposed a new model for disaster resilience which has three dimensions: time (before, during and after the disaster); space (community, town, country etc.); and attribute (economic, institutional, social and environment). On the other hand, Davoudi et al. (2012) argued that the resilience concept is often reduced to post-disaster emergency responses in the community resilience literature and policy reports. This causes a mis-measurement of the concept, since emergency responses focus on damage mitigation in the short term, while resilience is about constructing long-term adaptive capacity for cities or regions.

Compared with the first two scale levels, defining the urban resilience concept is more arguable. From a historical point of view, even though cities are vulnerable to human-made or natural disturbance, they also tend to survive destructions and exist afterwards (e.g. ancient cities such as Istanbul, Rome). Campanella (2006) asserts 'the persistence of place' view by claiming that modern cities are more durable and indestructible, and advocates that no major city has vanished since the nineteenth century. However, according to Ahern (2011), an urban system can only be considered resilient if it is able to retain the ability to adapt to unforeseen challenges. Ergo, the urban resilience concept appears to be more complicated than the ability to survive disasters or the ability to resist change.

A specific challenge in describing urban resilience derives from the long-standing debate about defining the *urban* area. The urban area can be identified as an administrative area or a functional economic area. However, in any case, with a reference to the geographical level, the urban (city) resilience concept is complex, dynamic, non-deterministic and uncertain in nature (Jabareen 2013). Since urban areas can be considered as adaptive socio-ecological systems, the social-ecological resilience approach is more suitable for the conceptualisation of urban resilience, which tends to emphasise transformation, learning, reorganisation, and renewal (Folke 2006). Yet, there are definitions of urban resilience in the literature which stress the 'bouncing back' concept in the context of single-state equilibrium also known as 'engineering resilience' (e.g. Wagner and Breil 2013; Campanella 2006). More recently, building upon the multi-state equilibrium resilience (ecological resilience), the equilibrium concept has evolved into a dynamic non-equilibrium notion which suggests there is no stable state to bounce back to at all. Following the trends in the debate on the equilibrium concept in the resilience literature, urban resilience is inclined to move to a multi- or non-equilibrium state, also known as evolutionary resilience (Pickett et al. 2004; Matyas and Pelling 2015; Meerow et al. 2016; Sharifi and Yamagata 2016; Figueiredo et al. 2018).

Regarding this discussion, Jabareen (2013) defined the resilient city in terms of 'the overall abilities of its governance, physical, economic and social systems and entities exposed to hazards to learn, be ready in advance, plan for uncertainties, resist, absorb, accommodate to and recover from the effects of a hazard in a timely and efficient manner'. Taking into account the non-static and complex characteristics of cities, UN-Habitat (2018) describes urban resilience as 'the measurable ability of any urban system, with its inhabitants, to maintain continuity through all shocks and stresses, while positively adapting and transforming toward sustainability'. More briefly, Leichenko (2011) defined urban resilience as 'the ability of a city or urban system to withstand a wide array of shocks and stresses'. Recently, Figueiredo et al. (2018) described urban resilience as 'the ongoing capacity of cities to absorb, adapt, transform and prepare for shocks and stresses along the economic, social, institutional and environmental dimensions, with the aim of maintaining the functions of a city and improving response to future shocks'. According to Meerow et al. (2016) who reviewed 172 publications with 25 definitions of urban resilience, a new, dynamic, and comprehensive but flexible definition of urban resilience is required. They define urban resilience as 'the ability of an urban system– and all its constituent socio-ecological and socio-technical networks across temporal and spatial scales– to maintain or rapidly return to desired functions in the face of a disturbance, to adapt to change, and to quickly transform systems that limit current or future adaptive capacity'.

Considering the multiple definitions of resilience from many disciplines which may lead to various policies and actions (Gunderson 2000), Rose (2017) argued the importance of a broader definition of resilience which unifies the various sets of definitions instead of only the intersections. According to Zhou et al. (2010), the heterogeneity in the definition of resilience originated from distinct epistemological orientations and methodological practices. On the other hand, Rose (2017) advocated that the existing discrepancy between the resilience definitions originates from the spatial dimension. Moreover, Jabareen (2013) stated that defining and measuring resilience is mostly related to capacity using quantitative indicators and claimed that the literature overlooks cities and space. As a solution, Cutter (2016) proposed an integration of the spatial sciences (planning and geography) with resilience concepts from different disciplines by considering their focus on the spatial need to integrate. By taking into account these existing attempts to define *urban resilience* in the literature, we describe it here as: 'a continuous learning ability of urban areas to absorb any kind of expected or unexpected disturbance or threat, to adapt, to evolve, and then to improve the distinctive features of urban areas in the face of probable future shocks'.

1.3 Dimensions of Urban Resilience

Urban resilience is a complex and multidisciplinary concept with many dimensions to consider (Sharifi and Yamagata 2016). Since it is not appropriate to neglect this multidimensional approach in order to frame urban resilience, the pillars of the concept have been investigated by many scholars. On the bases of a large body of works on urban resilience and its components, it can be argued that, amongst other dimensions, social, economic and institutional dimensions are prominent (Patel and Nosal 2016). The dimensions of urban resilience, including social, economic and institutional, have been named differently by researchers in the litera-

Table 1.2 Dimensions of urban resilience

Author/Year	Measure	Dimensions
ARUP (2014)	City resilience index	Health and well-being Economy and society Infrastructure and environment Leadership and strategy
Cutter et al. (2008)	Community resilience	Social vulnerability Built environment and infrastructure Natural systems and exposure Hazards mitigation and planning
Fu and Wang (2018)	Urban resilience capacity index	Ecological-physical conditions Economic conditions Institutional service Social capacity
Foster (2007)	Resilience capacity index	Economic capacity Socio-demographic capacity Community connectivity capacity
OECD (2014)	Urban resilience drivers	Economy Society Institution Environment
Wang et al. (2018)	Urban resilience	Economic Social Ecological
Yu et al. (2018)	Urban economic resilience evaluation index system	Economic growth index Opening up index Social development index Environmental protection index Natural condition index Technological innovation index
Kontokosta and Malik (2018)	Emergencies and disasters index	Social Infrastructure & Community Connectivity Physical infrastructure Economic strength Environmental conditions
Sharifi and Yamagata (2016)	Urban resilience dimensions	Materials and environmental resources Society and well-being Economy Built environment and infrastructure Governance and institution
Rus et al. (2018)	Urban resilience components	Buildings Infrastructure Community Open space

ture, but it is apparent that most of them are used as synonyms (Table 1.2). For instance, OECD (2014) addresses urban resilience with four strongly interconnected dimensions which are: economic, social, institutional and environmental dimensions, while Delgado-Ramos and Guibrunet (2017)'s *pyramid of urban resilience and sustainability* is composed of the ecological, economic, socio-cultural and governance dimensions. The World Bank (2012) defines urban resilience by breaking down its four components: economic, institutional, infrastructural and social, while Sharifi and Yamagata (2016) investigate urban resilience with its five main dimensions, namely materials and environmental resources; society and well-being; economy; built environment and infrastructure; and governance and institutions, in order to develop an urban resilience assessment tool. And finally, Kontokosta and Malik (2018) have developed an index to calculate regional resilience capacity from the dimensions: social infrastructure and community connectivity; physical infrastructure; economic strength and environmental conditions.

Another attempt to monitor urban resilience by creating an index with four key dimensions: health and well-being; economy and society; infrastructure and environment; and leadership and strategy, comes from The Rockefeller Foundation and ARUP (2014)'s study. Cutter et al. (2010) examine urban resilience based on social, economic, institutional, natural and physical dimension, whereas Wang et al. (2018) conceptualise urban resilience with three main aspects, including ecological, economic, and social resilience, which are all interrelated. Yet these studies fail to contain any spatial characteristics rather than a simple distinction between the urban and the rural area. More recently, Rus et al. (2018) divided complex urban systems into two basic components—physical (buildings, open space, infrastructure) and social (the community)—as well as the dynamic interactions between them in order to assess urban resilience to natural disasters, especially earthquakes. Based on their review of the assessment of urban system resilience, partial approaches (e.g. resilience of infrastructure, resilience of buildings) which neglect the links and interaction between the components can only present an incomplete view of an urban resilience level.

Considering the overlapping in assessing the dimensions of urban resilience in the related literature, we examine urban resilience with its five

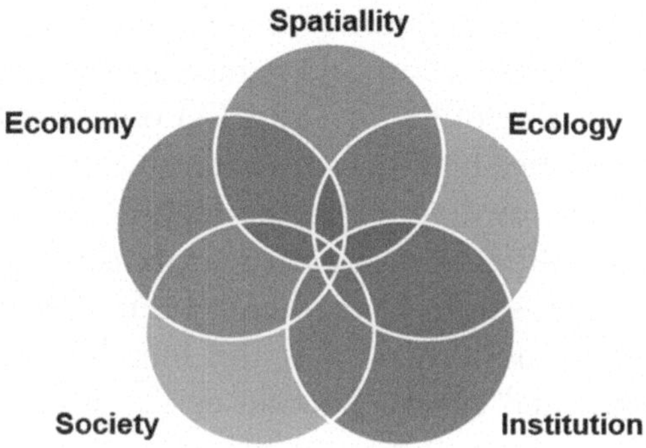

Fig. 1.1 The dimensions of urban resilience

dimensions including *economic*, *social*, *ecological* and *institutional* which are typical, and the *spatiality* dimension which is distinct from previous studies (Fig. 1.1). The spatiality dimension differs from the preceding physical or infrastructural dimensions by comprising the spatial characteristics of urban areas, such as urban morphology, urban size, transport networks, and location attributes of the urban areas, and bridging with the other four dimensions.

Urban morphology, which is the study of urban forms that include buildings, streets, and open spaces, is used to understand the spatial characteristics of the built environment (Schirmer and Axhausen 2016). In the discipline of urban planning, spatial characteristics affect the quality of the urban landscape and thus people's perception of it and that is why urban form is considered to promote a sense of community in an urban area (Eizenberg and Jabareen 2017). However, urban form has attracted attention in the literature mostly because of its relationship with sustainability and quality-of-life concepts, not with the resilience concept. Since Jacobs (1961), and Lynch (1984), it has been accepted that quality of life in an urban area is linked with its shape and the distribution of land uses. In the 1990s and early 2000s, the compact city and urban sprawl have been examined by focusing on urban development density to determine which urban forms are more sustainable and desirable. It is argued that in a compact city with high density and mix-land uses, it is easier to access services in a short time compared with a city with urban sprawl. Hege (2012) indicated that high-density space enhances walkability and social interaction, and reduces greenhouse emissions and thus increases the quality of life in a city. On the other hand, Dempsey and Jenks (2010) criticised high-density urban areas because of congestion and problems of overcrowding. However, high-density urban areas may create negative externalities but also positive externalities which are related to urban agglomerations from an economic point of view.

Another urban form study area is the link between urban forms and their environmental effects. Makido et al. (2012) investigated the relationship between urban form and energy consumption in Japanese cities, in order to calculate the effect of urban design on urban energy usage by using various spatial metrics. Another study by Xu et al. (2017) focused on urban morphology and climate change with a novel highly accurate satellite-based approach and claimed that high-density buildings create larger heat islands. However, the main aim of these studies is to understand the effect of urban morphology on sustainable urban living, and of enhancing sustainable cities for the future or the effect of urban form on resilience with a special focus on, for instance, energy (e.g. Yang and Quan 2016). Even though resilience invokes related terms, such as sustainability, adaptability and vulnerability, an integration of the urban resilience concept as a whole into urban morphology is missing in the literature.

For the case of the relationship between the transport network and resilience, Reggiani et al. (2015) observe that the studies that dominate transport network resilience in the literature interpret transport resilience in terms of robustness or reliability, which is similar to the single equilibrium approach of engineering resilience. However, the number of studies that measure network resilience with empirical applications or simulations is limited. Among them, Knoop et al. (2012) examine robustness, while Vromans et al. (2006) focus on the reliability issue for the Dutch road and railway network. However, it is also possible to state that interest in network resilience is increasing for all transport modes, for example, public transport networks, telecommunication, aviation, etc. at different scale levels with a special focus on shocks (Reggiani et al. 2015). To address transport network system resilience, accessibility—or connectivity—measures are used, but accessibility is also associated with the economic performance of an urban area, since higher accessibility creates lower transport costs, fosters agglomeration, and thus increases the productivity level of the area. Likewise, higher accessibility which emerges from transport infrastructure developments or land-use changes also increases the spatial interaction between places. But it is clear that accessibility varies in space, and is very sensitive to the spatial unit of analysis (Condeço-Melhorado et al. 2014).

To overcome the problem of an incomplete view of urban resilience, we propose to include the spatial characteristics of an urban area, as well as its interaction with other dimensions. The next step is quantifying urban resilience dimensions with the use of indicators and then creating an index for empirical analysis.

1.4 Measurement of Urban Resilience

The lack of consensus on both the definition and the measurement of resilience creates the danger of trivializing of the concept. One way to consider the resilience concept, not as a new buzzword or vague and umbrella concept for all desirable attributes, is to define it with measurable and observable attributes (Klein et al. 2003). This causes resilience to be seen by policy makers as an operational and practical concept. Thus, quantitative tools, indexes and indicators are preferred by policy makers to measure resilience and to formulate policies which enhance resilience.

In order to measure resilience, Reggiani et al. (2002) focused on Pimm's definition of resilience, which is more practical than Holling's, by taking into account the problems of measuring resilience in socio-economic terms. They applied the engineering resilience approach to identify non-resilient trends in regional labour markets in West Germany with the Lyapunov exponents method. Regional economic resilience was investigated by Chapple and Lester (2010) by looking at only one indicator: the changes in average real earnings per worker, from 1980, 1990 and 2000, while Swanstrom et al. (2009) investigated regional resilience in the face of foreclosures in three regions in the United States, and showed that resilience is diversified across space with different characteristics.

Table 1.3 Indicators of regional/urban economic resilience measurement

Author/Year	Spatial unit	Country	Indicator	Variable
Davies (2011)	10 countries	EU	Unemployment	Unemployment rate
Fingleton et al. (2012)	12 regions	UK	Employment	Employment growth
Lapuh (2018)	212 municipality	Slovenia	Output	Change in GVA per employee
Martin (2012)	12 regions	UK	Employment	Number of employees
Reggiani et al. (2002)	327 region	Germany	Employment	Number of employees
Chapple and Lester (2010)	191 metropolitan regions	USA	Income	Average earnings per worker
Di Caro (2014)	20 regions	Italy	Employment	Total employment Industrial employment
Swanstrom et al. (2009)	6 metropolitan regions	USA	Economic	Foreclosures
Simmie and Martin (2010)	2 city regions	UK	Economic	Employment growth Manufacturing employment Service sector employment Number of new firms

Recently Cai et al. (2018) synthesised 174 articles on disaster resilience measurement and found that the most common indicators for economic resilience are income and employment, and that only 17.8% of the articles had created a quantitative resilience index (Table 1.3).

Adger (2000), who relates social and ecological resilience, claims that different aspects of resilience have various indicators, and there is no single indicator to control resilience as a whole. Hence, he examined the social resilience with economic, demographic, and institutional variables. Likewise, Rose (2017) argued that the components of the existing resilience indicators in the literature are actually unimportant for the recovery process, and prior resilience indexes are not useful for the short run. He claimed that constructing a resilience index should serve both to study and to improve the recovery process, and instead of using a single resilience indicator, creating a resilience index is more popular. He constructed a resilience index (RI) for the recovery process from a disaster, while Girard (2011) defined qualitative and quantitative indicators for economic resilience criteria along with those for social and environmental resilience in order to make a multidimensional evaluation of resilient, creative and sustainable cities. Kontokosta and Malik (2018) developed the Resilience to Emergencies and Disasters Index (REDI) by integrating physical, natural and social systems measures in order to benchmark neighbourhood resilience. REDI consists of 24 indicators in order to calculate the regional resilience capacity for Hurricane Sandy. For monitoring disaster resilience in the case of the US counties, Cutter et al. (2010) created an index with social, economic, institutional, infrastructure and community dimensions. They underlined the presence of spatial variations in disaster resilience between urban and rural areas. However, Rose (2017) criticised the index derived by Cutter et al. (2010) for including indicators that are not based on a solid economic conceptual framework.

More recently, Sharifi and Yamagata (2016) aimed to address all urban system dimensions in an urban resilience assessment framework by creating five categories of criteria. The economic dimension of urban resilience is one of these five categories, and includes criteria for the economic structure, security and stability, and dynamism. They underlined the fact that the criteria for the different dimensions can be context-specific, and thus using all criteria for all contexts may not be meaningful (Sharifi and Yamagata 2016). Fu and Wang et al. (2018) criticise existing urban resilience capacity indicators for not being a comprehensive quantitative evaluation, but instead focus on resilience capacity enhancement. Thus, they develop a new urban resilience capacity index with currently available indicators extracted from the literature, instead of creating new resilience indicators. The study claims to create an index based on urban form and spatial attributes related to the urban planning discipline, but includes only a landscape shape index and a Shannon diversity indicator. More recently, Figueiredo et al. (2018) suggested a set of indicators to measure urban resilience based on four urban resilience dimensions. Eight out of 52 indicators are created for the economic dimension which focuses on innovation, diversity and employment aspects, whilst none of the indicators have a spatial reference. Similarly, for Chinese cities, Yu et al. (2018) use six dimensions which are: economic growth; opening up; social development; environmental production; natural condition; and technological innovation, and 25 indicators to measure urban economic resilience. However, except for the population density indicator of cities, the study ignores the spatial characteristics of the urban areas just like previous studies.

To date, the need to integrate spatial science into the resilience concept has not been successful, mainly because urban designers and urban planners opt to assess resilience with a qualitative conceptual framework rather than from a quantitative and measurable perspective (Cutter 2016; Rus et al. 2018). For example, Lu and Stead (2013) focus on the urban resilience concept in the spatial planning policies, and claim that planning strategies and the decision-making process can address the notion of resilience. They also emphasise that the resilience concept is important for cities to respond to uncertainty and to develop strategies to deal with change in cities. Similarly, to map out the characteristics of urban resilience, other studies (e.g. Sharifi and Yamagata 2016; Allan et al. 2013; Brand and Nicholson 2016) work on qualitative resilience attributes such as modularity, diversity, ecosystem services, variability, robustness, stability, flexibility, resourcefulness, redundancy, coordination, capacity, foresight capacity, independence, connectivity, collaboration, agility, adaptability, self-organisation, creativity, efficiency, equity, spare capacity, safe failure, rapid rebound and constant learning. In order to overcome the problem of the lack of spatial characteristics dimensions in the existing urban resilience literature, we believe that it is necessary to integrate the spatiality dimension with quantitative indicators into the urban resilience concept. Hence, we have created an urban resilience index with 5 main dimensions, and 14 subcategories using more than 50 indicators (Table 1.4). The spatiality dimension is composed of the subcategories urban size, urban sprawl, urban form, land use and transport network. With the development of GIS-based analysis and more utilisation of highly accurate

Table 1.4 Measuring urban resilience dimensions

Dimension	Category	Variable
Economy	Income and equality	GDP growth rate
		GDP per capita
		GINI coefficient
	Labour market	Employment rate
		Female employment rate
		Youth unemployment rate
	Innovation	R&D expenditure
		Number of patent applications
	Sector capacity	Economic diversity index
		Single-sector employment dependence
		High-tech industry ratio
		Number of new businesses
Society	Socio-demographic capacity	Population growth
		Life expectancy
		Number of doctors per 10,000
		Number of hospital beds per 100,000
		Insurance rate
		Adult literacy rate
		Education expenditures
		Pre-primary education ratio
		Percentage of homeownership
		Percentage of car ownership
	Community capacity	Poverty level
		Disabled population rate
		Elderly population rate
		Migration rate
		Accessibility index for services
		Households with access to broadband rate
Ecology	Environmental degradation	Population density
		Open space ratio
		Green area ratio
		Built-up area ratio
		Energy consumption per capita
		CO_2 emission rate
		Urban solid waste rate

(continued)

Table 1.4 (continued)

Dimension	Category	Variable
Institution	Civic infrastructure	Number of community organisations
		Number of local authorities
		Voter participation rate
	Government	Percentage of buildings with insurance
		Land-use plans for hazards
		Mitigation expenditure
Spatiality	Urban size	Urban density rate
		Urbanisation ratio
	Urban sprawl	Number of high-density peaks
		Percentage of population residing outside the high-density peaks
	Urban form	Medium block size
		Medium plot size
		Destination accessibility
	Land use	Simpson diversity index
		Dissimilarity index
	Transport network	Average streets per node
		Average street length
		Number of nodes and edges
		Space syntax

satellite images in land-use attributes, it is possible to measure urban size, urban sprawl, and urban form with temporal and spatial evolution included. By taking advantage of using population and land-use metrics with GIS-based methods, which generate more reliable dynamic spatial data on urban areas, one can observe the past and current state of the morphology of the urban areas. But in order to control the spatiality dimension, we also need more detailed spatial unit data, because the elements of urban form are not only streets and blocks, but also plots and buildings and their size and proportion. For the case of transport network connectivity, space syntax can play an important role in understanding the patterns of movement, interaction, and density.

Developing indicators for measuring urban resilience is problematic, since factors affecting urban resilience are miscellaneous, and these factors cause cities to have dissimilar capacities to adopt, recover and transform. Therefore, suggesting a one-size-fits-all approach is not relevant for the urban resilience concept, which is all about context. It is not appropriate to compare and rank different cities based on their inherent capacities by ignoring the need for a tailored/specified methodological approach for each case (Schiappacasse and Müller 2015). Using the standard internationally recognised indicators, such as the employment rate, creates sufficient conditions to compare different urban areas. However, standard metrics are too general and rigid to capture the local characteristics of cities. On the other hand, context- and space-specific indicators are able to control cities' own priorities and objectives more directly. Considering the differences in context, characteristics and size of the urban areas, it is more useful and proper to compile space-specific indicators and combine them with basic indicators which matter for all urban areas (Figueiredo et al. 2018; Winderl 2014; Yu et al. 2018).

Quantifying resilience by measuring it with created indexes and indicators, policy makers can enhance urban resilience. Many factors, including social, economic, geographical, and environmental, influence urban resilience and many indicators have been proposed in the literature to capture those factors. However, there is a need for weighting indicators that are used to measure urban resilience based on the priorities, problems and objectives of the city. Also bearing in mind that cities have different attributes and characteristics, the process of selecting the most appropriate indicators and weighting the indicators needs to be city-specific, rather than employing national resilience indexes which exclude place-specific indicators and local knowledge (Frazier et al. 2013). Taking into account the omission of differential weighting and the spatial context of resilience indicators, Frazier et al. (2013) examined spatial factors that were identified by the local focus groups and plans at the county level. Moran's I and LISA statistical analyses reveal that all spatial indicators vary across space and tend to show spatial clustering characteristics. The results give clear evidence that some indicators are more important in some areas than in others, and thus spatial autocorrelation between indicators should be considered (Frazier et al. 2013). Another important issue is controlling the spillover effects of the resilience indicator to give a clear answer to the question: Does a resilient urban area also affect the neighbouring regions' resiliency? With data from different scale levels, from plot size to satellite images, to measure the spatiality dimension, we assume it is possible to investigate not only the direct but also the indirect effects of each indicator on neighbouring regions. This would bring urban resilience into the realm of spatial statistics and econometrics.

1.5 Conclusion

Resilience has become a new and popular buzzword in the social sciences. This chapter has presented a new framework to understand the urban resilience concept at different scale levels and in terms of different dimensions. Based on our review of various definitions, dimensions and measurement types of urban resilience, we introduced a new dimension called 'spatiality' to capture the spatial characteristics of urban areas. It is clear that the existing literature overlooks space and its effects on other dimensions, and this partial approach can only lead to an incomplete view of urban resilience. As far as the authors know, this is the first study to underline the importance of spatial characteristics when conceptualising and measuring the notion of urban resilience and its interaction with other dimensions. In this study, we create—on the basis of a new comprehensive definition of urban resilience—a general index for the quantitative assessment of urban resilience by including urban form, urban size, and transport network categories. This index can be a useful tool for cities to examine their past and current state and thus prepare for all kinds of disturbance in the future. But it is crucial to stress that this index is only a first step for measuring resilience, and each city should consider and take into account its own special and unique conditions, and then combine them with this index to have a clearer idea of its degree of resilience. Resilience has both an analytical and a political meaning, and its use and relevance depends on various internal and external circumstances; against this background, one might speak of contextual resilience. Lastly, it is also worth mentioning that urban resilience variables vary across space and also affect neighbouring spatial units. Therefore, it would be more appropriate to look, on a broader scale, at not only the city itself but also its neighbours in order to analyse spillover effects. From an analytical perspective, there is a clear promising research agenda for urban resilience theory and methodology.

References

Adger, W. N. (2000). Social and Ecological Resilience: Are They Related? *Progress in Human Geography, 24*(3), 347–364.

Ahern, J. (2011). From Fail-Safe to Safe-to-Fail: Sustainability and Resilience in the New Urban World. *Landscape and Urban Planning, 100*(4), 341–343.

Allan, P., Bryant, M., Wirsching, C., Garcia, D., & Teresa Rodriguez, M. (2013). The Influence of Urban Morphology on the Resilience of Cities Following an Earthquake. *Journal of Urban Design, 18*(2), 242–262.

Allenby, B., & Fink, J. (2005). Toward Inherently Secure and Resilient Societies. *Science, 309*(5737), 1034–1036.

American Psychological Association (APA). (2019, February 12). The Road to Resilience. Retrieved from https://www.apa.org/helpcenter/road-resilience.

ARUP. (2014). *City Resilience Framework*. The Rockefeller Foundation.

Barasa, E., Mbau, R., & Gilson, L. (2018). What Is Resilience and How Can It Be Nurtured? A Systematic Review of Empirical Literature on Organizational Resilience. *International Journal of Health Policy and Management, 7*(6), 491.

Batabyal, A., Kourtit, K., & Nijkamp, P. (forthcoming). The Use of Resilience in Regional Science: Five Outstanding Issues, Entropy, Complexity and Spatial Dynamics. In A. Reggiani, L. Schintler, & D. Czamanski (Eds.). Cheltenham: Edward Elgar.

Berkes, F., & Folke, C. (Eds.). (1998). *Linking Social and Ecological Systems: Management Practices and Social Mechanisms for Building Resilience*. Cambridge: Cambridge University Press.

Berkes, F., Colding, J., & Folke, C. (Eds.). (2003). *Navigating Social-Ecological Systems: Building Resilience for Complexity and Change*. Cambridge University Press.

Bonanno, G. A., Westphal, M., & Mancini, A. D. (2011). Resilience to Loss and Potential Trauma. *Annual Review of Clinical Psychology, 7*, 511–535.

Boon, H. J., Cottrell, A., King, D., Stevenson, R. B., & Millar, J. (2012). Bronfenbrenner's Bioecological Theory for Modelling Community Resilience to Natural Disasters. *Natural Hazards, 60*(2), 381–408.

Brand, D., & Nicholson, H. (2016). Public Space and Recovery: Learning from Post-Earthquake Christchurch. *Journal of Urban Design, 21*(2), 159–176.

Cacioppo, J. T., Reis, H. T., & Zautra, A. J. (2011). Social Resilience. *American Psychologist, 66*(1), 43–51.

Cai, H., Lam, N. S., Qiang, Y., Zou, L., Correll, R. M., & Mihunov, V. (2018). A Synthesis of Disaster Resilience Measurement Methods and Indices. *International Journal of Disaster Risk Reduction, 31*, 844–855.
Campanella, T. J. (2006). Urban Resilience and the Recovery of New Orleans. *Journal of the American Planning Association, 72*(2), 141–146.
Cassidy, S. (2016). The Academic Resilience Scale (ARS-30): A New Multidimensional Construct Measure. *Frontiers in Psychology, 7*, 1787.
Chapple, K., & Lester, T. W. (2010). The Resilient Regional Labour Market? The US Case. *Cambridge Journal of Regions, Economy and Society, 3*(1), 85–104.
Coaffee, J. (2013). Rescaling and Responsibilising the Politics of Urban Resilience: From National Security to Local Place-Making. *Politics, 33*(4), 240–252.
Condeço-Melhorado, A., Reggiani, A., & Gutiérrez, J. (Eds.). (2014). *Accessibility and Spatial Interaction*. Edward Elgar Publishing.
Cutter, S. L. (2016). The Landscape of Disaster Resilience Indicators in the USA. *Natural Hazards, 80*(2), 741–758.
Cutter, S. L., Barnes, L., Berry, M., Burton, C., Evans, E., Tate, E., & Webb, J. (2008). Community and Regional Resilience: Perspectives from Hazards, Disasters, and Emergency Management. *Geography, 1*(7), 2301–2306.
Cutter, S. L., Burton, C. G., & Emrich, C. T. (2010). Disaster Resilience Indicators for Benchmarking Baseline Conditions. *Journal of Homeland Security and Emergency Management, 7*(1), 1–22.
Davies, S. (2011). Regional Resilience in the 2008–2010 Downturn: Comparative Evidence from European Countries. *Cambridge Journal of Regions, Economy and Society, 4*(3), 369–382.
Davoudi, S., Shaw, K., Haider, L. J., Quinlan, A. E., Peterson, G. D., Wilkinson, C., ... Davoudi, S. (2012). Resilience: A Bridging Concept or a Dead End? "Reframing" Resilience: Challenges for Planning Theory and Practice Interacting Traps: Resilience Assessment of a Pasture Management System in Northern Afghanistan Urban Resilience: What Does It Mean in Planning Practice? Resilience as a Useful Concept for Climate Change Adaptation? The Politics of Resilience for Planning: A Cautionary Note: Edited by Simin Davoudi and Libby Porter. *Planning Theory & Practice, 13*(2), 299–333.
De Montis, A., Ganciu, A., Cabras, M., Bardi, A., Peddio, V., Caschili, S., et al. (2019). Resilient Ecological Networks: A Comparative Approach. *Land Use Policy, 89*, 104207.

Delgado-Ramos, G. C., & Guibrunet, L. (2017). Assessing the Ecological Dimension of Urban Resilience and Sustainability. *International Journal of Urban Sustainable Development, 9*(2), 151–169.

Dempsey, N., & Jenks, M. (2010). The Future of the Compact City. *Built Environment, 36*(1), 116–121.

Di Caro, P. (2014). Recessions, Recoveries and Regional Resilience: Evidence on Italy. *Cambridge Journal of Regions, Economy and Society, 8*(2), 273–291.

Egeland, B., Carlson, E., & Sroufe, L. A. (1993). Resilience as Process. *Development and Psychopathology, 5*(4), 517–528.

Eizenberg, E., & Jabareen, Y. (2017). Social Sustainability: A New Conceptual Framework. *Sustainability, 9*(1), 68.

Figueiredo, L., Honiden, T., & Schumann, A. (2018). *Indicators for Resilient Cities* (No. 2018/02). OECD Publishing.

Fingleton, B., Garretsen, H., & Martin, R. (2012). Recessionary Shocks and Regional Employment: Evidence on the Resilience of UK Regions. *Journal of Regional Science, 52*(1), 109–133.

Folke, C. (2006). Resilience: The Emergence of a Perspective for Social–Ecological Systems Analyses. *Global Environmental Change, 16*(3), 253–267.

Foster, K. A. (2007). A Case Study Approach to Understanding Regional Resilience. Retrieved from https://www.econstor.eu/obitstream/10419/59413/1/592535347.pdf.

Fraser, M. W., Galinsky, M. J., & Richman, J. M. (1999). Risk, Protection, and Resilience: Toward a Conceptual Framework for Social Work Practice. *Social Work Research, 23*(3), 131–143.

Frazier, T. G., Thompson, C. M., Dezzani, R. J., & Butsick, D. (2013). Spatial and Temporal Quantification of Resilience at the Community Scale. *Applied Geography, 42*, 95–107.

Fu, X., & Wang, X. (2018). Developing an Integrative Urban Resilience Capacity Index for Plan Making. *Environment Systems and Decisions, 38*(3), 367–378.

Gillespie, B. M., Chaboyer, W., & Wallis, M. (2007). Development of a Theoretically Derived Model of Resilience Through Concept Analysis. *Contemporary Nurse, 25*(1–2), 124–135.

Girard, L. F. (2011). Multidimensional Evaluation Processes to Manage Creative, Resilient and Sustainable City. *Aestimum, 59*, 123–139.

Godschalk, D. R. (2003). Urban Hazard Mitigation: Creating Resilient Cities. *Natural Hazards Review, 4*(3), 136–143.

Gordon, J. E. (1978). *Structures*. Harmondsworth: Penguin Books.

Gunderson, L. H. (2000). Ecological Resilience—In Theory and Application. *Annual Review of Ecology and Systematics, 31*(1), 425–439.

Hege, H. (2012, October). Compact City Development: High Ideals and Emerging Practices. *European Journal of Spatial Development*, Refereed article No. 49.

Hegney, D. G., Buikstra, E., Baker, P., Rogers-Clark, C., Pearce, S., Ross, H., King, C., & Watson-Luke, A. (2007). Individual Resilience in Rural People: A Queensland Study, Australia. *Rural and Remote Health, 7*(4), 620.

Hill, E., Wial, H., & Wolman, H. (2008). *Exploring Regional Economic Resilience* (No. 2008, 04). Working Paper.

Holling, C. S. (1973). Resilience and Stability of Ecological Systems. *Annual Review of Rcology and Systematics, 4*(1), 1–23.

Holling, C. S. (1996). Engineering Resilience Versus Ecological Resilience. In P. E. Schulze (Ed.), *Engineering Within Ecological Constraints* (pp. 31–43). Washington, DC: National Academy Press.

Jabareen, Y. (2013). Planning the Resilient City: Concepts and Strategies for Coping with Climate Change and Environmental Risk. *Cities, 31*, 220–229.

Jacobs, J. (1961). *The Death and Life of Great American Cities*. New York: Random House.

Kimhi, S. (2016). Levels of Resilience: Associations Among Individual, Community, and National Resilience. *Journal of Health Psychology, 21*(2), 164–170.

Klein, R. J., Nicholls, R. J., & Thomalla, F. (2003). Resilience to Natural Hazards: How Useful Is This Concept? *Global Environmental Change Part B: Environmental Hazards, 5*(1), 35–45.

Knoop, V. L., Snelder, M., van Zuylen, H. J., & Hoogendoorn, S. P. (2012). Link-Level Vulnerability Indicators for Real-World Networks. *Transportation Research Part A: Policy and Practice, 46*(5), 843–854.

Kobasa, S. C. (1982). The Hardy Personality: Toward a Social Psychology of Stress and Health. In G. S. Sanders & J. Suls (Eds.), *Social Psychology of Health and Illness*. Hillsdale: Erlbaum.

Kontokosta, C. E., & Malik, A. (2018). The Resilience to Emergencies and Disasters Index: Applying Big Data to Benchmark and Validate Neighborhood Resilience Capacity. *Sustainable Cities and Society, 36*, 272–285.

Lang, T. (2010). Urban Resilience and New Institutional Theory – A Happy Couple for Urban and Regional Studies. In *German Annual of Spatial Research and Policy 2010* (pp. 15–24). Berlin and Heidelberg: Springer.

Lapuh, L. (2018). Socio-Economic Characteristics of Resilient Localities – Experiences from Slovenia. *Regional Studies, Regional Science, 5*(1), 149–156.

Leichenko, R. (2011). Climate Change and Urban Resilience. *Current Opinion in Environmental Sustainability, 3*(3), 164–168.

Levin, S. A., Barrett, S., Aniyar, S., Baumol, W., Bliss, C., Bolin, B., et al. (1998). Resilience in Natural and Socioeconomic Systems. *Environment and Development Economics, 3*(2), 221–262.

Lu, P., & Stead, D. (2013). Understanding the Notion of Resilience in Spatial Planning: A Case Study of Rotterdam, the Netherlands. *Cities, 35*, 200–212.

Lynch, K. (1984). *Good City Form*. MIT Press.

MacKinnon, D., & Derickson, K. D. (2012). From Resilience to Resourcefulness: A Critique of Resilience Policy and Activism. *Progress in Human Geography, 37*(2), 253–270.

Makido, Y., Dhakal, S., & Yamagata, Y. (2012). Relationship Between Urban Form and CO2 Emissions: Evidence from Fifty Japanese Cities. *Urban Climate, 2*, 55–67.

Martin, R. (2012). Regional Economic Resilience, Hysteresis and Recessionary Shocks. *Journal of Economic Geography, 12*(1), 1–32.

Masten, A. S. (2014). Global Perspectives on Resilience in Children and Youth. *Child Development, 85*(1), 6–20.

Matyas, D., & Pelling, M. (2015). Positioning Resilience for 2015: The Role of Resistance, Incremental Adjustment and Transformation in Disaster Risk Management Policy. *Disasters, 39*(s1), s1–s18.

Meerow, S., Newell, J. P., & Stults, M. (2016). Defining Urban Resilience: A Review. *Landscape and Urban Planning, 147*, 38–49.

Norris, F. H., Stevens, S. P., Pfefferbaum, B., Wyche, K. F., & Pfefferbaum, R. L. (2008). Community Resilience as a Metaphor, Theory, Set of Capacities, and Strategy for Disaster Readiness. *American Journal of Community Psychology, 41*(1–2), 127–150.

OECD. (2014). Meeting of the OECD Council at Ministerial Level 2014. Retrieved from https://www.oecd.org/mcm/C-MIN(2014)7-ENG.pdf.

Patel, R., & Nosal, L. (2016). *Defining the Resilient City*. United Nations University Centre for Policy Research, Working Paper, 6.

Pickett, S. T., Cadenasso, M. L., & Grove, J. M. (2004). Resilient Cities: Meaning, Models, and Metaphor for Integrating the Ecological, Socio-Economic, and Planning Realms. *Landscape and Urban Planning, 69*(4), 369–384.

Pimm, S. L. (1984). The Complexity and Stability of Ecosystems. *Nature, 307*(5949), 321.

Reggiani, A., De Graaff, T., & Nijkamp, P. (2002). Resilience: An Evolutionary Approach to Spatial Economic Systems. *Networks and Spatial Economics, 2*(2), 211–229.

Reggiani, A., Nijkamp, P., & Lanzi, D. (2015). Transport Resilience and Vulnerability: The Role of Connectivity. *Transportation Research Part A: Policy and Practice, 81*, 4–15.

Rose, A. (2017). *Defining and Measuring Economic Resilience from a Societal, Environmental and Security Perspective*. Springer.

Rus, K., Kilar, V., & Koren, D. (2018). Resilience Assessment of Complex Urban Systems to Natural Disasters: A New Literature Review. *International Journal of Disaster Risk Reduction, 31*, 311–330.

Sanchez, A. X., Van der Heijden, J., & Osmond, P. (2018). The City Politics of an Urban Age: Urban Resilience Conceptualisations and Policies. *Palgrave Communications, 4*(1), 25.

Schiappacasse, P., & Müller, B. (2015). Planning Green Infrastructure as a Source of Urban and Regional Resilience – Towards Institutional Challenges. *Urbani Izziv, 26*, S13–S24.

Schirmer, P. M., & Axhausen, K. W. (2016). A Multiscale Classification of Urban Morphology. *Journal of Transport and Land Use, 9*(1), 101–130.

Sharifi, A., & Yamagata, Y. (2016). Principles and Criteria for Assessing Urban Energy Resilience: A Literature Review. *Renewable and Sustainable Energy Reviews, 60*, 1654–1677.

Simmie, J., & Martin, R. (2010). The Economic Resilience of Regions: Towards an Evolutionary Approach. *Cambridge Journal of Regions, Economy and Society, 3*(1), 27–43.

Southwick, S. M., Bonanno, G. A., Masten, A. S., Panter-Brick, C., & Yehuda, R. (2014). Resilience Definitions, Theory, and Challenges: Interdisciplinary Perspectives. *European Journal of Psychotraumatology, 5*(1), 25338.

Sterk, M., van de Leemput, I. A., & Peeters, E. T. (2017). How to Conceptualize and Operationalize Resilience in Socio-Ecological Systems? *Current Opinion in Environmental Sustainability, 28*, 108–113.

Swanstrom, T. (2008). *Regional Resilience: A Critical Examination of the Ecological Framework* (No. 2008, 07). Working Paper.

Swanstrom, T., Chapple, K., & Immergluck, D. (2009). *Regional Resilience in the Face of Foreclosures: Evidence from Six Metropolitan Areas.* (No. 2009, 05). Working Paper, University of California, Institute of Urban and Regional Development (IURD), Berkeley, CA.

Thomas, S., Keegan, C., Barry, S., Layte, R., Jowett, M., & Normand, C. (2013). A Framework for Assessing Health System Resilience in an Economic Crisis: Ireland as a Test Case. *BMC Health Services Research, 13*(1), 450.

Ultramari, C., & Rezende, D. (2007). Urban Resilience and Slow Motion Disasters. *City & Time, 2*(3), 47–64.

UN-Habitat. (2018). City Resilience Profiling Tool. Retrieved from http://urbanresiliencehub.org/wp-content/uploads/2018/02/CRPT-Guide.pdf.

Van Breda, A. D. (2018). A Critical Review of Resilience Theory and Its Relevance for Social Work. *Social Work, 54*(1), 1–18.

Vromans, M. J., Dekker, R., & Kroon, L. G. (2006). Reliability and Heterogeneity of Railway Services. *European Journal of Operational Research, 172*(2), 647–665.

Wagner, I., & Breil, P. (2013). The Role of Ecohydrology in Creating More Resilient Cities. *Ecohydrology & Hydrobiology, 13*(2), 113–134.

Walker, B., & Salt, D. (2006). *Resilience Thinking: Sustaining Ecosystems and People in a Changing World.* Washington, DC: Island Press.

Walker, B., Holling, C. S., Carpenter, S. R., & Kinzig, A. (2004). Resilience, adaptability and transformability in social–ecological systems. *Ecology and Society, 9*(2), 5.

Walsh, F. (2006). *Strengthening Family Resilience* (2nd ed.). New York: Guilford Press.

Wang, Z., Deng, X., Wong, C., Li, Z., & Chen, J. (2018). Learning Urban Resilience from a Social-Economic-Ecological System Perspective: A Case Study of Beijing from 1978 to 2015. *Journal of Cleaner Production, 183*, 343–357.

Winderl, T. (2014). Disaster Resilience Measurements: Stocktaking of Ongoing Efforts in Developing Systems for Measuring Resilience. Retrieved from https://www.preventionweb.net/files/37916_disasterresiliencemeasurementsundpt.pdf.

World Bank. (2012). *Building Urban Resilience: Principles, Tools and Practice.* Washington, DC.

Xu, Y., Ren, C., Ma, P., Ho, J., Wang, W., Lau, K. K. L., et al. (2017). Urban Morphology Detection and Computation for Urban Climate Research. *Landscape and Urban Planning, 167*, 212–224.

Yang, P. P., & Quan, S. J. (2016). Urban Form and Energy Resilient Strategies: A Case Study of the Manhattan Grid. In *Urban Resilience* (pp. 153–172). Cham: Springer.

Yu, H., Liu, Y., Liu, C., & Fan, F. (2018). Spatiotemporal Variation and Inequality in China's Economic Resilience Across Cities and Urban Agglomerations. *Sustainability, 10*(12), 4754.

Zhou, H., Wan, J., & Jia, H. (2010). Resilience to Natural Hazards: A Geographic Perspective. *Natural Hazards, 53*(1), 21–41.

2

A Balanced Development? The Novel $\sigma-\mu$ Efficiency of Italian Regions

Salvatore Greco, Menelaos Tasiou, and Gianpiero Torrisi

2.1 Introduction

The concept of Local Economic Development (LED)—as opposed to economic growth—encompasses a variety of dimensions and stages (Feldman et al. 2016; Haller 2012; Todaro and Smith 2015; Thirlwall 2006). LED is intrinsically a multidimensional concept including aspects such as education, poverty, and health whereby "locally and regionally

S. Greco
Department of Economics and Business, University of Catania, Catania, Italy

Portsmouth Business School, Centre of Operations Research and Logistics, University of Portsmouth, Portsmouth, UK
e-mail: salvatore.greco@port.ac.uk

M. Tasiou
Portsmouth Business School, Centre of Operations Research and Logistics, University of Portsmouth, Portsmouth, UK
e-mail: Menelaos.Tasiou@port.ac.uk

S. Colombo (ed.), *Spatial Economics Volume II*,
https://doi.org/10.1007/978-3-030-40094-1_2

determined development models should not be developed independently of more foundational principles and values such as democracy, equity, internationalism and justice" (Pike et al. 2007). Moreover, it has been argued that 'development' is a process that involves the standards of living of societies and necessitates a balance between social and economic dimensions of regions, aiming at both a sustainable approach to production and the improvement in the quality of life of households (Huq et al. 2009). From a slightly different perspective, Ascani et al. (2012) pointed out how considerably high levels of unemployment and poverty testify that modern processes do not function solely on quantitative increases in activity, but that greater attention should be paid to social, cultural and human development within communities. Its multidimensionality, therefore, reverberates throughout both the development policies (Hansen 1965) and the measurement exercise (Greco et al. 2018). Interesting results emerge from the MAKSWELL (MAKing Sustainable development and WELL-being) frameworks work for policy analysis (www.makswell.eu) project which is a research project funded by the European Union's Horizon 2020 Programme with the aim to extend and harmonise the indicators able to capture the main characteristics of the beyond-GDP approach and to propose a new framework that includes them in the evaluation of the public policies. Indeed, preliminary findings of the projects highlight that 19 out of the 28 EU countries have put in place a framework to measure the well-being of their citizens according to a multidimensional perspective.

The measurement of the levels of LED, therefore, unavoidably goes beyond the Gross Domestic Product (GDP) and involves a variety of qualitative and quantitative measures in order to assess the extent to which the (GDP) growth translates into overall economic and social improvement. This is perhaps even more important in consideration

---

G. Torrisi (✉)
Department of Economics and Business, University of Catania, Catania, Italy

Economics and Finance, Portsmouth Business School, University of Portsmouth, Portsmouth, UK
e-mail: giatorri@unict.it

of the 'local' perspective. Indeed, the GDP or equally the Gross Value Added (GVA) approach, are not able to capture either regions' income or regional productivity (Dunnell 2009). The mounting criticism about GDP and other one-dimensional measures of economic performance (Kuznets 1934; Kubiszewski et al. 2013; Costanza et al. 2009; Stiglitz et al. 2009) has paved the way for use of composite indices to measure the level of economic development (Greco et al. 2018). "The key aim of Social Indicators Research is to create an all-inclusive measure of quality of life in countries that is akin to Gross National Product in Economic Indicator Research" (Veenhoven 1996, p. 1). It is worth noticing that this evidence is in line with the general trend seeing composite indicators gaining astounding popularity in all areas of research (Greco et al. 2019a). For example, in Bandura (2005), over 400 official composite indices that rank or assess a country according to some economic, political, social or environmental measures are reviewed. More recently, Yang (2014) documents over 100 composite measures of human progress.

Within this general trend, the between-country perspective is coupled with within-country exercises aiming to measure the economic development at subnational levels. In accordance with this subnational perspective, in turn, emphasis is given to different aspects ranging from more precise ones such as 'competitiveness', for example, European Union (EU) Regional Competitiveness Index (RCI) (Annoni and Kozovska 2010; Dijkstra et al. 2011), to overall quality of life such as the Organisation for Economic Co-operation and Development (OECD)'s initiative 'How is life in your region?', proposing the Better Life Index (BLI) (OECD 2014). Overall, the subnational approaches share the aim to somewhat address the criticism about the neglected distributional aspects related to a single-country measure. Indeed, the substantial limits of a single value to represent the distribution of, for example, education, health and living standards, especially among vast countries (Sagar and Najam 1998; United Nations (UN) 2018), have been pointed out. Put differently, the uneven spatial distribution of the economic development within countries is deemed an aspect that can no longer be neglected. In this regard, an interesting initiative concerns the computation of the well-known Human Development Index (HDI) at subnational level (UN 2018). The Subnational Human Development Index (SHDI) aims to measure the variation in human development among geographic regions within countries in a globally comparable way. Similarly, the EU (Bubbico and Dijkstra 2011) has realised a 'regional focus' analysing the Human Development Index (HDI) and Human Poverty Index (HPI) as published in the Fifth Cohesion Report (EC 2010) at regional level based on a slight variation of the methodology developed by the United Nations Development Programme (UNDP).

An important single-country attempt to measure economic development at the local level is represented by the Italian index called *Benessere Equo e Sostenibile* (BES, equitable and sustainable well-being) proposed by the ISTAT (*Instituto Nazionale di Statistica*). The BES (ISTAT 2018) offers an overall picture of the main economic, social and environmental phenomena through the analysis of a wide set of indicators divided into 12 domains. This experience is of particular interest because since 2016 the BES is part of the official stages of economic planning. Indeed, Law no. 163/2016 stated that a selection of BES indicators should contribute to defining those economic policies which largely affect some fundamental dimensions for the quality of life. In 2018, the Italian Economic and Financial Document (*Documento di Economia e Finanza*, DEF) considered the list of 12 BES indicators.[1] Consequently, the very recent DEF 2019 includes BES indicators[2] in reporting both the trend and the programmatic forecast of the effects of Italian budgetary policy.

Undoubtedly, the inclusion of a multidimensional measure of development alongside the mainstream GDP emphasises some interesting points about the aggregation procedure (especially in terms of weighting) and its representativeness. Indeed, all the attempts to measure (local) economic development according to a multidimensional perspective share issues regarding the aggregation of the multiple aspects considered. As Greco et al. (2018, p. 591) cogently point out,

> [. . .] mainstream composite indices of regional socioeconomic performance do not allow for differences in the weighting system and are

[1]While eight out of the 12 indicators were analysed in their recent evolution, the remaining four were estimated for the following three years.

[2]See http://www.mef.gov.it/documenti-allegati/2019/def/DEF_2019_Allegato_BES_16_04_19_H_19_30.pdf. Retrieved: 22/08/2019.

> thus effectively maintaining an unwarranted mask of objectivity. They implicitly assume equal weighting, which may not be justified with respect to the preferences of different groups of individuals. The equal weighting assumption runs counter to a policy world that values local preferences, and hence runs counter to the seminal contributions founded on their importance. These relate to different preferences for sets of local public goods according to the Tiebout (1956) model and further developments in fiscal federalism building upon the work of Oates (1972).

In this regard, it is worth noticing that both the BES and the OECD BLI share the deliberate methodological choice of refusing to adopt a single weighting system, with different nuances. Indeed, the OECD proposes overcoming the weighting issue by (1) presenting a set of headline indicators[3] rather than a single composite index (OECD 2014) for 362 OECD regions and then (2) giving to the single user the possibility to set his or her own set of weights in order to get her personalised composite indicator. The BES, instead, does not allow achieving a single measure as each domain is presented separately. Arguably, both approaches, while avoiding the issue of providing a single set of weights, are potentially even more difficult to communicate to the public and decision-makers alike (Greco et al. 2018).

To the best of our knowledge, the work proposed by Greco et al. (2018) represents the first attempt to overcome the weighting issue by adopting the Stochastic Multiobjective Acceptability Analysis (SMAA) (Lahdelma et al. 1998) to the measurement of local economic development. Their work builds upon the possibility that the SMAA method allows considering the whole set of possible weights. However, the application of the SMAA method has pros and cons. On the one hand, it can make a substantial contribution to achieve a better balance in the trade-off between a composite index and a range of indicators as it allows for maximum variety in the relative evaluation of each dimension of development. On the other hand, it does not produce a single composite indicator value. Furthermore, the SMAA has been mainly (if not exclusively) used to provide ordinal information through probabilistic rankings or an

[3] Currently 11. See http://www.oecdbetterlifeindex.org/. Retrieved: 22/08/2019.

expected overall ranking. The aforementioned study of Greco et al. (2018) does not represent an exception in this respect.

Nonetheless, very recently Greco et al. (2019c) proposed the use of SMAA in an innovative way—called $\sigma-\mu$ *efficiency analysis* (hereafter $\sigma-\mu$)—in order to encapsulate a more holistic evaluation in a single value providing information about the magnitude of the performance of each alternative. The next section briefly illustrates the methodology proposing a possible application with reference to the measurement of LED. Section 2.3 will apply the methodology to the Italian regional case. Section 2.4 concludes.

2.2 The σ–μ Analysis as Applied to the Measurement of the Local Economic Development

As already noted, the consideration of multiple views in measuring the levels of LED according to a multidimensional perspective is a crucial issue, especially in order to highlight differences in the spatial distribution of benefits eventually arising from the narrower economic growth. Put differently, a multidimensional measure of LED should be able to consider not only the multiple dimensions of LED, but also the different views about the relative importance of each dimension of development. Although on the conceptual grounds the above argument is widely accepted, on the practical side a convincing methodological approach is far from being achieved. Composite indicators are the natural candidate to perform the task. Yet, the aggregation procedure(s) cannot achieve unanimity. It is worth stressing how this aspect is significant in the measurement of well-being related to different levels of development as shown by Greco et al. (2019b) by means of a 'multidimensional spatial model' using the data from the OECD BLI.

In this regard, the aforementioned $\sigma-\mu$ expressly stands "by the principle that a meaningful composite indicator should ideally reflect a multiplicity of viewpoints" (Greco et al. 2019c, p. 945), rejecting the idea of the allegedly representative agent in favour of the consideration of the variety of preferences between citizens and/or clusters of them (e.g. practitioners, experts, households). Departing from the currently available methodology, however, the $\sigma - \mu$ is able to provide also a final single measure encapsulating both the multiple dimensions and the multiple preferences in a single measure of efficiency and, therefore, in the case at hand, of development. While the reader is referred to Greco et al. (2019c), especially section 3 at pp. 945–950 on which this section draws heavily, for the technicalities of the procedure, in what follows we report the intuition behind it with particular regard to the goal of the measurement of levels of LED.

The starting point of the $\sigma - \mu$ analysis is the outcome of a SMAA exercise applied to the normalised dimension of LED considered in the analysis (e.g. health, education, work conditions). Therefore, within the SMAA setting a random sampling of q vectors of weights $w_h = [\, w_{1h}, \ldots, w_{mh} \,]$, with $h = 1, \ldots, q$, such that w_{ih} is non-negative for all i and for all h, and $w_{1h} + \ldots + w_{mh} = 1$ for all h is used to aggregate m dimensions. The q random extracted weight vectors w_h, $h = 1, \ldots, q$, constitute a representative sample of the whole set of feasible weights vector. They can be collected in the following $m \times q$ **RW** matrix:

$$\underset{m \times q}{\mathbf{RW}} = \begin{pmatrix} w_{11} & w_{12} & \cdots & w_{1q} \\ w_{21} & w_{22} & \cdots & w_{2q} \\ \vdots & \vdots & \cdots & \vdots \\ w_{m1} & w_{m2} & \cdots & w_{mq} \end{pmatrix}$$

Observe that we can assume that the feasible weight vectors w_h have to satisfy some constraints representing the importance assigned to the considered dimensions by the individuals of the considered population. For example, if the first dimension is at least as important as the second, that, in turn, is at least as important as the third and so on, the following constraints have to be satisfied:

$w_{1h} \geq w_{2h} \geq \ldots \geq w_{mh}$,
for all $h = 1, \ldots, q$.

Then, using the weight matrix **RW**, a composite indicator
$CI(\mathbf{x}_i, \mathbf{w}_h) = w_{1h}x_1 + w_{2h}x_2 + \ldots + w_{mh}x_m$
can be computed for each local economy (e.g. region) i and each weight vector w_h. Hence, the results can be ordered in the following $n \times q$ matrix **CI:**

$$\underset{n\times q}{\mathbf{CI}} = \begin{pmatrix} CI\left(\mathbf{x}_1, \mathbf{w}_1\right) & CI\left(\mathbf{x}_1, \mathbf{w}_1\right) & \cdots & CI\left(\mathbf{x}_1, \mathbf{w}_q\right) \\ CI\left(\mathbf{x}_2, \mathbf{w}_1\right) & CI\left(\mathbf{x}_2, \mathbf{w}_2\right) & \cdots & CI\left(\mathbf{x}_2, \mathbf{w}_q\right) \\ \vdots & \vdots & \cdots & \vdots \\ CI\left(\mathbf{x}_n, \mathbf{w}_1\right) & CI\left(\mathbf{x}_n, \mathbf{w}_2\right) & \cdots & CI\left(\mathbf{x}_n, \mathbf{w}_q\right) \end{pmatrix}$$

The following step consists in using the values collected in **CI**, for each economy i to compute the approximated values $\tilde{\mu}_i$ and $\tilde{\sigma}_i$ for the mean μ_i and the standard deviation σ_i of the composite indicator $CI(x_i, w)$ in the whole set of feasible weight vectors:

$$\tilde{\mu}_i = \frac{1}{q}\sum_{h=1}^{q} CI\left(\mathbf{x}_i, \mathbf{w}_h\right), \tilde{\sigma}_i = \sqrt{\frac{1}{q}\sum_{h=1}^{q}\left(CI\left(\mathbf{x}_i, \mathbf{w}_h\right) - \tilde{\mu}_i\right)^2}.$$

These two—μ and σ—are the parameters of interest where μ_i is intended to be maximised, because it represents the average evaluation of the level of economic development of a local economy taking into account the variability of the weight vectors **w**. Instead, σ_i has to be minimised, as it exhibits the instability in the overall evaluations of the LED achieved with respect to the variability of weights.[4] The economic rationale for this stems from the literature about inequality. Indeed, σ is the multidimensional projection of the inequality in the GDP economics discussion (Piketty 2014). Moreover, once interpreted within a neo-Benthamite beyond GDP perspective, σ is just a common measure of

[4]For a detailed discussion on this point including the economic rationale the reader is referred to Greco et al. (2019c, p. 946).

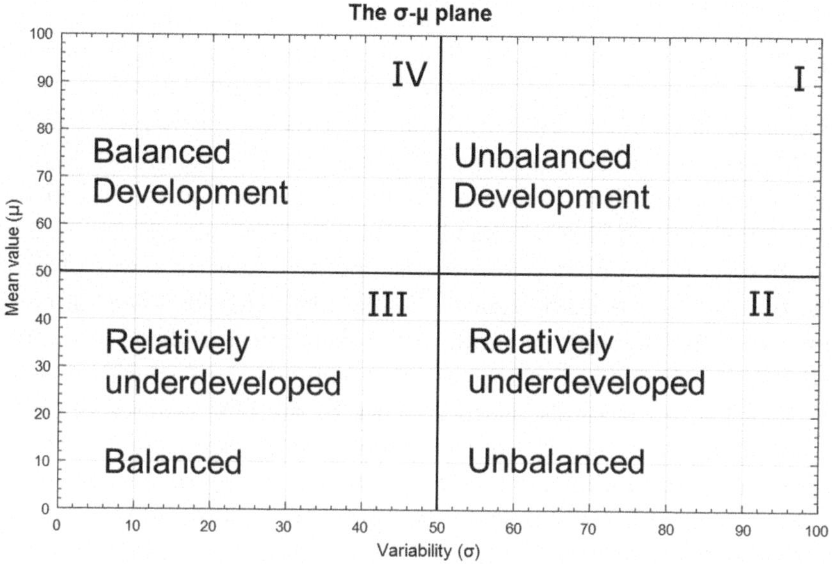

Fig. 2.1 The σ–μ plane of local economic development. (Source: adapted from Greco et al. (2019c))

inequality and, as such, has to be minimised (Atkinson 1970, 2015). The point can be further illustrated with the help of the following so-called $\sigma-\mu$ plane reported in Fig. 2.1 below.

In the above figure, quadrants I–IV refer to cases of economic development differing for both the overall performance (as measured by μ, reported on the y-axis) and the dispersion between the individual evaluations according to different sets of weights (as measured by σ, reported on the x-axis). Indeed, cases belonging to the first quadrant show relatively high levels of overall performance (i.e. above the threshold put at 50 for the sake of illustration); however, those relatively high levels of development are coupled with a relatively high degree of variability in the evaluations, due to different preferences about the importance of the considered aspects of development considered. This might be the case of unbalanced development where the policy focuses on a few dimensions while missing an overall harmonious development path. For example, Hansen (1965) pointed out as those persons who benefited most by Social

Overhead Capital may be unsatisfied and eventually migrate to other regions in the absence or in case of unsatisfactory levels of supplementary policy measures. Such a high variation might reflect just the preferences of those unsatisfied by the strong imbalance between implemented policies.

Quite symmetrically, cases reported in the second quadrant while sharing the above unbalance between different individuals in the considered population, are not able to overall perform as good as cases reported in the above I quadrant. It is worth recalling here how, in terms of local development, it has been argued that the unbalance between different dimensions is (not only an undesirable situation but also) a situation making the given local economy more vulnerable to shocks. Martin (2011, p. 14), for example, with reference to the UK, pointed out how an unbalanced development of the economy and, "especially the relative dependence on production industry, is generally regarded as having a major influence on the sensitivity of regional economies to recessionary shock".

The following quadrant (III) includes cases of balanced relative underdevelopment. Put differently, this quadrant refers to cases of relatively low levels of overall development coupled with a relative balance between the evaluations of different individuals in the considered population. Finally, the IV quadrant refers to the desirable balance between different components of economic development able to provide relatively high levels of overall performance. These cases, therefore, represent combinations of balanced development whereby the trade-off between the multiple components of economic development achieves a balance able to satisfy a variety of viewpoints potentially belonging to different stakeholders.

Undeniably, the comparative static reported in Fig. 2.1 can potentially be extended to include the dynamic case. That is to say, building upon Barro and Sala-i Martin's (1992) seminal contribution in terms of convergence in terms of GDP, a given set of local economies could be evaluated at regular intervals to check whether a more balanced multidimensional performance is occurring over time.

In both, static and dynamic cases, the σ–μ framework allows defining both a concept of Pareto–Koopmans dominance between local economies based on the uneven spatial LED and a set of local and global efficiency scores. Those scores, once applied to the case at hand, can be easily interpreted as a holistic score of LED.

As for the former, the σ–μ Pareto–Koopmans dominance relation on the set of economies to compare can be defined as follows: a unit $i \in I$ (the set of all units, local economies in case at hand) is σ–μ Pareto–Koopmans efficient if there is no convex combination of $\mu_{i'}$ and $\sigma_{i'}$ of the remaining units, $i' \neq i$, with a mean value μ that is not smaller, and a standard deviation σ that is not greater, with at least one of these inequalities being strict. It is worth noticing here that the above is just an extension of the Pareto-efficiency whereby for all i, $i' \in I$, unit i is Pareto dominating unit i' if $\mu_i \geq \mu_{i'}$ and $\sigma_i \leq \sigma_{i'}$, with at least one of the two inequalities being strict (and where a unit $i \in I$ is σ–μ Pareto-efficient if there is no other unit dominating it). The proposed extensive application allows for the possibility to combine different units. Then, the set of all Pareto efficient units constitutes the Pareto frontier and, similarly, the set of all σ–μ Pareto–Koopmans efficient units constitutes the σ–μ Pareto–Koopmans frontier.

Removing the first PKF from the set of units to be evaluated and computing again the PKF efficiency frontier for the remaining units results in the second σ–μ PKF (PKF_2), and so on until all PKFs have been computed. The recursive calculation of Pareto–Koopmans Frontiers (PKF) can be used to provide a more plausible benchmark for spatial units. Indeed, it might be argued that it makes little sense to compare a single spatial unit remote from the frontier to units belonging to the (first) frontier, as they could be potentially implausible benchmarks. Rather, comparing units that are closer in the σ–μ plane constitute a more realistic exercise. This can be the case, for example, of regions belonging to different areas in countries characterised by a significant spatial divide such as the UK or Italy. Consequently, our methodology allows for the comparison of units closer in terms of their development, even regardless of their spatial proximity. In any case, the efficiency is related to the considered frontiers, so that we pass from one absolute to a relative concept of efficiency.

Moreover, taking into account the whole set of PKF(s), in turn, allows for both a 'local' and an 'overall' measure of efficiency. As for the former, it can be defined as follows:

$$\delta_i^* = \text{Max}\,\delta$$
$$s.t.$$
$$\begin{cases} \alpha\mu_i - \beta\sigma_i \geqslant \sigma\mu_{i'} - \beta\sigma_{i'} + \delta, \forall i' \neq i \\ \alpha, \beta \geqslant 0 \\ \alpha + \beta = 1 \end{cases}$$

To determine δ_i^* requires the solution of the above Linear Programming (LP) problem. In words, the LP problem verifies that once an evaluation $\alpha\mu_{i'}-\beta\sigma_{i'}$, with α, $\beta \geq 0$ and $\alpha + \beta = 1$,[5] is assigned to all units $i' \in I$, a pair (α, β) exists, for which unit $i \in I$ receives an evaluation—in our case in terms of multidimensional measure of economic development—that is not worse than the remaining local economies, $i' \neq i$, that is, $\alpha\mu_i-\beta\sigma_i \geq \alpha\mu_{i'}-\beta\sigma_{i'}+\delta$.

Once applied to the measurement of LED, δ_i^* can be interpreted as a measure of overall economic development of the local economy *i*. More in detail, while for the units belonging to the $\sigma-\mu$ PKF, it represents the margin that can be *subtracted* from the overall evaluation $\alpha\mu_i-\beta\sigma_i$ of the local economy *i* maintaining the maximality of its evaluation with respect to all other units $i' \neq i$, for all local economies $i \in I$ that *do not belong to* the $\sigma-\mu$ PKF. Consequently, the greater the absolute value of δ_i^*, the greater the margin that has to be *added* to $\alpha\mu_i-\beta\sigma_i$, in order to attain the evaluation $\alpha\mu_{i'}-\beta\sigma_{i'}$ of at least one unit belonging to the $\sigma-\mu$ PKF.

[5]It is worth noticing how the non-negative coefficient α for the mean $\mu_{i'}$ and the non-positive coefficient $-\beta$ for the standard deviation $\sigma_{i'}$ are coherent with the idea that $\mu_{i'}$ is intended to be maximised and $\sigma_{i'}$ is intended to be minimised. Therefore, the greater $\alpha\mu_{i'}-\beta\sigma_{i'}$, the better the unit i′ performs with respect to $\mu_{i'}$ and $\sigma_{i'}$.

As for the local multidimensional measure of economic development (δ_{ik},), for each PKF$_k$ and for each unit i it can be defined as follows:

$$\delta_{ik} = \text{Max } \delta$$
$$s.t.$$
$$\begin{cases} \alpha\mu_i - \beta\sigma_i \geqslant \sigma\mu_{i'} - \beta\sigma_{i'} + \delta, \forall i' \in I \backslash \bigcup_{h=1}^{k-1} \text{PKF}_h \\ \alpha, \beta \geqslant 0 \\ \alpha + \beta = 1 \end{cases}$$

Hence, similar to the 'overall' case, the above Linear Programming (LP) problem checks whether there exists a pair (α, β), for which economy $i \in I$ receives an evaluation ($\alpha\mu_i - \beta\sigma_i$)—that is, once more, in the case at hand, a level of multidimensional local development—which is not worse than the analogous level of development of the rest of the units belonging to the k-th σ–μ Pareto–Koopmans efficiency frontier, or to a better σ–μ Pareto–Koopmans efficiency frontier. This happens if $\delta_{ik} \geq 0$. Instead, if $\delta_{ik} < 0$, then unit i belongs to a σ–μ PKF worse than PKF$_k$—that is, it belongs to a set of units characterised by a significant lower level of development. Put differently, similar to the global case, for the units in the k-th σ–μ PKF frontier or better, $\delta_{ik} \geq 0$ represents the margin that can be subtracted from the overall evaluation $\alpha\mu_i - \beta\sigma_i$ of the local economy i maintaining an evaluation that is superior to all economies in the k-th σ–μ PKF or worse.

Finally, in order to explicitly take into account the multiplicity of PKFs a 'global' development score, denoted by sm_i, reflecting the level of development of each local economy with respect to all frontiers can be defined as follows:

$$sm_i = \sum_{k=1}^{p} \delta_{ik}.$$

Hence, sm_i represents a more holistic measure of local development extending the classic concept of context-dependent DEA (Seiford and

Zhu 2003). The next section will apply this methodological framework to the multidimensional measurement of the development of Italian regions.

2.3 An Application to Italian Regions

This section shows how the σ–μ analysis can be applied to the measurement of levels of economic development of Italian regions. The Italian setting characterised by a marked and persistent North–South divide represents an interesting showcase for the measurement of the spatial divide according to a multidimensional perspective as proposed by the novel methodology at hand. Indeed, the analysis allows unveiling how the spatial divide in terms of GDP translates into an uneven economic development considering both the multidimensional nature of the spatial disparities and the multiplicity of preferences (or standpoints) from which those disparities can be considered. While the multidimensional approach to the spatial divide is in line with the extant literature (see, between others, Cannari et al. 2009; Torrisi et al. 2015; Stanickova and Melecký 2018), the consideration of a multiplicity of weights represents only a very recent contribution (Greco et al. 2018). Moreover, to the best of our knowledge, this is the first attempt to consider the multiplicity of weights at the same time as achieving a single global measure of regional economic development.

In order to apply the σ–μ analysis to the measurement of the level of development of Italian regions we consider the full set of variables collected along with the 12 main categories[6] (or, in ISTAT's terms, *domini*) and made available by the ISTAT within the BES initiative. It is worth noticing here that the BES initiative represents, to date, the most comprehensive attempt to measure well-being according to a multidimensional approach across the EU member states. Indeed, the 130 BES indicators represent the maximum number of indicators considered

[6]The categories are: health, education, working conditions, economic well- being, social relationships, quality of government and institutions, safety, individual wellbeing, heritage, environment, R&D, quality of public services (own translation). Available at https://www.istat.it/it/archivio/224669. Retrieved: 29/08/2019.

by national initiatives (with the seven Hungarian indicators representing the minimum number of dimensions considered).[7]

Table 2.1 reports the results of the analysis performed according to the methodology illustrated in Sect. 2.3 for each of the 20 Italian regions (with separate calculation also for the autonomous provinces of Trento and Bolzano). More in detail, the second column of Table 2.1 reports the overall performance (μ) achieved across different weights assigned to the considered 130 BES dimensions. The third column reports the dispersion (σ) across the different evaluation depending on the relative importance assigned to each dimension (i.e. weights assigned). The fourth column reports the single measure of (efficiency in terms of) economic development (*sm*). Columns from 5th to 12th report the relative performance of each region according to a set of eight different PKFs (δ_{ik}).

The figures concerning μ, σ, and *sm* are mapped in Figs. 2.2, 2.3, and 2.4, respectively.

The results concerning the overall performance according to the different weights (μ) substantially confirm the well-known North–South divide characterising the Italian case. Moreover, in line with Greco et al. (2018), the empirical evidence obtained according to the multidimensional perspective shows that the spatial divide in Italy is much wider than the one measured in terms of GDP. Put differently, the sharp spatial divide between northern and southern regions goes well beyond the strict (GDP) growth sphere to pervade all aspects of development, creating a generalised picture of relative underdevelopment. The widespread underdevelopment, in turn, unavoidably affects the whole development path contributing to the persistence of the spatial divide (Fujita 2007). This evidence is confirmed by the global measure of development reported, for the sake of completeness, in Fig. 2.4.

Moreover, by disentangling the spatial divide into the overall performance and the disparities arising from different preferences about the multiple dimensions of development, one can have insights about the depth of the divide both within and between regions. Generally

[7] See https://www.istat.it/it/files//2018/12/BES2018-intro.pdf and https://www.makswell.eu/attached_documents/output_deliverables/deliverable_1.1_draft.pdf. Retrieved: 29/08/2019.

Table 2.1 Results of the σ–μ analysis of regional economic development of Italian regions

Region	μ^a	σ^a	sm^b	δ_i							
				(1)	(2)	(3)	(4)	(5)	(6)	(7)	(8)
Piemonte	0.16	−1.17	0.3894	−0.0012	0.0001	0.0015	0.0058	0.0274	0.0785	0.1293	0.1492
Valle d'Aosta	0.62	1.04	0.5035	−0.0107	−0.0102	0.0018	0.0156	0.0640	0.1151	0.1659	0.1858
Liguria	−0.03	−1.54	0.3440	0.0018	0.0018	0.0030	0.0067	0.0124	0.0630	0.1138	0.1336
Lombardia	0.6	0.39	0.5012	−0.0075	−0.0070	0.0017	0.0138	0.0622	0.1133	0.1641	0.1840
Trentino-AA	1.79	−0.42	1.0000	0.0048	0.0104	0.0935	0.1091	0.1575	0.2086	0.2594	0.2793
Bolzano	1.79	1.17	0.9967	0.0001	0.0105	0.0936	0.1092	0.1576	0.2087	0.2595	0.2794
Trento	1.66	−0.21	0.9875	−0.0014	0.0641	0.0831	0.0986	0.1471	0.1982	0.2490	0.2689
Veneto	0.42	−0.44	0.4499	−0.0040	−0.0031	0.0006	0.0035	0.0478	0.0990	0.1498	0.1696
Friuli-VG	0.86	−0.92	0.6149	−0.0004	0.0010	0.0190	0.0345	0.0830	0.1341	0.1849	0.2048
Emilia-R	0.43	0.3	0.4805	−0.0076	−0.0068	−0.0028	0.0484	0.0484	0.0996	0.1504	0.1702
Toscana	0.31	−0.7	0.4223	−0.0031	−0.0021	0.0004	0.0043	0.0389	0.0900	0.1408	0.1607
Umbria	0.15	−0.87	0.3801	−0.0028	−0.0015	0.0004	0.0043	0.0260	0.0772	0.1280	0.1478
Marche	0.07	−1.19	0.3638	−0.0014	0.0001	0.0015	0.0055	0.0199	0.0710	0.1218	0.1417
Lazio	−0.18	0.91	0.2873	−0.0124	−0.0107	−0.0094	−0.0057	0.0316	0.0511	0.1019	0.1218
Abruzzo	−0.56	−1.12	0.2228	−0.0021	−0.0003	0.0013	0.0023	0.0065	0.0206	0.0714	0.0913
Molise	−0.69	−0.76	0.1898	−0.0040	−0.0022	−0.0018	0.0036	0.0044	0.0099	0.0607	0.0806
Campania	−1.56	1.31	0.0238	−0.0145	−0.0127	−0.0123	−0.0105	−0.0077	−0.0040	0.0026	0.0113
Puglia	−1.27	−0.21	0.0932	−0.0068	−0.0050	−0.0046	−0.0028	0.0021	0.0038	0.0145	0.0343
Basilicata	−0.82	0.53	0.1768	−0.0105	−0.0087	−0.0084	−0.0066	−0.0023	0.0508	0.0508	0.0707
Calabria	−1.45	1.97	0.0191	−0.0178	−0.0160	−0.0157	−0.0139	−0.0111	−0.0073	0.0086	0.0199
Sicily	−1.7	1.72	0.0000	−0.0166	−0.0148	−0.0144	−0.0126	−0.0098	−0.0060	−0.0021	0.0000
Sardegna	−0.57	0.21	0.1928	−0.0089	−0.0071	−0.0066	−0.0041	0.0014	0.0196	0.0703	0.0902
North[c]	0.81	−0.25	1	0.0499	0.1703	–	–	–	–	–	–
Centre[c]	0.23	−0.81	0.5662	0.0017	0.1203	–	–	–	–	–	–
South[c]	−1.15	1.16	0	−0.0061	0	–	–	–	–	–	–

Source: Authors' elaboration on data from BES (ISTAT 2018)
[a]values are expressed as z-scores
[b]values are normalised in the [0, 1] interval
[c]Macro-areas composition reported in Appendix

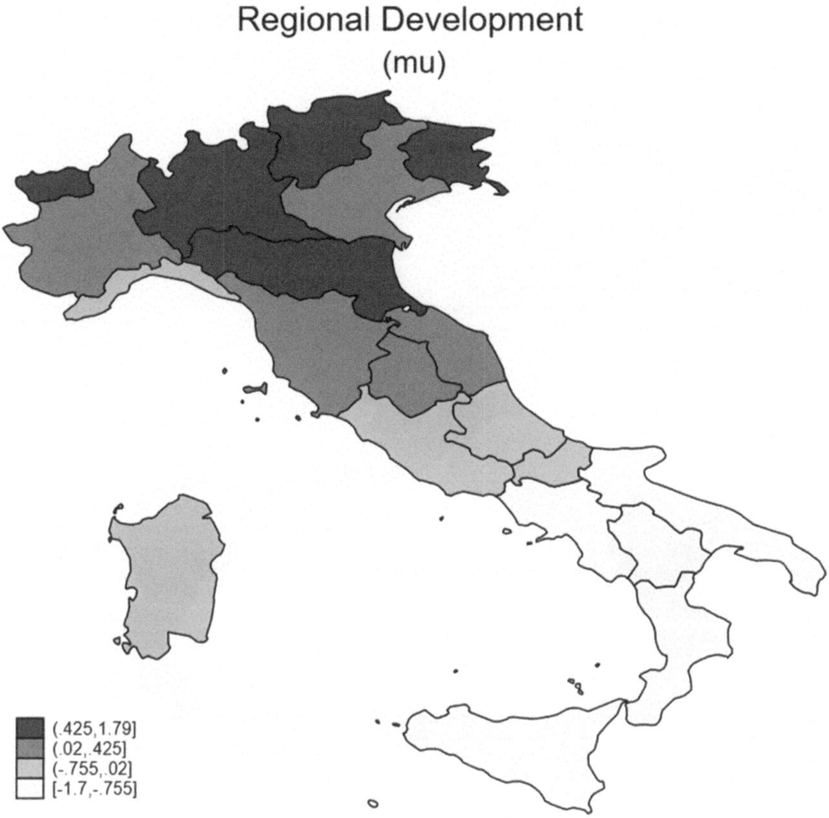

Fig. 2.2 Regional development (μ). (Source: Authors' elaboration on data from BES (ISTAT 2018))

speaking, Fig. 2.3 shows that the southern part of Italy is characterised by higher levels of σ. This evidence read through the lenses of the scheme introduced in Fig. 2.1 shows that the south is characterised by 'unbalanced relative underdevelopment (II quadrant)'. In other words, the southern part of Italy shows a low performance under both the μ and the σ measures considered here. Therefore, the level of development from which the southern citizens are benefiting is both (1) substantially lower than that of the northern counterpart and (2) unevenly distributed across its dimensions. It is worth stressing that this evidence is able to generate

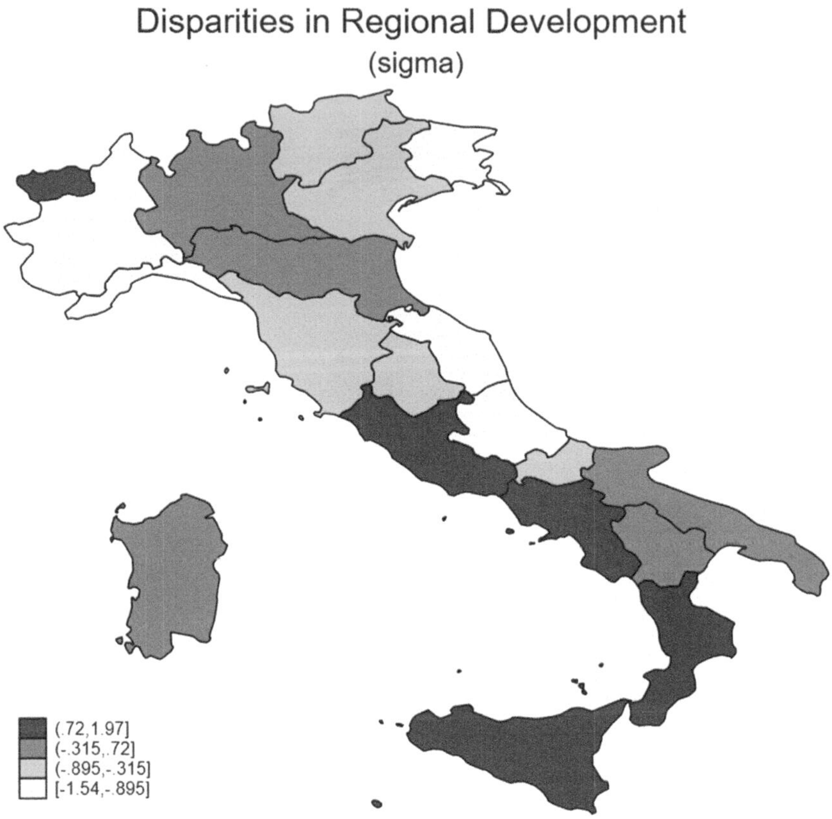

Fig. 2.3 Disparities in regional development (σ). (Source: Authors' elaboration on data from BES (ISTAT 2018))

differences in individual well-being that are much wider than those that can be detected by making reference to the allegedly representative agent using an equal weights framework to aggregate the multiple dimensions of (regional) economic development.

By continuing to make use of the scheme proposed in Fig. 2.1, a more granular picture does emerge in Fig. 2.5.

Indeed, by plotting the Italian regions in the σ–μ plane, it can be shown that Trentino-Alto Adige (with Bolzano, but excluding Trento) and Liguria belong to the first (highest) PKF. The above two regions

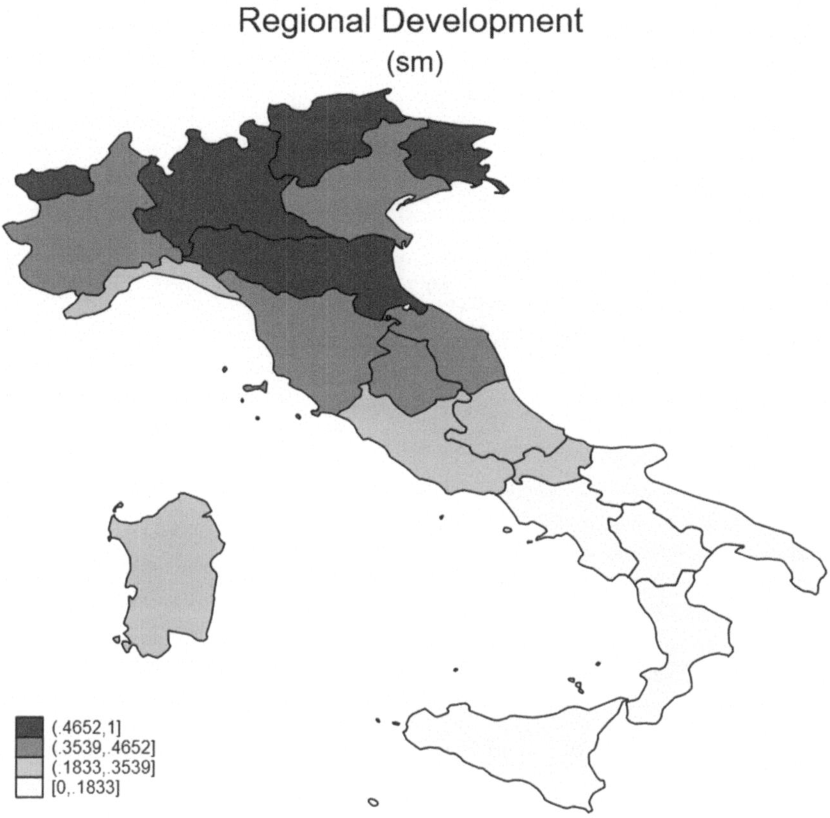

Fig. 2.4 Regional development (*sm*). (Source: Authors' elaboration on data from BES (ISTAT 2018))

(even if Liguria is a borderline case) along with Piemonte, Friuli, Marche, Toscana, Veneto and Umbria are the only eight regions out of the 20 Italian regions showing relatively high levels of development coupled with relatively low levels of dispersion across dimensions (i.e. 'balanced development', quadrant IV in Fig. 2.1), though spreading across four different PKFs. Quite interestingly, Lombardia —the Italian region with the highest level of GDP (about 381.000 million EUR in 2017[8]) belongs

[8]Eurostat, regional gross domestic product by NUTS 2 regions, retrieved: 01/09/2019.

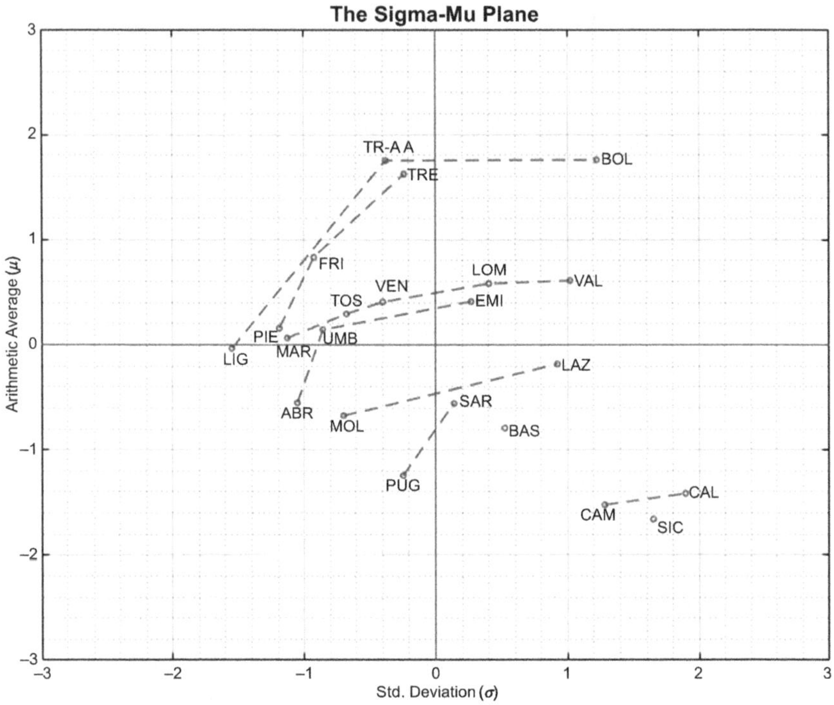

Fig. 2.5 The σ–μ plane of Italian regions. (Source: Authors' elaboration on data from BES (ISTAT 2018))

neither to the first PKF nor to the group of regions with balanced development. Indeed, Lombardia with Emilia Romagna and Valle d'Aosta are characterised by 'unbalanced development'. Similarly, the same province of Bolzano, even belonging to the PK1 is characterised by the same 'unbalanced development'. To what extent this evidence is linked with the (debated) trade-off between *growth and basic needs* (Hicks 1979) is difficult to ascertain and goes well beyond the scope of the current work. Nonetheless, the σ–μ approach seems to be an interesting methodological starting point for further research also in this regard.

None of the southern regions belong to either the I or the IV quadrants as a further confirmation of the aforementioned sharp spatial divide. Within the same pattern of relative development, however, different nuances can be detected. While Abruzzo, Molise and Puglia represent

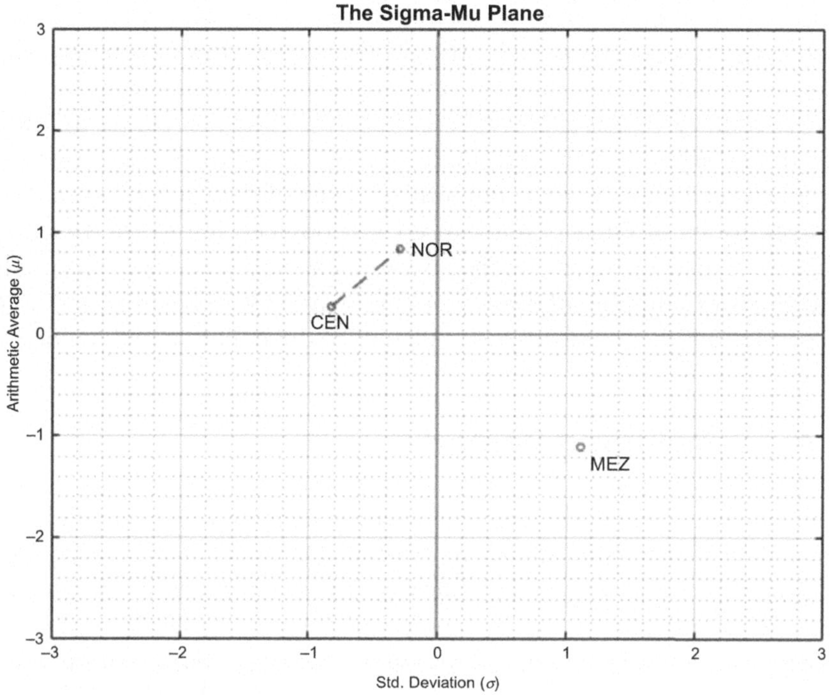

Fig. 2.6 σ–μ plane of macro-areas. (Source: Authors' elaboration on data from BES (ISTAT 2018))

cases of 'balanced relative underdevelopment', Sardegna, Basilicata, Campania, Calabria, and Sicily suffer from both relative underdevelopment and an imbalance between the different dimensions considered (i.e. 'unbalanced underdevelopment'). The same status characterises the central Lazio.

To further explore the Italian spatial divide, according to the proposed methodology, a tripartite perspective has been adopted considering the North, Centre and South macro-areas.[9] Such a choice by collapsing the 20 regions into three macro-areas allows for a sharper picture of the spatial development across Italy. Figure 2.6 graphically reports the results of the analysis for macro-areas.

[9]For macro-areas composition the reader is addresses to Appendix.

Figure 2.6 shows that in the tripartite scheme of Italian regional development (Bagnasco 1984), the divide between the Centre and the North is much smaller than the one separating the South from the rest of the country (Putnam 1993; Vecchi 2011). While the Centre and the North can be both grouped within the same PKF and can be characterised by a balanced development, the southern part of the country, overall, is sharply distant in a state of unbalanced development. It is worth stressing, once more, despite based on single two-dimensional space, that this result encompasses a number of dimensions, as high as 130. Therefore, it is able to provide a rather comprehensive picture of the Italian spatial divide.

2.4 Concluding Remarks

This work addressed the issue of measurement of LED according to a novel approach using the σ–μ method. Departing from the current common practice, the main tenets of the σ–μ method consists in considering the plurality of preferences in terms of dimensions of LED jointly with a single measure of overall performance. Furthermore, such an approach allowed separating of cases of balanced and unbalanced (under-)development. The analysis shows a more nuanced view of LED at the regional level. By disentangling the overall performance from the balance between the considered components the analysis does show potential for an important contribution in the field of spatial analysis at least to the extent that it allows unveiling complex patterns of uneven socio-economic performance. For instance, both Puglia and Sardegna sharing the same (higher) frontier, register a better performance than geographically confining regions such as Basilicata, Calabria, Campania, and the other big island Sicily, respectively. Besides, moving from the consideration that such a pattern is not fully confirmed in terms of GDP, the current σ–μ analysis seems to be able to methodologically contribute to the analysis concerning the existence of trade-offs and synergies between GDP and overall socio-economic performance.

Finally, a macro-areas analysis depicted a sharp spatial divide where the southern part of the country is significantly distant from the remaining part of the country according to a rather comprehensive point of view.

Therefore, by considering three separate macro-areas (North, Centre and South), the analysis shows that the divide is moving from the tripartite North–Centre–South division to a bipartite Centre/North–South one, even considering a much broader set of socio-economic indicators. Hence, it shows that the divide is much deeper and generalised than the extent to which it is captured by spatial differences in GDP only.

A.1 Appendix

North	
Piemonte	PIE
Valle d'Aosta	VAL
Liguria	LIG
Lombardia	LOM
Trentino Alto-Adige	TR-AA
Provincia Autonoma Bolzano	BOL
Provincia Autonoma Trento	TRE
Veneto	VEN
Friuli-Venezia Giulia	FRI
Emilia-Romagna	EMI
Centre	
Toscana	TOS
Umbria	UMB
Marche	MAR
Lazio	LAZ
South	
Abruzzi	ABR
Molise	MOL
Campania	CAM
Puglia	PUG
Basilicata	BAS
Calabria	CAL
Sicily[a]	SIC
Sardegna[a]	SAR

[a]Islands

References

Annoni, P., & Kozovska, K. (2010). *EU Regional Competitiveness Index 2010*. European Commission, Joint Research Centre.

Ascani, A., Crescenzi, R., & Iammarino, S. (2012). Regional Economic Development: A Review. WP1.

Atkinson, A. B. (1970). On the Measurement of Inequality. *Journal of Economic Theory, 2*(3), 244–263.

Atkinson, A. (2015). *Inequality*. Harvard University Press.

Bagnasco, A. (Ed.). (1984). *Tre Italie. La problematica territoriale dello sviluppo italiano*. Bologna: Il Mulino.

Bandura, R. (2005). *Measuring Country Performance and State Behavior: A Survey of Composite Indices*. New York: Office of Development Studies, United Nations Development Programme (UNDP).

Barro, R. J., & Sala-i-Martin, X. (1992). Convergence. *Journal of Political Economy, 100*(2), 223–251.

Bubbico, R. L., & Dijkstra, L. (2011). The European Regional Human Development and Human Poverty Indices. *Regional Focus, 2*, 1–10.

Cannari, L., Magnani, M., & Pellegrini, G. (2009). *Quali politiche per il Sud? Il ruolo delle politiche nazionali e regionali nell'ultimo decennio*. Banca d'Italia.

Costanza, R., Hart, M., Talberth, J., & Posner, S. (2009). *Beyond GDP: The Need for New Measures of Progress*. The Pardee Papers.

Dijkstra, L., Annoni, P., & Kozovska, K. (2011). *A New Regional Competitiveness Index: Theory, Methods and Findings*. European Commission. Directorate-General for Regional Policy.

Dunnell, K. (2009). National Statistician's Article: Measuring Regional Economic Performance. *Economic & Labour Market Review, 3*(1), 18–30.

European Commission, 2010, Fifth report on economic, social and territorial cohesion. http://ec.europa.eu/regional_policy/sources/docoffic/offic

Feldman, M., Hadjimichael, T., Lanahan, L., & Kemeny, T. (2016). The Logic of Economic Development: A Definition and Model for Investment. *Environment and Planning C: Government and Policy, 34*(1), 5–21.

Fujita, N. (2007). Myrdal's Theory of Cumulative Causation. *Evolutionary and Institutional Economics Review, 3*(2), 275–284.

Greco, S., Ishizaka, A., Matarazzo, B., & Torrisi, G. (2018). Stochastic Multi-Attribute Acceptability Analysis (SMAA): An Application to the Ranking of Italian Regions. *Regional Studies, 52*(4), 585–600.

Greco, S., Ishizaka, A., Tasiou, M., & Torrisi, G. (2019a). On the Methodological Framework of Composite Indices: A Review of the Issues of Weighting, Aggregation, and Robustness. *Social Indicators Research, 141*(1), 61–94.
Greco, S., Ishizaka, A., Resce, G., & Torrisi, G. (2019b). Measuring Well-Being by a Multidimensional Spatial Model in OECD Better Life Index Framework. *Socio-Economic Planning Sciences, 70*, 1–10.
Greco, S., Ishizaka, A., Tasiou, M. and Torrisi, G. (2019c). Sigma-Mu efficiency analysis: A methodology for evaluating units through composite indicators. *European Journal of Operational Research, 278*(3), 942–960.
Haller, A. P. (2012). Concepts of Economic Growth and Development Challenges of Crisis and of Knowledge. *Economy Transdisciplinarity Cognition, 15*(1), 66.
Hansen, N. M. (1965). Unbalanced growth and regional development. *Economic inquiry, 4*(1), 3.
Hicks, N. L. (1979). Growth vs Basic Needs: Is There a Trade-Off? *World Development, 7*(11–12), 985–994.
Huq, M. M., Clunies-Ross, A., & Forsyth, D. (2009). *Development Economics*. London: McGraw Hill.
Istituto Nazionale di Statistica (ISTAT). (2018). *BES 2018: The Equitable and Sustainable Well-Being*. Rome: ISTAT.
Kubiszewski, I., Costanza, R., Franco, C., Lawn, P., Talberth, J., Jackson, T., & Aylmer, C. (2013). Beyond GDP: Measuring and Achieving Global Genuine Progress. *Ecological Economics, 93*, 57–68.
Kuznets, S. (1934). National Income, 1929–1932. In *National Income, 1929–1932* (pp. 1–12). NBER.
Lahdelma, R., Hokkanen, J., & Salminen, P. (1998). SMAA-Stochastic Multiobjective Acceptability Analysis. *European Journal of Operational Research, 106*(1), 137–143.
Martin, R. (2011). Regional Economic Resilience, Hysteresis and Recessionary Shocks. *Journal of Economic Geography, 12*(1), 1–32.
Oates, W. E. (1972). Fiscal federalism. Books.
OECD Publishing. (2014). *How's Life in Your Region?: Measuring Regional and Local Well-Being for Policy Making*. OECD Publishing.
Pike, A., Rodríguez-Pose, A., & Tomaney, J. (2007). What Kind of Local and Regional Development and for Whom? *Regional Studies, 41*(9), 1253–1269.
Piketty, T. (2014). *Capital in the Twenty-First Century*. Cambridge, MA: Harvard University Press.

Putnam, R. D. 1993. *Making Democracy Work: Civic Traditions in Modern Italy*, Princeton 1993 (trad. it. La tradizione civica nelle regioni italiane, Milano.
Sagar, A. D., & Najam, A. (1998). The Human Development Index: A Critical Review. *Ecological Economics, 25*(3), 249–264.
Seiford, L. M., & Zhu, J. (2003). Context-dependent data envelopment analysis—measuring attractiveness and progress. *Omega, 31*(5), 397–408.
Stanickova, M., & Melecký, L. (2018). Understanding of Resilience in the Context of Regional Development Using Composite Index Approach: The Case of European Union NUTS-2 Regions. *Regional Studies, Regional Science, 5*(1), 231–254.
Stiglitz, J., Sen, A. K., & Fitoussi, J. P. (2009). *The Measurement of Economic Performance and Social Progress Revisited: Reflections and Overview*. OFCE Working Paper. New York, NY: Columbia University.
Thirlwall, A. P. (2006). *Growth and Development* (8th ed.). Basingstoke: Palgrave Macmillan.
Tiebout, C. M. (1956). A pure theory of local expenditures. *Journal of political economy, 64*(5), 416–424.
Todaro, M. P., & Smith, S. C. (2015). *Economic Development* (12th ed.). New York: Pearson.
Torrisi, G., Pike, A., Tomaney, J., & Tselios, V. (2015). (Re-) Exploring the Link Between Decentralization and Regional Disparities in Italy. *Regional Studies, Regional Science, 2*(1), 123–140.
United Nations. (2018). *The Subnational Human Development Index: Moving Beyond Country-Level Averages*. Retrieved August 21, 2019, from http://hdr.undp.org/en/content/subnational-human-development-index-moving-beyond-country-level-averages.
Vecchi, G. (2011). *In ricchezza e in povertà: il benessere degli italiani dall'unità a oggi*. Bologna: Il Mulino.
Veenhoven, R. (1996). Happy Life-Expectancy. *Social Indicators Research, 39*(1), 1–58.
Yang, L. (2014). *An Inventory of Composite Measures of Human Progress*. Occasional Paper on Methodology.

Part II

Growth

3

Modelling and Forecasting Regional Growth: The MASST Model

Roberta Capello and Andrea Caragliu

3.1 Introduction

The need for anticipatory and far-seeing strategies on economic dynamics has always induced economists to look for reliable methodologies with which to produce insights on what the future will look like. With this aim, several regional forecasting growth models have been created. Among these models, the MAcroeconomic, Sectoral, Social, Territorial (MASST) model is among the longest-standing in present-day regional economics.

The MASST model was conceived with the aim to fill a gap in the existing literature on forecasting regional growth models. In fact, the landscape of available toolboxes was made up of two classes of models. On the one hand, some forecasting regional growth models were based on a distributional logic whereby national growth rates simulated or forecasted in macro models were reassigned to regions constituting the countries modelled using regional GDP and employment shares as weights. In

R. Capello · A. Caragliu (✉)
ABC Department, Politecnico di Milano, Milan, Italy
e-mail: roberta.capello@polimi.it; andrea.caragliu@polimi.it

S. Colombo (ed.), *Spatial Economics Volume II*,
https://doi.org/10.1007/978-3-030-40094-1_3

more sophisticated versions, this redistribution could take place by means of input-output linkages. On the other hand, other forecasting regional growth models focused on the purely regional component, relatively ignoring the important consequences that macro shocks could exert on regional growth rates.

MASST was conceived as a way to overcome this dichotomy and interpret regional growth as both a top-down and bottom-up process. This implied, from a theoretical perspective, a marriage between two opposing views on regional growth; a bottom-up/top-down regional growth view, on the one hand, and a demand-side/supply-side view, on the other hand. In other words, it had the aim to create a new model whereby national and regional growth would have to feed back to one another, thus truly striking a balance between the two theoretical approaches.

The MASST model has now reached its fourth generation and provides a valuable toolbox for assessing possible future growth patterns of European regions within complex scenario frameworks. This paper presents the original structure of the model, and a critical overview of the evolution of the MASST model, highlighting the reasons that led to four generations for this toolbox. Each new version, in fact, superseded the previous one by answering the need to interpret specific stylized facts taking place in Europe. The main goal of each version is to update the model with a more comprehensive structure of interrelated equations, capable of modeling new causal changes emerging from new stylized facts, so as to guide policy makers in replying the most urgent European debates emerging over time.

When the model first appeared, a clear gap existed in the forecasting tools, that is, the lack of models able to integrate the regional and national components driving regional growth, and this happened despite stylized facts suggesting the paramount importance of both regional and national aspects. For instance, in 2015, the first year with full availability of data for all EU28 Countries, Luxembourg produced per capita roughly 5.6 times as much as Bulgaria, the most and least productive Country in the EU, respectively.[1] These differences were reflected in econometric exercises in

[1]Source of raw data: EUROSTAT. Productivity measured as per capita GDP in PPS.

which the national effects explained at least around 50% of the regional growth variance, suggesting that regional growth is first of all the result of a national trend. At the same time, also regional differentials should be explained in front of data suggesting that the average inhabitant of the most productive region in Europe (Inner London) produced 21.2 times more than its peer in the Bulgarian region of Severozapaden, and that also within the same Country, regional disparities could be quite staggering: London itself produced ten times as much as the least productive region in the UK (southern Scotland).

The first version of the MASST model provided an original and comprehensive toolbox to interpret regional growth as the result of both national dynamics and local competitiveness. The subsequent advances of the model were mainly driven by the reinforcement of interpretative elements that were left in the shades in this first version of the model and that instead became fundamental in specific periods of time for modelling urgent policy issues (e.g. the debate on the need for reindustrialization of the European Union, and the role of large versus small-medium-sized cities in European growth) and the new events that were destined to change the cause–effect relationships in an economic system (e.g. the economic crisis, and Brexit). As an example, the industrial dimension was reinforced when the debate on the need for the reindustrialization of Europe started. Instead, on the national side, the need to endogenize the dynamics of public expenditure and the mechanisms of its funding became evident with the appearance of the 2007–2008 crisis provoking spatially heterogeneous impacts. For instance, 2008–2017 per capita GDP growth grew on average by 8% in the region of southern Ireland, but decreased by 3.35% in the Greek region of Voreio Aigaio. These differences appear quite robust and stable over the medium term and are difficult to reconcile with (in particular spatial) general equilibrium models that work under several assumptions of equilibrium clearance of all markets and of perfect information on relative prices.

This chapter explains in depth the stages of the evolution of the MASST model, and its functioning. In Sect. 3.2, the theoretical framework within which the MASST model was first conceived is presented. Next, Sects. 3.3, 3.4, 3.5 and 3.6 present the advances of the model for each of the major steps it developed through. The chapter concludes in Sect. 3.7, hinting at possible research directions for the next generation of the MASST model.

3.2 Regional Growth Theories: The Scientific Debate and the Positioning of the MASST Model

Over the past century, forecasting regional growth models have always remained on top of the agenda in applied regional economics research. Different forecasting models[2] embrace different regional growth theories, and reflect the evolution of the economic thinking and the debate that came with it.

Two main debates in the way in which regional growth is foreseen influenced the creation of regional growth forecasting models. The first debate relates to whether regional growth is to be seen as a bottom-up or a top-down process. The second debate pertains instead to the dichotomy between supply-side and demand-side approaches to regional growth.

The debate whether growth is a bottom-up or a top-down process is a long-standing dispute in regional science. This dichotomy translates into two opposing fields (Richardson 1969): advocates of top-down approaches believe that regional growth is the result of a national growth that is, ex post, allocated among regions according to their participation in the national economy. This way of reasoning translates into focusing on national factors of growth, allocating to regions a national growth on the basis of their weight in the national economy (Stevens and Moore 1980). Supporters of bottom-up approaches hold instead that regional economic performance is mostly a matter of local economic factors, in a process of spatial competition for resources eventually causing the most efficient areas to excel, and, thus, grow faster than other regions and the

[2]The most celebrated regional growth forecasting models include the GMR model, the RHOMOLO and REMI models, and the MASST model presented in this chapter. For a critical review of these models, see Brandsma et al. (2015); Gori and Paniccià (2015); Varga and Sebestyén (2017); and Capello et al. (2017).

nation itself (Stöhr and Taylor 1980). In this view, national growth is the result of the weighted sum of the growth of single regions belonging to the nation.

This dichotomy translates into a major bifurcation in the way regional growth is interpreted. In the first case, the explanation lies exclusively in the national dynamics, in that regional economic performance is mostly due to the pull effect exerted by the Country and by rest of the world, leaving exogenous factors explaining regional growth. In the second case, the other extreme circumstance takes place, and national growth plays no role in interpreting regional dynamics, for local endogenous factors represent the sources of regional competitiveness. In this sense, it is clear that a more balanced approach is needed, so as to accommodate both national and regional elements in regional growth modelling.

A second fundamental dichotomy in the way regional growth models interpret and explain growth patterns is due to the focus on the supply-side or the demand-side as the main driver of regional economic performance. Advocates of bottom-up approaches believe regional growth is mostly due to the presence in a region of growth-enhancing factors, what in the literature has been termed *territorial capital*, a term defining all tangible and intangible endogenous assets, of public and private nature, that constitute the development potentials of an area (Camagni 2009). On the contrary, supporters of demand-side approaches believe that regional economic performance is mostly due to external demand factors that, through consumption multiplier effects on local income, drive regional economic performance (for a debate, see Capello 2015).

Models of regional growth based on external demand are built upon a Keynesian approach to economic theory. The classical textbook example is the economic base model (North 1955), whereby external demand triggers regional economic performance through a local multiplier effect. Another celebrated class of demand-driven models includes the Myrdal-Kaldor-Dixon-Thirlwall model, where a cumulative demand–supply causal effect of growth is explained, leading to divergent regional trends (Myrdal 1957; Kaldor 1970; Dixon and Thirlwall 1975).[3]

[3]For a thorough discussion of the features of demand-driven models, see Cochrane and Poot (2014).

Both theoretical debates translate into different approaches to modelling regional growth for forecasting purposes, in which the two dichotomies are intertwined. When a demand-side theoretical approach is embraced, forecasting regional growth models are produced, which portray regional economic dynamics as the result of positive external demand shocks, and therefore as the counterpart of macro systems' growth.[4] When a supply-side, bottom-up theoretical approach is instead embraced, regional growth forecasting models are built in which regional economic dynamics is obtained as the result of endogenous forces, and the national growth is obtained as the weighted sum of regional growth.[5]

Over time, an effort has been made in the economic literature on how to endogenize sources of economic growth in formalized aggregate (neoclassical) economic growth models as drivers of growth. The celebrated Solow–Swan model (Solow 1956; Swan 1956)—driven by exogenously determined capital accumulation rates and technological levels—has in fact been extended to accommodate the role of endogenous growth drivers such as human capital accumulation (Romer 1986), entrepreneurship (Aghion and Howitt 1992), learning by doing (Young 1993), and technological progress of nearby regions through spillovers effects (Ertur and Koch 2007).[6] This last extension allowed conceptualizing regions not as isolated islands, but as parts of larger economic systems, whose single constituents influence one another. The main channel of inter-regional interdependence was at first highlighted in the geographical proximity among regions; in later elaborations, inter-linkages were expected to occur also through non-geographical proximities, like cognitive, social and sectoral proximities, through channels such as reverse engineering or commuting (Boschma 2005; Caragliu 2015).

Although these theories made an advancement by identifying endogenous forces and interdependence in regional growth models, they did not adopt a solid territorial approach to regional growth. In the endogenous growth theory, the laws for a cumulative local growth are definitely a-

[4]For this kind of forecasting models, see, e.g. the RHOMOLO model (Lecca et al. 2019).

[5]For this kind of forecasting models, see, e.g. Cappellin (1975, 1976).

[6]These theoretical models have been translated into micro-founded testable growth equations by Mankiw et al. (1992).

spatial, in that they work in the same way, irrespective of the type of area (region or city) where they take place.

Instead, theories able to interpret territorial capital elements in regional dynamics pertain to local endogenous development models, conceptualized already in the 1970s (Becattini 1975, 1979). These models emphasize the role of territory as an active resource for local development, through agglomeration economies explaining the static and efficiency gains of a local area, and through local context specificities explaining regional differentials with respect to a national trend. However, they do this by neglecting the formalized nature of growth theories, and by denying a role to the macroeconomic environment in which a region lies (Capello 2019).

Since its inception, the MASST model has aimed at filling these gaps. Firstly, it combines bottom-up with top-down approaches, on the one hand, and supply-side with demand-side ones, on the other hand. Secondly, it merges the insightful interpretation of the complexity of economic phenomena taking place at territorial (local) level provided by qualitative local development models with the rigour and precision of the formalized analytical macroeconomic models. In so doing, the model is able to interpret regional growth through local context specificities without neglecting the macroeconomic environment in which a region lies. The result is a tool with an unprecedented interpretative power: the MASST model.

3.3 Merging Macroeconomic and Territorial Drivers of Regional Growth: The MASST1 Model

The MASST model is a macroeconometric regional growth model built to simulate regional growth in the medium and the long run.[7] The acronym contains the different dimensions—Macroeconomic, Sectoral, Social and Territorial—on which the model is built. Regional growth

[7]The first version of the model is presented in detail in Capello (2007).

is in fact explained by macroeconomic elements that play a prominent role in national growth trajectories, capturing the national/global demand framework which involves all regions. However, macroeconomic conditions are only part of the story, and in particular regional competitiveness, that is, the supply-side of growth, is explained by the sectoral, social and territorial aspects characterizing the region. In particular, regional competitiveness is explained by:

- *Single quantified tangible and intangible elements*: different assets of territorial capital, especially those with an intangible nature, linked to the ways in which actors' perceptions, to relational elements, and to cooperation attitudes that arise and grow due to local socio-economic specificities present in the local context explain regional competitiveness
- *Territorial complexity*: the set of context specificities and synergies that characterize regional growth, like differentiated territorial patterns of innovation, regional urban structure, net agglomeration economies, urban structural dynamics are captured through specific regional equations explaining, in their turn, regional competitiveness

The model runs across two stages. In an estimation stage, structural relations between explanatory and dependent variables in various national and regional equations are estimated over a long-run time span through a set of equations included in the model. In the simulation stage, instead, estimated coefficients are employed for simulating likely future growth patterns (usually, over a 15–20 years' horizon), and given an internally coherent sets of assumptions forming regional growth scenarios.

Figure 3.1 presents the structure of the model in its most updated version. Figure 3.1 also shows the evolution of the structure that took place over time, by highlighting the different sets of equations that were added at the time of the different versions of the model. The dashed shapes in Fig. 3.1 mark the first and basic structure of the model. The model merges national and regional growth-enhancing factors by explaining regional

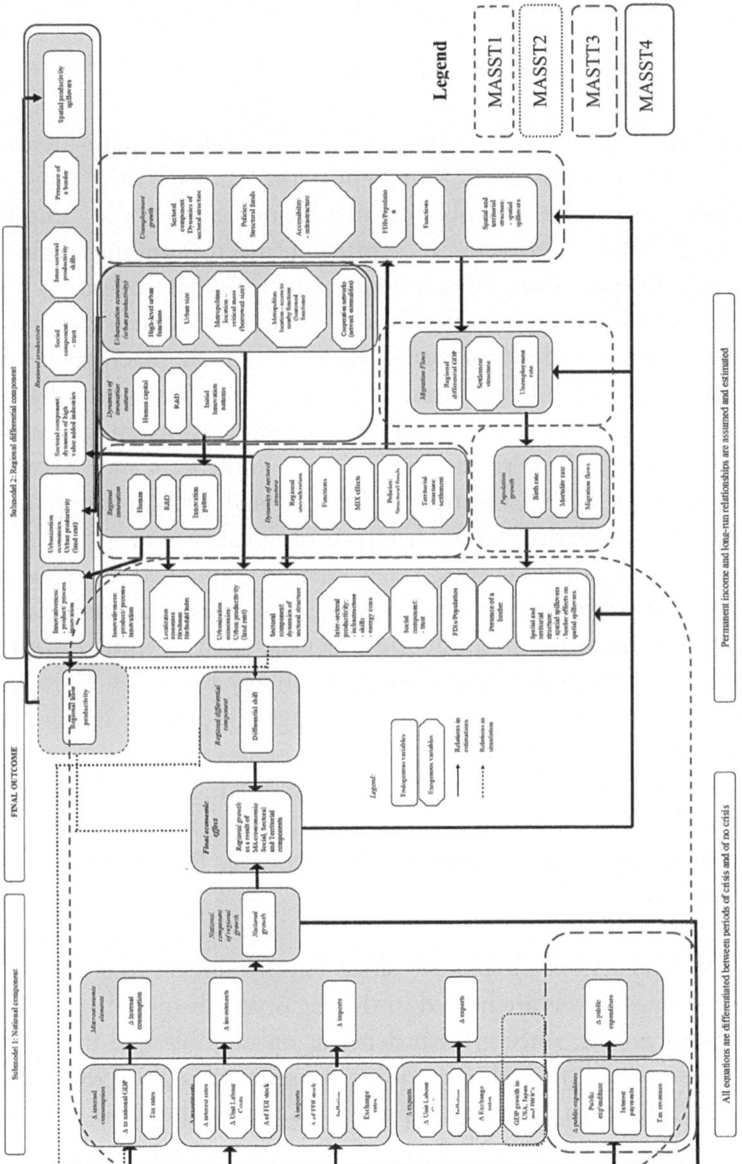

Fig. 3.1 Structure of the MASST4 model. (Source: Capello and Caragliu (2020), Authors' elaboration)

growth (ΔY_r) as a decomposition between a national growth rate (ΔY_N) and a regional differential shift (s) (Eq. 3.1) (Capello 2007):

$$\Delta Y_N = \Delta Y_N + s; r \in N \tag{3.1}$$

The national sub-model is based on a Keynesian quasi-identity, whereby GDP growth (ΔY_N) depends on the growth rates of consumption, investment, public expenditure, export and import. The national sub-model aims at capturing macroeconomic/national determinants of regional growth within a partial equilibrium setting. This part of the model captures macroeconomic (national) effects generated by exogenous trends and/or policies for regional growth; macroeconomic policies and trends in interest rates, in public expenditure, in inflation rates, in investment rates differ radically among European Countries (especially between Eastern and Western Countries, and between Northern and Southern Countries). The national growth component allows capturing individual Country effects on local growth.

The regional differential shift (s) is instead explained by regional competitiveness, measured as efficiency of local resources, increases in the quality and quantity of production factors, such as human capital and population, infrastructure endowment, energy resources, European funds, and, finally, interregional spatial linkages, capturing the growth externalities that influence a region located close to fast-growing areas.

This first generation of MASST already embeds several features of the present-day model, and is characterized by the effort to merge the separated blocks of theories discussed in Sect. 3.2. Regional growth is here interpreted as:

1. A *competitive bottom-up process*, since supply-side aspects defining competitiveness levels are hosted in the regional sub-model.
2. A *territorial process*, since growth depends on tangible and intangible regional assets and on agglomeration economies (Aydalot 1986; Camagni 1991). Territorial features represent in fact at the same time the propulsive forces of regional growth and the factors that explain local responses to exogenous aggregate trends.

3. A *spatial process*, in that the model conceptualizes regional dynamics as the result also of the influence the region receives from its surroundings (other regions) via growth spillovers.
4. An *interactive process* between regional and national growth. National macroeconomic trends generate an effect on both national and regional growth; at the same time regional elements affect both regional and national performance in an interactive national-regional manner. Complex vertical feedbacks between the regional and national economy are taken into consideration without imposing a complex system of interlinked equations.
5. An *endogenous process*, being local, growth takes place as the effect of endogenous mechanisms and forces behind local competitiveness.

Because of this structure, the MASST model is top-down and bottom-up at the same time, through horizontal feedbacks (among regions, in the form of growth spillovers) and vertical ones (between nations and their regions, and vice versa). National shocks influence national GDP growth rates through the national GDP growth (Fig. 3.2, link I). National shocks propagate to the regional level since regional GDP growth is obtained as the sum of the national GDP growth and the regional differential GDP growth (Fig. 3.2, links II). The latter is distributed differently among regions via spillover effects and territorial dummies. Regional shocks, and regional feedbacks, propagate on regional GDP growth thanks to the shift equation: regional shocks differ among regions thanks to spillovers dummy variables and different levels of the control variables (Fig. 3.2, link III). Regional shocks propagate to the national level through the sum of the regional GDP levels which defines the annual national GDP growth (Fig. 3.2, link IV) (Capello 2015).

This structure allows to model competitiveness and cooperation among regions at the same time. Regions compete since they grow thanks to their internal characteristics. At the same time, cooperation is modelled through the presence of growth spillovers: a region grows because of the economic performance of nearby regions, and vice versa.

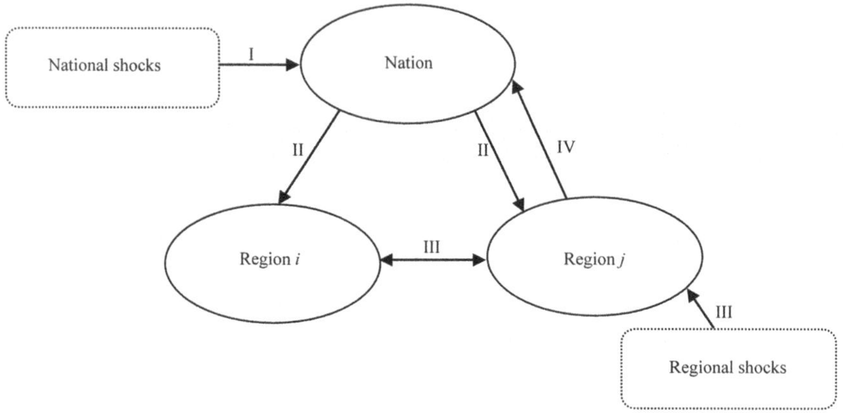

Fig. 3.2 National-regional linkages in MASST. (Source: Capello 2015)

3.4 Strengthening the Role of Industrial Specialization and Intangible Elements in Regional Growth: The MASST2 Model

The MASST model mostly advances our capacity of forecasting regional growth with the substantial focus on the regional side. In its first generation, this aspect was still in its infancy; for this reason, a second generation (Capello and Fratesi 2012; Capello et al. 2011) of the model offers some relevant advances, identified with dotted shapes in Fig. 3.1.

The main improvement in this second generation lies in the extension of the industry composition of the employment equation of the model, influenced by the debate on the need of a reindustrialization process for Europe, also known as the *Industrial Renaissance* of the European Union (BCG 2013; Foresight 2013; European Commission 2013) to counterbalance the unbundling process (Baldwin 2016) that was taking place since many years. Within the first version of MASST, in fact, employment was modelled in one equation highlighting the determinants of employment growth taken altogether. From the second generation of the model, instead, MASST is capable of capturing the differentiated effects on the manufacturing or service industry to external shocks (Autor et al. 2013), by providing simulation outputs separately for manufacturing and service employment growth rates.

Moreover, within each of the two equations describing manufacturing and service employment growth rates, initial specialization levels of various industries within each region allow the MASST model to encompass within-industry effects (in classical regional growth models, these are labelled MIX effects). Maintaining inter-sectoral productivity elements (i.e. the DIF component in the classical shift-share analysis), the second generation of the MASST model became capable of breaking down sources of regional growth with a structure following the classical Hoover classification of localized externalities (scale, specialization, and urbanization economies, respectively; Hoover 1937).

With this major advance, a mechanism to readjust predicted employment levels in the simulation stage became needed. This mechanism has been built through the simulation of the constant term in both the manufacturing and service employment growth rates, as described in Eq. (3.2):

$$\text{const}_r = \text{const}_r^0 + \sum\nolimits_i \left(\frac{E_i}{E_{EU}}\right) LQ_{ir} \Delta E_{iEU} + s \qquad (3.2)$$

where E_i is total employment in industry i at the European level and E_{EU} is total employment in the EU. Equation (3.2) decomposes the increase of total manufacturing (service) employment within each region into an exogenous increase in European employment growth rates within industry i (ΔE_{iEU}), weighted by the specialization of the region in industry i and the relative importance of industry i on total EU employment. Within the classical shift-share approach, Eq. (3.2) represents the so-called MIX effect.

In the simulation stage, the addition of this important module in the MASST model allows simulating the impact of exogenous industry-specific shocks—important at the time this was introduced, even more important right now, given the increasing pervasiveness of general purpose technologies and the shift to a new technological paradigm, labeled Industry 4.0 (Autor and Dorn 2013; Acemoglu and Autor 2011; Capello et al. 2019).

In the second generation of the MASST model, another important improvement lies in an extended role played by external (to the EU) demand for goods. This is formally modelled by including the growth rates of the United States and Japan's GDP in the exports equation within the national sub-model. In fact, even the European economy reacts to external demand shocks which enhance, or hamper, the growth rates of its national economies.

Lastly, the MASST2 model also allows regional trust, as a proxy for social capital, to play a role in determining the regional differential shift. This addition is also relevant in that it further strengthens the capacity of the model to interpret regional growth as a territorial process, one based on place-specific features characterized by imperfect mobility.

3.5 Between Competitiveness and Austerity: The MASST3 Model

When the MASST2 model reached maturity, a major breakthrough in world economies took place, namely the financial crisis that took off in 2008 from the United States after the closure of Lehman Brothers and rapidly extended to the rest of the world (Hausman and Johnston 2014). The financial crisis turned quickly into an economic crisis, which brought several macroeconomic factors to the center of the stage, while also showcasing structural breaks in economic relations, which could no longer be modelled on the basis of pre-crisis structures. This prompted research on a third generation of the MASST model, capable of better modelling the regional distribution of exogenous shocks at the Country level.

Among the many risk factors in the renewed financial climate emerging from one of the largest global crises after the 1929 stock crash (Bordo and Landon-Lane 2010), one major feature is the breakdown of the expectations channel on Eurozone public debts, leading to the (downward) convergence of ten-year government bonds towards German Bunds, typically considered as the risk-free benchmark.

Prior to the crisis, and since when the Euro was created in 1999, interest rates on public debts in Countries members of the Eurozone quickly converged towards the low levels until then recorded only for historically solvable countries, such as Germany. This happened mainly because of the elimination of exchange rate risk and the adoption of a common monetary policy (Ehrmann et al. 2011). The 2007–2008 crisis exposed instead some potential weaknesses in this mechanism. Markets suddenly stopped believing that the Eurozone as a whole would be solvable in case of Country-specific debt crises; consequently, the cost of servicing public debt in several EU economies rose to substantially higher levels (although for many of them, interest rates never reached pre-crisis levels). Eventually, one such Country (Greece) applied a partial (50%) haircut to its nominal public debt, in order to avoid full bankruptcy.

Consequences of this major global event are still visible more than ten years after the inception of the crisis. Several EU economies still register levels of debt substantially higher than pre-crisis levels, while others have not yet recovered pre-crisis per capita GDP levels. While the role of territorial features in explaining the geographical breakdown of crisis effect cannot be ignored (Capello et al. 2015), the MASST model needed a major restructuring in order to strengthen the national sub-component and enhance the model's interpretative and simulation power when dealing with macroeconomic shocks.

This main goal was pursued with MASST3 (Capello et al. 2017). In its third generation, the MASST model has been enhanced with two major improvements, namely the inclusion of the estimates for the period of crisis, and the endogenization of public expenditure in the national sub-model (Fig. 3.1, long dashed shapes).

In order to model the crisis, MASST3 was re-estimated to cover two time periods, the pre-crisis and the crisis ones. In the new estimates, a dummy variable for the crisis period was added and interacted with other independent variables, so as to capture differences in the relationships among economic variables in ordinary or crisis periods. In addition, the simulation procedure was modified to allow modellers to choose the pre-crisis or crisis coefficients, according to assumptions on the length of the crisis formulated in each scenario.

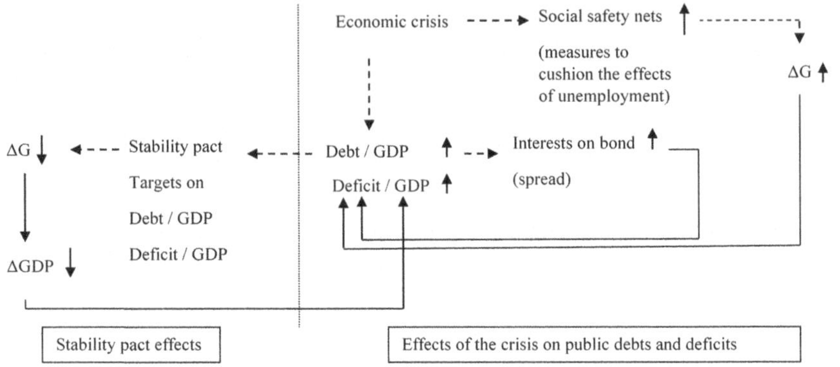

Fig. 3.3 Logic of the endogenization of public expenditure in MASST3. (Source: Capello et al. 2017)

The endogenization of public expenditure is summarized in Fig. 3.3. As Fig. 3.3 illustrates, public budget (net deficit or debt) has on purpose not been fully endogenized in the model. This structure allows the modeller to hold control of fundamental public policy instruments. This in particular applies to macroeconomic variables such as national tax rates, EU targets in national public deficits, and interests on public bonds; however, the effects of these exogenously determined levers on public expenditure and national GDP are in MASST3 fully endogenous to the model.

The dual (bottom-up and top-down) nature of MASST allows breaking down of the potential effects of exogenous shocks to the macro component of the model into simulated regional impacts, through the regional differential shift linkage between the macro and regional submodels.

Despite the paramount importance of this additional component of the model, MASST3 also presents advances with respect to prior generations of the model along several regional dimensions. In particular, on the regional side, the model was strengthened in order to take into account the territorial complexity that characterizes local economic patterns, by highlighting the set of context specificities and synergies that characterize regional growth.

In this vein, the model attributes a distinctive role to context conditions that give rise to different innovation growth patterns (Capello and Lenzi 2013a, b). The idea behind this approach is to spatially break down the possible variants of the knowledge/invention/innovation/development logical path, on the basis of the local endowment of preconditions for knowledge creation, knowledge attraction, and innovation. In this way, peculiarities in the mode regions innovate are highlighted. The dependent variable of this additional module of the MASST model, that is, regional innovation, becomes a fully endogenous explanatory factor of the simulated regional differential shift, explained through differentiated regional innovation patterns stemming from different local context conditions.

Moreover, the model attributes a distinctive role to advantages stemming from an urban environment: advantages which, in their turn, depend on the specificities of single cities, and of the regional urban system as a whole. This source of externalities is included in the model through a sub-model which defines an equilibrium size for each city reached as marginal location costs equal marginal location benefits (Camagni et al. 2013). Both benefits and costs depend, in their turn, on the specificities of single cities: amenities, industrial diversity, and high-level functions explain the benefits, while urban land rent, social conflicts and sprawl explain the costs (Rosen 1979; Roback 1982).

A last important addition to the regional sub-model is related to the endogenization of unemployment rates. This advance nicely fits with the regionalization of the macroeconomic shocks also modelled by means of endogenizing public expenditure, and provides a convenient lever to identify the spatial distribution of macroeconomic impacts of major Country- and EU-wide shocks.

Taken together, the three additions to the regional sub-model imply a major surge in the interpretative power of the MASST model. Still, as a chiefly territorial tool, the MASST model is amenable to several tweaks to the regional component, some of which have been undertaken in the fourth generation.

3.6 Reinforcing Territorial Determinants of Regional Growth: The MASST4 Model

The main goal of MASST4 has been to strengthen the link between macroeconomic and regional components with respect to both prior versions of the model and other similar macroeconometric regional growth models.[8] When the MASST3 version came to its maturity, a post-crisis period was reached, and an update of the estimates was needed. The updating exercise came with a substantial improvement also of the regional side of the model and its territorial characteristics, along with a further integration with the national sub-model. Integration took place through several substantial additions to the complexity of the structure of the model: this section details these advances, identified with continuous shapes in Fig. 3.1.

The update of the model for the first time allowed MASST4 to be estimated in panel form both for the national (with yearly data from 1995 to 2018) and for the regional (in three periods: pre-crisis, crisis, and after-crisis) sub-models. This has allowed testing, for both sub-models, the assumption that EU economies exited the crisis quite differently from how they entered it, and that these changes had a structural nature.

The first structural break identified by means of these panel estimates relates to what has been termed[9] the *4.0 industrial revolution*. While prior to the crisis, and following global trends in advanced Countries, Europe had been deindustrializing (Rodrik 2016), after the end of the crisis (by convention identified in MASST4 in 2012 for all EU Countries), several EU economies witnessed a renewed acceleration in manufacturing employment growth, driven by the new technological paradigm labeled *Industry 4.0*. The new paradigm is shifting the technological frontier in a few selected hotspots capable of both efficient production and diffusion of these new technologies centred on general purpose technologies whose adoption cuts across several manufacturing industries. In MASST4, this process is modelled with an enhanced component of the regional sub-

[8]The MASST4 version is presented in details in Capello and Caragliu (2020).
[9]Possibly a bit of an overstatement.

model explaining the probability of a region to experience a structural evolution in its territorial innovation patterns (Sect. 3.5; Capello and Lenzi 2018).

The second major trend that can be detected in post-crisis estimates refers to the strain through which economic and political institutions in several EU Countries are presently walking. The most important example is the relatively recent decision by the UK to leave the European Union (henceforth, *Brexit*). After holding a close-call referendum on June 23, 2016, UK decided to withdraw its membership of the European Union, which it had achieved after roughly 12 years of negotiations beginning in 1961 and ending in 1973 with the UK's admission to the EU (UK and EU 2018). The MASST4 model has been updated in order to allow the modeller to assess the regional effects of Brexit, while also leaving the chance to model similar events for other EU Countries (Capello et al. 2018).

A third and fundamental trend is related to the growing role of cities as engines of national growth. After a two-decade renaissance of research on empirical urban economics and in particular on the nature and extent of agglomeration economies, a relatively recent debate has been sparked over whether large (capital) cities catalyze economic growth, which then diffuses to the rest of their Countries, or whether instead these large agglomerations, more directly hit by the crisis, actually slow down full recovery at Country level (Parkinson et al. 2015; Capello et al. 2015; Dijkstra et al. 2015).

MASST4 incorporates this debate and models the role of cities in stimulating national economies through their capability to meet new challenges. Empirically, this translates into estimating an additional equation whereby urban agglomeration economies (measured by urban land rent) depend on high-quality functions hosted, on the quality of local institutions, and on the capability of cities to cooperate with other cities (Camagni et al. 2016). Agglomeration economies estimated by this module enter then the regional differential shift as an additional explanatory factor.

One last relevant addition to the regional sub-model represents a landmark in the evolution of MASST. In fact, until the third generation, labour productivity was exogenously determined by the modeller and represented a lever that exogenously determined the simultaneous covariation between employment and GDP growth. MASST4 made a significant leap forward in endogenizing regional labour productivity, with major normative implications: from a regional economics perspective, employment and wages adjust to national and global shocks through a geographical reallocation that guarantees spatial equilibrium. This crucial determinant of the observed spatial variability in economic growth rates is now fully absorbed by the model.

3.7 Conclusions and Future Research Avenues

The MASST model has now reached its fourth generation, and has gained a firm reputation among other important regional growth models used to interpret regional growth in European Countries. Its interpretative power has been tested through its application to a baseline scenario forecasting GDP growth for 2030 that was run at the end of 2013. In this simulation, the MASST model forecasted the emerging trend of divergence in GDP growth among European regions, in a period in which macroeconomic forces were forcing superior (but regionally differentiated) constraints to all regions (national fiscal crises, austerity measures, exchange rate devaluations and *internal* devaluations). Secondly, comparing two scenarios driven respectively by mega-cities and by medium and medium-large cities, the latter scenario proved to be at the same time the most expanding and the most cohesive (Camagni et al. 2015). In the same vein, MASST has been applied to several scenario-building exercises, from the costs of an enduring crisis (Capello et al. 2015, 2016), to the costs of a dismembering process in the EU (Capello et al. 2018), providing sound messages and raising awareness of the risks embedded in political and economic turmoil.

This chapter has documented several advances of the model, each of which supersedes previous versions by filling gaps or by complexifying the structure of the model in order to endogenize additional economic relations. Nevertheless, future challenges lie ahead, which promise to deliver further enhances of the model.

A first possible research avenue relates to the endogenization of markets that at present are not formalized in the model. While the objective of this exercise cannot be to reach the status of full Computable General Equilibrium (CGE) model, which would change the very nature of the MASST model, the latter can still endogenize some markets that are typically very important for interpreting the geographical distribution of economic growth. The labour market is one such example, since, even in presence of imperfect labour mobility, relocation decisions represent an important mechanism for regional economies to adjust to national and global demand shocks. The medium to long-run periods covered by MASST allow to safely assume that some relocation could take place both locally (across sectors) as well as nationally (or at the supranational level) in response to the increase (or decrease) of demand in some industries, both because of local supply-side (technological) shocks, as well as due to increased global demand.

A second market that could be considered for clearing is the money one. At national level, the pervasive importance of monetary policies, especially with the abundance of savings and in a context of limited growth in advanced Countries, represents a relevant context condition that is shaping the debate on economic growth even after the 2007–2008 financial crisis ceased to exert its (sharpest) effects. This second possibility walks on an edge, though, since the way money is presently managed as a scenario lever in the model allows the modeller to keep partial control of the logical chain behind macro shocks.

A third possible future development of the model is linked to the possibility of running individual simulations on single markets, in order to assess the likely effects of individual policies, that are instead presently difficult to model with MASST because of its very nature of scenario building model. This third point is a direct consequence of the full endogenization of specific markets hinted at earlier.

With its fifteen years of history, and with the possible enlargements just mentioned, MASST appears to be getting close to full maturity. Regional growth still presents many important issues to be explained and interpreted, and MASST will likely provide many additional insights in the years to come.

References

Acemoglu, D., & Autor, D. (2011). Skills, Tasks and Technologies: Implications for Employment and Earnings. In O. Ashenfelter & D. Card (Eds.), *Handbook of Labor Economics* (Vol. 4B, pp. 1043–1171). San Diego, CA: Elsevier.

Aghion, P., & Howitt, P. (1992). A Model of Growth Through Creative Destruction. *Econometrica, 60*(2), 323–351.

Autor, D., & Dorn, D. (2013). The Growth of Low-Skill Service Jobs and the Polarization of the US Labor Market. *American Economic Review, 103*(5), 1553–1597.

Autor, D., Dorn, D., & Hanson, G. (2013). The China Syndrome: Local Labor Market Effects of Import Competition in the United States. *American Economic Review, 103*(6), 2121–2168.

Aydalot, P. (Ed.). (1986). *Milieux innovateurs en Europe*. Paris: GREMI.

Baldwin, R. (2016). *The Great Convergence*. Cambridge, MA: Harvard University Press.

BCG. (2013). *Plan estratégico para el fortalecimiento y desarrollo del sector industrial en España*. Informe para el Ministerio de Industria, Energía y Turismo del Gobierno de España.

Becattini, G. (Ed.). (1975). *Lo sviluppo economico della Toscana. Con particolare riguardo all'industrializzazione leggera*. Istituto regionale per la programmazione economica della Toscana-Irpet.

Becattini, G. (1979). *Dal settore industriale al distretto industriale. Alcune considerazioni sull'unità di indagine dell'economia industriale*. Bologna: Il Mulino.

Bordo, M. D., & Landon-Lane, J. S. (2010). The Global Financial Crisis of 2007-08: Is It Unprecedented? *National Bureau of Economic Research WP w16589*. Retrieved September 30, 2019, from https://www.nber.org/papers/w16589.

Boschma, R. (2005). Proximity and Innovation: A Critical Assessment. *Regional Studies, 39*(1), 61–74.

Brandsma, A., Kancs, D. A., Monfort, P., & Rillaers, A. (2015). RHOMOLO: A Dynamic Spatial General Equilibrium Model for Assessing the Impact of Cohesion Policy. *Papers in Regional Science, 94*, S197–S221.

Camagni, R. (1991). Local 'Milieu', Uncertainty and Innovation Networks: Towards a New Dynamic Theory of Economic Space. In R. Camagni (Ed.), *Innovation Networks: Spatial Perspectives* (pp. 121–144). London: Belhaven.

Camagni, R. (2009). Territorial Capital and Regional Development. In R. Capello & P. Nijkamp (Eds.), *Handbook of Regional Growth and Development Theories* (pp. 118–132). Cheltenham: Edward Elgar Publishing.

Camagni, R., Capello, R., & Caragliu, A. (2013). One or Infinite Optimal City Sizes? In Search of an Equilibrium Size for Cities. *The Annals of Regional Science, 51*(2), 309–341.

Camagni, R., Capello, R., Caragliu, A., & Fratesi, U. (2015). Territorial Scenarios in Europe: Growth and Disparities Beyond the Economic Crisis. *Europa Regional, 21*(4), 190–208.

Camagni, R., Capello, R., & Caragliu, A. (2016). Static vs. Dynamic Agglomeration Economies. Spatial Context and Structural Evolution behind Urban Growth. *Papers in Regional Science, 95*(1).

Capello, R. (2007). A Forecasting Territorial Model of Regional Growth: The MASST Model. *The Annals of Regional Science, 41*(4), 753–787.

Capello, R. (2015). *Regional Economics*. London: Routledge.

Capello, R. (2019). Regional Development Theories and Formalised Economic Approaches: An Evolving Relationship. *Italian Economic Journal, 5*(1), 1–16.

Capello, R., & Caragliu, A. (2020). Merging Macroeconomic and Territorial Determinants of Regional Growth: The MASST4 Model. *The Annals of Regional Science*, 1–38.

Capello, R., & Fratesi, U. (2012). Modelling Regional Growth: An Advanced MASST Model. *Spatial Economic Analysis, 7*(3), 293–318.

Capello, R., & Lenzi, C. (Eds.). (2013a). *Territorial Patterns on Innovation: An Inquiry on the Knowledge Economy in European Regions*. London: Routlegde.

Capello, R., & Lenzi, C. (2013b). Territorial Patterns of Innovation and Economic Growth in European Regions. *Growth and Change, 44*(2), 195–227.

Capello, R., & Lenzi, C. (2018). The Dynamics of Regional Learning Paradigms and Trajectories. *Journal of Evolutionary Economics, 28*(4), 727–748.

Capello, R., Fratesi, U., & Resmini, L. (2011). *Globalization and Regional Growth in Europe: Past Trends and Future Scenarios*. Berlin: Springer Verlag.

Capello, R., Caragliu, A., & Fratesi, U. (2015). Spatial Heterogeneity in the Costs of the Economic Crisis in Europe: Are Cities Sources of Regional Resilience? *Journal of Economic Geography, 15*(5), 951–972.

Capello, R., Caragliu, A., & Fratesi, U. (2016). The Costs of the Economic Crisis: Which Scenario for the European Regions? *Environment and Planning C: Government and Policy, 34*(1), 113–130.

Capello, R., Caragliu, A., & Fratesi, U. (2017). Modeling Regional Growth Between Competitiveness and Austerity Measures: The MASST3 Model. *International Regional Science Review, 40*(1), 38–74.

Capello, R., Caragliu, A., & Fratesi, U. (2018). The Regional Costs of Market Size Losses in a EU Dismembering Process. *Papers in Regional Science, 97*(1), 73–90.

Capello, R., Laffi, M., & Lenzi, C. (2019, August 27–30). *Spatial Trends in 4.0 Technologies Across European Regions: New Islands of Creative Innovation*. Paper presented at the 59th ERSA conference, Lyon.

Cappellin, R. (1975). La Struttura dei modelli econometrici regionali. *Giornale degli Economisti ed Annali di Economia, 25*(5–6), 423–452.

Cappellin, R. (1976). Un Modello Econometrico dell'Economia Lombarda. *Giornale degli Economisti ed Annali di Economia, 25*(5–6), 263–290.

Caragliu, A. (2015). *The Economics of Proximity: Regional Growth, Beyond Geographic Proximity.* Ph.D. Dissertation, VU University Amsterdam.

Cochrane, W., & Poot, J. (2014). Demand-Driven Theories and Models of Regional Growth. In M. Fischer & P. Nijkamp (Eds.), *Handbook of Regional Science* (pp. 259–276). Berlin: Springer.

Dijkstra, L., Garcilazo, E., & McCann, P. (2015). The Effects of the Global Financial Crisis on European Regions and Cities. *Journal of Economic Geography, 15*(5), 935–949.

Dixon, R., & Thirlwall, A. P. (1975). A Model of Regional Growth-Rate Differences on Kaldorian Lines. *Oxford Economic Papers, 27*(2), 201–214.

Ehrmann, M., Fratzscher, M., Gürkaynak, R. S., & Swanson, E. T. (2011). Convergence and Anchoring of Yield Curves in the Euro Area. *The Review of Economics and Statistics, 93*(1), 350–364.

Ertur, C., & Koch, W. (2007). Growth, Technological Interdependence and Spatial Externalities: Theory and Evidence. *Journal of Applied Econometrics, 22*(6), 1033–1062.

European Commission. (2013). *Competing in Global Value Chains*. EU Industrial Structure Report 2013. Publication Office of the European Union. Luxembourg.

Foresight. (2013). *The Future of Manufacturing: A New Era of Opportunity and Challenge for the UK*, Project Report. The Government Office for Science, London.

Gori, G. F., & Paniccià, R. (2015). A Structural Multisectoral Model with New Economic Geography Linkages for Tuscany. *Papers in Regional Science, 94*, S175–S196.

Hausman, A., & Johnston, W. J. (2014). Timeline of a Financial Crisis: Introduction to the Special Issue. *Journal of Business Research, 67*(1), 2667–2670.

Hoover, E. M. (1937). *Location Theory and the Shoe and Leather Industries*. Cambridge, MA: Harvard University Press.

Kaldor, N. (1970). The Case for Regional Policies. *Scottish Journal of Political Economy, 17*(3), 337–348.

Lecca, P., Christensen, M., Conte, A., Mandras, G., & Salotti, S. (2019). Upward Pressure on Wages and the Interregional Trade Spillover Effects Under Demand-Side Shocks. *Papers in Regional Science*. https://doi.org/10.1111/pirs.12472.

Mankiw, N. G., Romer, D., & Weil, D. N. (1992). A Contribution to the Empirics of Economic Growth. *The Quarterly Journal of Economics, 107*(2), 407–437.

Myrdal, G. (1957). *Economic Theory of Under-Developed Regions*. London: General Duckworth & Co.

North, D. (1955). Location Theory and Regional Economic Growth. *Journal of Political Economy, 63*(3), 243–258.

Parkinson, M., Meegan, R., & Karecha, J. (2015). City Size and Economic Performance: Is Bigger Better, Small More Beautiful or Middling Marvellous? *European Planning Studies, 23*(6), 1054–1068.

Richardson, H. W. (1969). *Regional Economics; Location Theory, Urban Structure, Regional Change*. New York: Praeger Publishers

Roback, J. (1982). Wages, Rents, and the Quality of Life. *Journal of Political Economy, 90*(6), 1257–1278.

Rodrik, D. (2016). Premature Deindustrialization. *Journal of Economic Growth, 21*(1), 1–33.

Romer, P. M. (1986). Increasing Returns and Long-Run Growth. *Journal of Political Economy, 94*(5), 1002–1037.

Rosen, S. (1979). Wage-Based Indexes of Urban Quality of Life. In P. Mieszkowski & M. Straszheimand (Eds.), *Current Issues in Urban Economics* (pp. 74–104). Baltimore, MD: John Hopkins University Press.

Solow, R. M. (1956). A Contribution to the Theory of Economic Growth. *The Quarterly Journal of Economics, 70*(1), 65–94.

Stevens, B. H., & Moore, C. L. (1980). A Critical Review of the Literature on Shift-Share as a Forecasting Technique. *Journal of Regional Science, 20*(4), 419–437.

Stöhr, W., & Taylor, D. R. F. (Eds.). (1980). *Development from Above or Below? A Radical Reappraisal of Spatial Planning in Developing Countries*. London: Wiley.

Swan, T. W. (1956). Economic Growth and Capital Accumulation. *Economic Record, 32*(2), 334–361.

UK and EU. (2018). *When Did Britain Decide to Join the European Union?* Retrieved July 17, 2018, from http://ukandeu.ac.uk/fact-figures/when-did-britain-decide-to-join-the-european-union/.

Varga, A., & Sebestyén, T. (2017). Does EU Framework Program Participation Affect Regional Innovation? The Differentiating Role of Economic Development. *International Regional Science Review, 40*(4), 405–439.

Young, A. (1993). Invention and Bounded Learning by Doing. *Journal of Political Economy, 101*(3), 443–472.

4

On the Spatial Determinants of Firm Growth: A Microlevel Analysis of the Italian SMEs

Giuseppe Arbia, Maria Michela Dickson, Roberto Gabriele, Diego Giuliani, and Flavio Santi

4.1 Introduction

The New Economic Geography reckons that localization economies and urbanization economies are important phenomena (Krugman 1991; Glaeser et al. 1992; Arbia 2001; Audretsch and Dohse 2007), but empir-

G. Arbia (✉)
Università Cattolica del Sacro Cuore, Rome, Italy
e-mail: giuseppe.arbia@unicatt.it

M. M. Dickson · R. Gabriele · D. Giuliani
D.E.M. Department of Economics and Management, University of Trento, Trento, Italy
e-mail: mariamichela.dickson@unitn.it; roberto.gabriele@unitn.it; diego.giuliani@unitn.it

F. Santi
Department of Economics, University of Verona, Verona, Italy
e-mail: flaviosanti@univr.it

S. Colombo (ed.), *Spatial Economics Volume II*,
https://doi.org/10.1007/978-3-030-40094-1_4

ical studies adopting this framework do not offer clear insights on how such spatial effects differently affect firms that are not comparable in terms of structural dimensions and behavioral aspects (Fujita et al. 1999; Frenken et al. 2014). A few exceptions relate to studies that take into account the location of the firm and the nature of geographical interactions among firms in a local context (Duschl et al. 2011; Barbosa and Eiriz 2011; Antonietti et al. 2013).

Indeed, the presence of positive externalities in a region does not guarantee that all the firms in that region benefit from them, or at least not to the same extent. More specifically, externalities can produce different effects on growth dynamics if we consider (a) small firms (SMFs) as opposed to large ones and (b) young firms as opposed to older ones (Brown and Rigby 2010).

Firms growth, as measured by employment growth, is often the objective variables in this field of research (Beaudry and Swann 2009; Beaudry and Schiffauerova 2009; Raspe and Van Oort 2008, 2011).[1] Theoretically, location within a geographically concentrated area, or an agglomeration, may result into greater firm efficiencies due to labor market pooling, to the provision of non-traded inputs, or to the development of specialized intermediate goods knowledge externalities and knowledge spillovers. These locational advantages may foster regional growth supporting the expansion of individual firm (Audretsch and Dohse 2007). In addition, vertical relationships in downstream markets can entail the expansion of firms—in particular small firms—driving the growth of sales. Taking into account the dynamics of innovation processes, we can postulate that the diversity of complementary economic activity is more conducive to growth than specialization (Glaeser et al. 1992; Feldman and Audretsch 1999). Indeed, we expect that localization economies stimulate incremental and process innovations, thus leading to higher productivity. In contrast, Jacobs economies are expected to spur more radical innovations through the recombination of existing knowledge, thus leading to the creation of new employment (Frenken et al. 2007). This effect, in turn,

[1]The other largely studied dependent variable is the productivity growth (see Andersson and Lööf 2011). Findings for the two set of objectives variables can be very different (Beaudry and Schiffauerova 2009).

would imply that employment growth would benefit from diversification, while productivity would increase with specialization of industrial activities. Despite the richness of theoretical paradigms, however, there is still little empirical evidence on the impact of location on growth at the firm level (Acs and Armington 2004).

The present chapter proposes a new approach to empirically assess the role of localization and agglomeration economies in shaping the patterns of firm growth. In particular, our method is based on the use of firm-level measures of specialization and diversity (based on the local K-function; see Getis 1984) associated to the specification of a quantile regression.

In line with a recent stream of literature which makes use of distance-based measures (see Duranton and Overman 2005; Espa et al. 2013; Arbia et al. 2010, 2012; Marcon and Puech 2010), the Getis local K-function (Getis 1984; Getis and Franklin 1987) can be used to define firm-level indicators able to endogenize the emergence of spatial externalities and to overcome two methodological shortcomings of region-level measures, namely (a) the arbitrary definition of the spatial observational units (such as provinces, regions and municipalities) and (b) the restrictive assumption of spatial homogeneity within regions. We argue in favor of the use of the local K-function to empirically distinguish between Marshall-Arrow-Romer externalities (MAR) and Jacobs externalities (JAC). The former refers to knowledge spillovers accruing to firms operating in the same industry, while the latter are pure agglomeration economies arising from knowledge spillover external to the industry in which the local firm operates. Moreover, the local K-function-based measure allows us to detect (separately, but simultaneously) the two types of externalities. This is of primary importance given that previous studies have shown that both kinds of externalities can coexist and can differently affect business enterprises (Beaudry and Schiffauerova 2009).

The empirical analysis reported in this chapter is found on a database of limited liabilities, single-unit manufacturing firms located in Italy in the period 1994–2006. The individual level of observation allows us to effectively study the organic growth of firms and the role of spatial and geographical factors. In particular, we aim at disentangling how much the different kinds of geographical externalities (MAR and JAC externalities) are in place for the different kind of firms of our sample in the time window under investigation.

Our investigation produced a series of interesting results that can be summarized as follows. First of all, small firms experiencing a growth rate above the average benefit more from MAR externalities at long range than from JAC externalities at shorter distance. Secondly, these small firms grow faster than other firms because the effect of MAR externalities on them is bigger. Thirdly, small firms that shrink do not benefit at all from MAR, but only benefit from medium range JAC externalities. Fourthly, small firms that perform extremely bad in terms of employment growth, suffer from short-range MAR. Finally, MAR and JAC externalities bear negligible effects on both medium and large firms.

The rest of the present chapter is organized as the following. Section 4.2 discusses the literature about geographical determinants of firm growth. Section 4.3 explains the methodologies employed for the investigation. Section 4.4 describes the database used. Results are presented in Sect. 4.5. Section 4.6 concludes.

4.2 The Spatial Determinants of Firm Growth

There are two kinds of reasons why location can be postulated to play a crucial role on the growth of firms. On one side, industries can specialize geographically, due to the fact that proximity (1) favors the intra-industry transmission of knowledge, (2) reduces transport costs of inputs and outputs and (3) allows firms to benefit from a more efficient labor market. Firstly, introduced by Marshall (1890), this approach was further developed into the Marshall–Arrow–Romer (MAR) model (Glaeser et al. 1992; Henderson et al. 1995).

The MAR model states that concentration of an industry in a geographical context facilitates knowledge spillovers between firms and promotes innovation. Indeed, the sectoral specialization encourages the transmission and exchange of tacit or codified knowledge and information that depend on distance (Griliches 1992). Knowledge spillovers are geographically bounded in the place where the knowledge is created (Autant-Bernard 2001; Feldman and Audretsch 1999), alongside the imitation activity, the business interactions and the interfirm circulation of skilled workers. Moreover, economies of scale can be generated from input-sharing activity (e. g. labor equipment and infrastructure) among firms of the same industry (Krugman 1991). All these phenomena can be labeled as localization externalities (or MAR externalities), and they are likely to arise when an industry is relatively large with respect to the whole economy (Frenken et al. 2007).

On the other side, Jacobs (1969) suggests that the sources of knowledge spillovers are external to the industry. Indeed, according to Jacobs (1969) it is the diversity of knowledge within a geographical context which is relevant, because the variety of industries within a geographic region promotes knowledge externalities and innovative activity and leads to economic growth. In this respect, the urban agglomerations play a key role. Therefore, a diversified local production structure gives rise to diversification externalities (called "Jacobs externalities").[2]

Spatial concentration may affect both the productivity and the growth of firms. Nonetheless, productivity and growth are shaped in a different way by MAR and JAC externalities. Employment growth and innovation would benefit from diversification, while productivity would increase with specialization of industrial activities. In particular, Jacobs economies should spur radical innovations and product innovation (recombination and cross-fertilization of existing knowledge) that lead to new employment creation (Frenken et al. 2007).

Empirical evidence on the effect of localization economies and MAR externalities on the one side and urbanization economies and Jacobs externalities on the other produced different evidences (Frenken et al. 2014). Beaudry and Swann (2009) found, for UK industries, a positive effect of own-sector employment. Maine et al. (2010) find that in the high-technology sectors, firm growth is negatively related to the distance of each firm from the top-ten firms in a cluster (localization diseconomies). Furthermore, younger, and particularly new, firms benefit more from

[2]The literature identifies a third type of externality. It refers to Porter's (1990) argument, and it is associated with Jacobs idea that competition is better for growth. Strong competition in the same geographical market provides incentives to innovate which, in turn, accelerate the technical progress, the productivity, and, finally, the growth.

localization economies in terms of growth than older firms (Rosenthal and Strange 2005; Brown and Rigby 2010). Wennberg and Lindqvist (Wennberg and Lindqvist 2010) find evidence of localization economies both in manufacturing and in services sectors. Raspe and Van Oort (2008) study on Dutch firms suggests that agglomeration economies have a positive effect on firm growth in an R&D-intensive environment. Finally, Staber (2001) shows that MAR externalities are present in sectors where knowledge spillovers are present, for example high technology sectors.

Empirical studies concerning Italian firms have mainly focused on size, age and R&D activities (Del Monte and Papagni 2003) as major determinants of growth. They have neglected, at least partially, the second group of determinants. Contini and Revelli (1988) find a negative impact of extant size over the employment growth of manufacturing firms located in the Northern Italy over the period 1980–1986. Similarly, Becchetti and Trovato (2002) estimate a negative growth-size relationship for small and medium-sized Italian manufacturing firms that survive during the 1995–1997 period. Nevertheless, when non-surviving firms are included in the sample, they obtain a significant effect of size on growth rates only for companies employing between 10 and 50 employees, while the workforce expansion of firms with more than 100 employees seems to be independent of size. Del Monte and Papagni (2003) strengthen this last finding by showing that the independence assumption postulated in Gibrat's Law (Gibrat 1931) is empirically validated in a sample of more than 650 large manufacturing firms examined over the period 1989–1997. Lotti et al. (2003) provide a comprehensive picture of growth patterns for a sample of 1570 manufacturing firms born in January 1987 and tracked until 1993. The study outlines that, in five of the six industrial sectors considered, smaller firms grew faster than their larger counterparts over the entire period 1987–1993, as well as in the year that immediately followed the start-up. Nonetheless, as soon as new entrants approach an acceptable size that shields them from the risk of failure, Gibrat's Law seems to be reestablished, thus implying no significant difference in the growth behavior between small and large firms.

4.3 Methodology

This study proposes a series of firm-level regression models in order to investigate the role of internal and external factors on firms growth rates. In particular, we use a quantile regression approach in which the dependent variable is represented by the firm growth rate regressed against internal, external and spatial determinants of growth. Internal and external factors of growth are selected according to the existing literature, while spatial factors are investigated using firm-level measures of agglomeration and localization, that allow us to overcome the limitations arising from the use of aggregate indices and traditional spatial econometric models. Moreover, we estimate separate quantile regression models for small firms (less or equal to 50 employees) and medium and large firms (more than 50 employees) to uncover variations in the impact of spatial factors on firms of different size.

4.3.1 Measures of Spatial Interaction

4.3.1.1 The Limits of Regional and Aggregate Measures

We argue that the locational measures commonly used by researchers—such as the Gini (Gini 1912, 1921), Hirschman-Herfindahl (Hirschman 1945), Location Quotient (Florence 1939) and Ellison-Glaeser (Ellison and Glaeser 1997) indices—may not be adequate. In particular, they are computed on regional aggregates built on arbitrary definitions of the spatial observational units (such as provinces, regions and municipalities). Hence, they introduce a statistical bias arising from the discretionally chosen definition of space (i.e., the so-called *modifiable areal unit problems* bias; see Arbia 1989). As an evidence of that, in reviewing the relevant literature, Beaudry and Schiffauerova (2009) found that the emergence and intensity of agglomeration externalities are strictly dependent on the level of spatial aggregation of data.

4.3.1.2 A Firm-Level Measure of MAR Externalities

To build up an indicator that opportunely captures Marshall externalities, we rely on the well-established idea in the literature (Glaeser et al. 1992) that the degree of specialization of an industry (rather than its size) can better embody the potential for Marshall externalities in that it expresses the intensity and the density of interactions among firms (Beaudry and Schiffauerova 2009). Accordingly, we build a firm-level distance-based measure of industry specialization that captures the firm's potential for Marshall externalities. We propose the use of the Getis local K-function (Getis 1984), a statistical measure assessing the degree of spatial interactions among geo-referenced locations. Indeed, in the context of micro-geographic data, which are identified by maps of point events (as represented by their longitude/latitude coordinates), Getis local K-function is an explorative tool that summarizes the characteristics of a spatial distribution of point events relative to its location. If the events of interest are firms (as in our case), this measure allows to statistically test if a given individual firm is localized into a cluster.

For the given ith firm located in a geographical area, the local K-function can be defined as follows:

$$K_i(d) = E\left[\sum_{j \neq i} I\left(d_{ij} \leq d\right)\right] / \lambda \tag{4.1}$$

where $E\{.\}$ indicates the expectation operator; the term d_{ij} is the Euclidean distance between the ith and jth firms' locations; $I(d_{ij} \leq d)$ represents the indicator function such that $I = 1$ if $d_{ij} \leq d$ and 0 otherwise; d is a threshold distance and λ represents the mean number of firms per unitary area: a parameter called *spatial intensity*. Given definition (1), the term $\lambda K_i(d)$ can be interpreted as the expected number of further firms located up to a distance d from the ith firm. The local K-function quantifies the degree of spatial interaction between the ith firm and all other firms at each possible distance d, and hence can be exploited to develop a proper locational measure of industry specialization.

Henderson (2003) established that both the number of firms and the level of employment in a region are key determinants of the generation of spillovers within the region. For this reason, we introduce weights in Eq. (4.1) so as to be able to account for the number of employees in each firm. Thus, we obtain the following weighted version of the local K-function,

$$WK_i(d) = E\left[\sum_{j\neq i} e_i e_j I\left(d_{ij} \leq d\right)\right] / \lambda\mu^2 \tag{4.2}$$

where e_i and e_j denote the number of employees of the ith and jth firms, respectively, and μ is the mean number of employees per firm. Therefore, the term $\lambda\mu^2 WK_i(d)$ can be interpreted as the mean of the sum of the products formed by the number of employees of the ith firm and the number of employees of all other firms located up to a distance d of the ith firm.

Turning now to the estimation aspects, following Getis (1984), Getis and Franklin (1987) and Penttinen (2006), a proper unbiased estimator of $WK_i(d)$ for a study area containing n firms is given by:

$$W\hat{K}_i(d) = \left(\sum_{j\neq i}^{n} e_i e_j w_{ij} I\left(d_{ij} \leq d\right)\right) / (n-1)\hat{\lambda}\hat{\mu}^2 \tag{4.3}$$

where $\hat{\lambda}$ is the estimated spatial intensity[3] and $\hat{\mu}$ is the mean number of employees per firm computed on the n observed firms. Due to the presence of edge effects arising from the bounded nature of the study area, an adjustment factor, say w_{ij}, is introduced, thus avoiding potential biases in the estimates close to the boundaries.[4] The adjustment factor w_{ij} expresses the reciprocal of the proportion of the surface area of a circle centered on the ith firm's location, passing through the jth firm's location, which lies within the area A (Boots and Getis 1988).

[3] $\hat{\lambda} = n/|A|$, where A is the study area and $|A|$ denotes its surface.

[4] Firms located near the boundary of the study area may be close to unobserved firms located outside the study area. Neglecting this circumstance may lead to a biased estimate.

As the last step, we use the function expressed in Eq. (4.3) to obtain a measure of industry specialization with the possibility of specifying a benchmark value allowing to assess if the *i*th firm is located in a specialized or despecialized industrial area. The most popular approach in the literature (see e.g. Beaudry and Schiffauerova 2009) has been to refer to a relative benchmark, in which an industry in a region is considered specialized (or, alternatively, despecialized) if it is overrepresented (or underrepresented) within the region with respect to the entire economy. A relative measure allows to control for the presence of spatial heterogeneity in the study area and hence is able to identify industry specialization due to the interactions among economic agents (see e.g. Arbia et al. 2012 and Espa et al. 2013).

In light of these considerations, in order to measure firm-level relative industry specialization, we can use the following statistics:

$$Kmar_i(d) = W\hat{K}_{i,\text{sector}}\frac{(d)}{W\hat{K}_{i,\text{all}}}(d) \qquad (4.4)$$

where $W\hat{K}_{i,\text{sector}}(d)$ is the weighted local *K*-function estimated on the firms belonging to the same sector of activity of the *i*th firm and $\hat{K}_{i,\text{all}}(d)$ is the weighted local *K*-function estimated on all firms of the dataset. If, at a given distance *d*, $Kmar_i(d)$ tends to be close to 1, then the *i*th firm is located in an area (with a spatial extension of radius *d*) where economic activities are randomly and independently located from each other, implying absence of industry specialization. *W*, at a given distance *d*, the functional expressed in Eq. (4.4), is greater than 1, the *i*th firm is located in a cluster with a spatial extension of *d* where the firms of its sector of activity are more concentrated than all firms of the dataset, implying presence of industry specialization. Conversely, when at a given distance *d*, $Kmar_i(d)$ is less than 1, the *i*th firm is located in a dispersed area, where the firms of its sector of activity are less concentrated than all firms of the dataset, implying presence of industry despecialization.

The functional expressed in Eq. (4.4) thus represents a relative measure in that the benchmarking value of random localization is represented by the spatial distribution of all economic activities. Hence, a specific sector exhibits specialization (or despecialization) if its spatial distribution is more concentrated (or dispersed) than the spatial distribution of all economic activities. Therefore, it represents a micro-geographic firm-level version of the Location Quotient and, hence, a proper measure to assess the working of MAR externalities.

4.3.1.3 A Firm-Level Measure of Jacobs Externalities

Let's now turn to discuss how to properly measure Jacobs' externalities. There is a wide consensus in the literature that a proper way to capture this second typology of externalities is through variables representing the extent of diversity of spatially close industries (see Beaudry and Schiffauerova 2009 among others). Coherently, in order to assess the effect of Jacobs externalities, we propose a firm-level distance-based measure of relative locational diversity. Similar to the case of the industry specialization index, we rely on the weighted local K-function. However, here we argue that a proper diversity measure may be provided by the following expression:

$$Kjac_i(d) = W\hat{K}_{\overline{i,\text{sector}}} \frac{(d)}{W\hat{K}_{i,\text{all}}}(d) \tag{4.5}$$

where $W\hat{K}_{\overline{i,\text{sector}}}(d)$ is the weighted local K-function estimated on the firms which do not belong to the same sector of activity of the ith firm and $W\hat{K}_{i,\text{all}}(d)$ is the local K-function estimated on all firms of the dataset.

Clearly, $Kjac_i(d) = 1$ represents the benchmark value corresponding to the case of absence of locational diversity. As a result, when $Kjac_i(d) > 1$ the ith firm is located in a cluster with a spatial extension of d where the firms of the other sectors of activity are more concentrated than all firms of the dataset, implying presence of locational diversity.

Conversely, when $Kjac_i(d) < 1$, the ith firm is located in a dispersed area, where the firms of the other sectors of activity are less concentrated than all firms of the dataset, implying presence of locational uniformity. We argue that $Kjac_i(d)$ represents a proper measure to assess the working of Jacobs externalities and it is a micro-geographic firm-level version of the Hirschman–Herfindahl index.

4.3.2 The Model

In this section, we will use the quantile regression approach to present a model linking the locational effects to firm growth. Indeed, it is well known that the growth rates distribution of firms departs significantly from the normal distribution (Bottazzi et al. 2007) so that a standard linear regression model does not seem appropriate because, in this case, the residuals would depart from the assumption of normality. As a consequence, the linear regression model may provide, at best, point estimates of the average effect of the independent variables on the "average firm." However, the focus on the average firm could hide important features of the underlying relationship given the existence of fat tails in the growth rates distribution (Coad 2007; Coad and Rao 2008). In particular, we aim at investigating the role of firms that have different size and exhibit different abilities to grow (Birch and Medoff 1994).

The quantile regression approach (Koenker and Hallock 2001) permits to estimate the differential effects of a series of independent variables on an objective variable for different quantiles of the distribution of the dependent variable.

We estimate two sets of quantile regressions separately for small and medium-large firms (MLFs) because the literature suggests that the growth behavior of the two groups might be very different (Haltiwanger et al. 2013). In the case of our working dataset, indeed, the range of growth rates for the two groups is very diverse: growth rates of small firms range from around—16% in the lower quantile (20% of all the sample of small firms) to 16.7% in the upper quantile, whereas medium-large firms appear to be more inertial in terms of contractions as measured by the number of employees—they contract at most of around 10%—and grow on average less than smaller firms—15.8% the upper quantile.

We concentrate on regressions of the following quantiles of the growth rate distribution: *q25, q50* and *q90.* The full model is based on the common econometric model used to evaluate the growth performance of business firm (Hall 1987; Audretsch and Dohse 2007; Coad and Rao 2008) but is “augmented” with a set of firm-level indicators that allow to investigate the different aspects of spatial and geographical distribution of firms:

$$\Delta s_{i,t} = \alpha_i + \sum_{d=5,50,100} \gamma_{MAR}{}' Kmar_{i,t}(d) + \sum_{d=5,50,100} \gamma_{JAC}{}' Kjac_{i,t}(d) + \\ + \beta'_1 SP_{i,t} + \beta_2 X_{i,t-1} + \beta'_3 Z_{i,t} + \varepsilon_{i,t} \tag{4.6}$$

where the dependent variable $\Delta s_{i,\,t}$ represents the rate of growth of the *i-th* firm from year *t*−*1* to year *t* calculated as difference in logs of size of firm *i* at year *t* and size of firm *i* at year *t*−*1*. In addition, in Eq. (4.6) the terms $Kmar_{i,\,t}(d)$ and $Kjac_{i,\,t}(d)$ represent the two measures of externalities introduced in the preceding Sect. 4.3.1. In particular, $Kmar_{i,\,t}(d)$ (for $d = 5, 50$ and 100 km) represents the firm-specific measures of industry specialization used to assess the effect of Marshallian externalities at short, medium and long range, while $Kjac_{i,\,t}(d)$ (for $d = 5, 50$ and 100 km) are the firm-specific measures of locational diversity used to assess the Jacobian externalities (agglomeration effects) related with the economies of urbanization at different distance ranges.

Among the other regressors SP_i represents a vector of additional aggregate measures of spatial interactions. Indeed, it should be noted that the specialization and locational diversity explanatory variables to capture agglomeration externalities are firm level and hence computed using data deriving from the firms of our sample. As already mentioned, our sample excludes the multiplant firms, which typically consist of big multinational corporations. This exclusion may cause an underestimation of the two variables and, as a result, a downward bias in the estimate of the associated regression parameters. In order to control for this potential bias, we cover the whole extent of economic activity, and proxy for the latent information about the multiplant firms, using regional aggregated data. In particular, we compute region-level indicators of specialization and diversity. As an indicator of specialization, we employ the common “location quotient” (*LQ*) which, for a certain combination of region and industry, is given by the ratio of the region’s share of industry employment to the region’s share of total employment. As an indicator of diversity, we employ the inverse of the Krugman specialization index (McCann 2001; de Vor and de Groot 2010) (*KRUG*), which, for a certain region, indicates how much the employment pattern of the region deviates from the employment pattern of the whole economy. For both indicators, regions are NUTS III regions and industries are defined according to the *NACE* Rev. 2 classification. We include a dummy (*Distr*) to signal that firm belongs to a district—as defined by ISTAT—because such administrative agglomeration of companies could benefit from specific policies that are not captured by our measures.

Finally, going back to the description of the regressors in Eq. (4.6), we have that $X_{i,t}$ is a vector of "standard" determinants of growth that include the following:

- The $Log(age_{i,t})$ that measures the number of years since the firm was established;
- The size of firm given by the logarithm of number of employees ($Log(\text{size}_{i,t-1})$);
- A proxy for financial constraints as measured by the cash flow (*Cash* $flow_{t-1}$);
- $Z_{I,t}$ is a vector of three systems of dummy variables to control for year, sector of activity and geographical area of activity. Disturbance terms are given by $\varepsilon_{i,\,t}$.

4.4 Data

The empirical analysis carried out in this chapter draws on a database containing information for about 8300 Italian limited liabilities manufacturing companies active in the time window from year 1996 to year 2004. The unit of observation is the single location firm and, consequently, results can be easily interpreted and directly compared with those deriving from studies conducted at an establishment level. The primary source of data is the Italian section of Bureau Van Dijk's database, which provides financial and balance sheet information together with geographic localization information and employment figures. In particular, our sample includes only firms active in the whole period 1996–2004 and operating only in one location.

Employment figures are corrected using the National Social Security Institution—INPS—archives, in particular the monthly social security declarations. This procedure allows to control for the reliability of information about the number of employees, a feature that is considered necessary to undertake a sound analysis of firms' dynamics involving employment dynamics (Haltiwanger et al. 2013; Neumark et al. 2011). The "adjusted" average number of employees of a firm is given by the yearly average number of employees present in the firm.

The key characteristic that distinguishes our dataset from other similar studies on the growth of Italian firms is the use of single location firms. This level of analysis helps to shed light on the determinants of "organic" growth.

4.5 Empirical Results

The quantile regressions are first run splitting the sample into small firms (SMFs) and medium-large firms (MLFs) and then into low-tech and high-tech firms. Moreover, we run quantile regression referring to positional means of growth rates given by: 0.25 quantile (q25 henceforth), 0.50 quantile (q50 henceforth) and 0.90 quantile (q90 henceforth).

Table 4.1 reports some descriptive statistics of the variables included in the analysis.

First of all, notice that the average size of the firms is 50 employees while the median size is 34, with a strong evidence of a negative skew. Firms are 21 years old on average. The 0.90 quantile of the firm age (38) years shows that the firms in our sample are relatively young.

A particular attention is devoted to the study of the distribution of the growth rates of firms. Indeed, as mentioned before, the standard regression techniques can lead to incorrect inference about the coefficients if their distribution departs from normality. In order to investigate the shape of growth rate distribution, we estimated a series of normality tests: (a) for all the years separately for small and medium-large firms; (b) pooling together all the years separately for small and medium-large firms.

Table 4.1 Descriptive statistics of the variables used in the regression analysis

Variable name	Variable description	*N*	min	max	mean	sd
$\Delta s_{i,\,t}$	Growth rate in terms of number of employees	66,896	−1.91	3.01	0.01	0.15
Kmar(5)	Getis K function within sector at 5 km	74,133	0.00	144.16	2.70	5.33
Kmar(50)	Getis K function within sector at 50 km	74,133	0.00	21.90	1.48	1.32
Kmar(100)	Getis K function within sector at 100 km	74,133	0.00	8.12	1.25	0.75
Kjac(5)	Getis K function (all firms) at 5 km	74,133	0.00	118.86	1.16	2.81
Kjac(50)	Getis K function (all firms) at 50 km	74,133	0.00	713.14	1.23	8.37
Kjac(100)	Getis K function (all firms) at 100 km	74,133	0.00	104.15	1.09	2.00
LQ	Location Quotient	74,133	0.00	33.19	1.08	1.17
KRUG	Krugman agglomeration index	74,133	0.21	21.03	2.26	1.67
Distr	Dummy industrial districts	75,258	0	1	0.51	0.49
$size_{i,t-1}$	Number of employees	75,258	2.00	920.00	49.68	54.65
$age_{i,t}$	Age of firm	75,258	0.00	132.00	21.83	12.78
$Cash\ flow_{t-1}$	Proxy for financial constraints	75,258	−1.50	1.05	0.02	0.05
Low-tech sector	Dummy for OECD low sector firms	75,258	0	1	0.41	0.49
Low-medium tech sector	Dummy for OECD low-medium sector firms	75,258	0	1	0.31	0.46
mid-high tech sector	Dummy for OECD medium-high sector firms	75,258	0	1	0.25	0.43
High-tech sector	Dummy for OECD high sector firms	75,258	0	1	0.03	0.17
Du_area_1	Dummy northeast of Italy	75,258	0	1	0.41	0.49
Du_area_2	Dummy northwest of Italy	75,258	0	1	0.36	0.48
Du_area_3	Dummy center of Italy	75,258	0	1	0.17	0.38
Du_area_4	Dummy south of Italy	75,258	0	1	0.06	0.23

Table 4.2 Normality tests for the distribution of growth rates (z values and significance level)

	Shapiro-Wilk	Sahpiro-Francia
Years	All firms	
All years (pooled)	21.297***	23.743***
1997	16.862***	16.825***
1998	15.897***	15.884***
1999	16.674***	16.640***
2000	15.341***	15.345***
2001	15.487***	15.478***
2002	15.163***	15.167***
2003	14.793***	14.801***
2004	15.879***	15.864***
Small firms (<=50 employees)		
All years (pooled)	19.794***	21.575***
Medium-large firms (>50 employees)		
All years (pooled)	19.614***	20.381***

Legenda: *** $p < 0.001$

The battery of tests leads us to reject the null hypothesis of normality in all the cases (Table 4.2).

The presence of spatial variability may lead to the violation of the assumption on which Model (6) is based: the independence of growth rates, which in turn results in spatial autocorrelation of model residuals. The proper diagnostic tool for verifying whether the residuals of a micro-geographic firm-level model are spatially correlated is the variogram (Schabenberger and Gotway 2005). For the standardized model residuals the empirical variogram ordinates are the quantities $v_{ij} = \frac{1}{2}(r_i - r_j)^2$, where r_i and r_j are the standardized residuals corresponding to the firms at the locations x_i and x_j, respectively (Diggle and Ribeiro Jr 2007). A plot of v_{ij} against the corresponding distance $d_{ij} = \|x_i - x_j\|$ compared with the envelope of empirical variograms computed from random permutations of the residuals, holding their locations fixed, allows the detection of spatial autocorrelation.

A separate variogram has to be computed on the residuals for each single year t. As a way of illustration, Fig. 4.1 shows a variogram envelope obtained from 999 independent random permutations of the standardized residuals for year $t = 2000$ for each of the 10th quantile and 90th

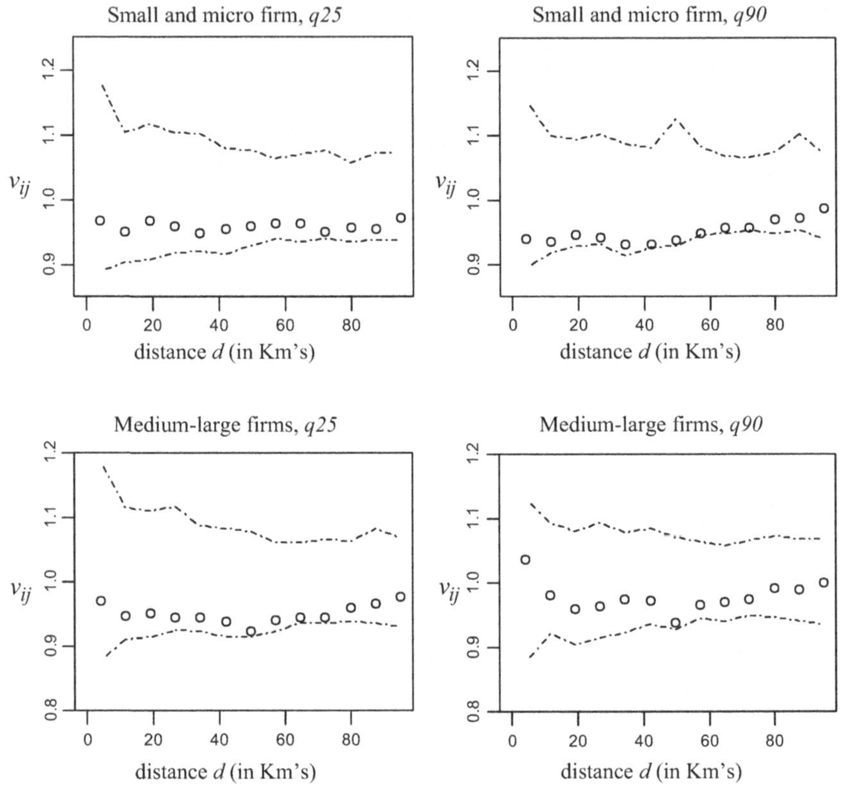

Fig. 4.1 Monte Carlo envelopes for the variogram of the Model (6) standardized residuals (dashed lines) and empirical variogram of residuals (circles) for year $t = 2000$ and 25th and 90th quantiles

quantile regression models, with values averaged within distance bands. Since all the empirical variogram ordinates are within the Monte Carlo simulation envelopes, we can conclude that there is no spatial dependence amongst these model's residuals.[5]

[5]The same graphical test of spatial correlation has been performed on the model residuals for all the other years and quantiles as well, leading to the same conclusion of absence of spatial correlation. The results are available upon request to the authors.

Table 4.3 presents the results of two separate regressions referring to small (less than or equal to 50 employees) and medium-large firms (more than 50 employees), and Table 4.4 presents the results of the separate regressions for high-tech and low-tech firms. The technological sectors are defined according to the definition provided by OECD ISIC REV.3.

For each of these four subsets of firms, the 25th, 50th and 90th quantile regressions have been estimated. In particular, columns 1–3 of Table 4.3 report the results for the small firms, columns 4–6 for the medium-large firms; columns 7–9 of Table 4.4 for the high-tech firms and columns 10–12 for the low-tech firms. We split the sample according to the firm size and level of technology starting from the assumption that they are important mediators in the relationship between the spatial determinants and the growth of firm. The results reported below seem to confirm this intuition.

The first important evidence emerging from the results reported in Table 4.3 is that the way agglomeration externalities (both MAR and JAC) exert their effects on firm growth, strongly depends on the spatial dimension of the industrial site in which firm is located. It can indeed be seen that the regression coefficients associated with the variables *Kmar(d)* and *Kjac(d)*, (at distance $d = 5, 50, 100$) can have different signs, different values and different levels of significance depending on the value of the distance *d*. In particular, from the exam of Table 4.3 it clearly emerges that the small and low-tech firms in 0.90 quantile benefit from positive JAC externalities at a distance of 50 km, while, on the contrary, they are affected by negative JAC externalities at a distance of 100 km. Therefore, a firm may have both a positive and a negative effect from agglomeration externalities at the same time. This implies that when we try to estimate the effect of agglomeration externalities using region-level locational measures (i.e., we refer to a fixed arbitrarily defined spatial scale), what we estimate is indeed more likely to be the combined result of different effects observed at different spatial scales. The opportunity of using firm-level distance-based measures, such as those proposed, is then confirmed. In Sect. 4.3.1, in order to better assess the effects of agglomeration externalities in their whole complexity.

Table 4.3 Results of the quantile regressions for small firms and medium-large firms

	Small firms (≤ 50 employees)			Medium-large firms (>50 employees)		
	(1)	(2)	(3)	(4)	(5)	(6)
Quantiles of growth distribution	q25	q50	q90	q25	q50	q90
	−0.074	0.000	0.167	−0.045	0.012	0.158
Kmar(5)	−0.0001	0.0000	0.0001	−0.0003*	−0.0002	−0.0002
	0.0000	*0.0000*	*0.0000*	*0.0000*	*0.0000*	*0.0000*
Kmar(50)	−0.0008	−0.0009	0.0005	*0.0000*	0.0005	−0.0007
	0.001	*0.001*	*0.001*	*0.001*	*0.001*	*0.001*
Kmar(100)	0.0012	0.0009	0.0007	0.0007	−0.0002	0.0030***
	0.001	*0.001*	*0.001*	*0.001*	*0.001*	*0.001*
Kjac(5)	−0.0039	−0.0028	0.0042	−0.0013	0.0094**	0.0113***
	0.003	*0.003*	*0.003*	*0.006*	*0.004*	*0.004*
Kjac(50)	−0.0013	0.0101	0.0696***	0.0188	0.0256	0.0788
	0.017	*0.017*	*0.015*	*0.03*	*0.027*	*0.056*
Kjac(100)	0.0041	−0.0065	−0.0657***	−0.003	−0.0144	−0.07
	0.018	*0.016*	*0.013*	*0.03*	*0.025*	*0.055*
LQ	0.0025***	0.0033**	0.0004	−0.0023	0.0002	−0.0014
	0.001	*0.001*	*0.002*	*0.002*	*0.002*	*0.002*
KRUG	0.0025***	0.0015**	0.0022	0.0008	0.0021***	0.0040**
	0.001	*0.001*	*0.001*	*0.001*	*0.001*	*0.002*
Distretto	0.0081**	0.0058**	−0.0068	0.0011	−0.0013	−0.0002
	0.003	*0.003*	*0.004*	*0.005*	*0.003*	*0.006*
Log(age$_{i,t}$)	−0.0018	−0.0221***	−0.0534***	−0.0247***	−0.0479***	−0.1096***
	0.003	*0.002*	*0.003*	*0.004*	*0.003*	*0.008*

Log(size$_{i,t-1}$)	−0.0892***	−0.1167***	−0.2548***	−0.1408***	−0.1236***	−0.1500***
	0.003	*0.003*	*0.006*	*0.005*	*0.004*	*0.007*
Cash flow$_{t-1}$	0.3841***	0.2908***	0.1246**	0.4389***	0.4402***	0.4058***
	0.031	*0.032*	*0.058*	*0.049*	*0.056*	*0.058*
Constant	0.1042***	0.4050***	1.2064***	0.5824***	0.6853***	1.2772***
	0.02	*0.019*	*0.031*	*0.026*	*0.017*	*0.045*
Sector controls	Y	Y	Y	Y	Y	Y
Year controls	Y	Y	Y	Y	Y	Y
Geographic area controls	Y	Y	Y	Y	Y	Y
Observations	33,772	33,772	33,772	15,650	15,650	15,650

Dependent variable: one-year growth rate
Notes: Standard errors in italics. *** $p < 0.01$, ** $p < 0.05$, * $p < 0.1$

Table 4.4 Results of the quantile regressions for low-technology firms and high-technology firms

	Low-technology firms			High-technology firms		
	(7)	(8)	(9)	(10)	(11)	(12)
Quantiles of growth distribution	q25	q50	q90	q25	q50	q90
	−0.074	0.000	0.167	−0.045	0.012	0.158
Kmar(5)	−0.0001	0.0004	0.0012**	−0.0002	−0.0001	−0.0001*
	0.0000	*0.0000*	*0.001*	*0.0000*	*0.0000*	*0.0000*
Kmar(50)	−0.0026***	−0.0025***	−0.003	−0.0002	−0.0005	0.0008
	0.001	*0.001*	*0.002*	*0.001*	*0.001*	*0.001*
Kmar(100)	0.0047*	0.0029	0.0052	0.0003	0.0004	0.0009
	0.003	*0.003*	*0.003*	*0.001*	*0.001*	*0.001*
Kjac(5)	0.0054	0.0073	−0.0049	−0.0035	−0.0027	0.0043
	0.018	*0.013*	*0.032*	*0.003*	*0.003*	*0.004*
Kjac(50)	−0.0815	−0.0675	−0.0353	0.0048	0.0295*	0.0712***
	0.079	*0.08*	*0.101*	*0.023*	*0.017*	*0.013*
Kjac(100)	0.2176	0.1691	0.2438	−0.0065	−0.0299*	−0.0701***
	0.167	*0.154*	*0.158*	*0.021*	*0.016*	*0.013*
LQ	0.0071***	0.0063**	0.0032	0.0023***	0.0037*	0.0009
	0.002	*0.003*	*0.003*	*0.001*	*0.002*	*0.002*
KRUG	0.0038***	0.0039***	0.0011	0.0025**	0.0015	0.0026
	0.001	*0.001*	*0.002*	*0.001*	*0.001*	*0.002*
Distretto	0.0014	0.0037	−0.0165**	0.0096**	0.0033	−0.0048
	0.005	*0.005*	*0.007*	*0.004*	*0.002*	*0.005*
Log($age_{i,t}$)	−0.0071	−0.0331***	−0.0633***	0.0026	−0.0173***	−0.0506***
	0.007	*0.007*	*0.01*	*0.004*	*0.003*	*0.005*

Log(size$_{i,t-1}$)	−0.0884***	−0.1189***	−0.2918***	−0.0900***	−0.1148***	−0.2419***
	0.006	*0.005*	*0.014*	*0.003*	*0.005*	*0.005*
Cash flow$_{t-1}$	0.3492***	0.2999***	0.1169	0.4125***	0.2855***	0.1405***
	0.043	*0.06*	*0.093*	*0.047*	*0.043*	*0.053*
Constant	−0.0523	0.3237***	1.1518***	0.1182***	0.4038***	1.1698***
	0.145	*0.106*	*0.146*	*0.018*	*0.018*	*0.017*
Year controls	Y	Y	Y	Y	Y	Y
Geographic area controls	Y	Y	Y	Y	Y	Y
Observations	33,772	33,772	33,772	15,650	15,650	15,650

Dependent variable: one-year growth rate

Notes: Standard errors in italics. *** $p < 0.01$, ** $p < 0.05$, * $p < 0.1$

Having in mind this general consideration, we can now look at the results in a greater detail. To start with, let us consider the MAR externalities. According to the level of significance of the parameters associated with the variables *Kmar(d)*, it seems that the annual growth of small firms is not affected by MAR externalities. On the other hand, this type of externality is relevant for the medium-large firms. Indeed, shrinking medium-large firms (*q25*) are weakly negatively affected by MAR externalities at small distances ($d = 5$ km) while high growth firms (*q90*) are positively affected at long distances ($d = 90$ km). Therefore, medium-large firms tend to suffer from congestion related with the presence of firms of the same industry in the neighborhood and to benefit from large spatial-scale industry specialization.

If we condition the analysis to the technological level of firms, the pattern of MAR externalities is even more complex and produce a rich set of further considerations. MAR externalities are not substantially relevant for low-tech firms, if we exclude only a very weak negative effect observed in the firms characterized by a high level of growth. On the contrary, they tend to have an important role for the high-tech firms. These firms are, indeed, positively affected on the short and long distances (5 and 100 kms, respectively) and negatively affected on the medium distances (50 km), thus suggesting that the effect of MAR externalities is strongly nonlinear in space.

Turning now to the role of JAC externalities, among the small firms, they are relevant only for the *q90* firms and exert a positive influence at 50 kms and a negative influence at 100 kms. This very same pattern of nonlinearity in space applies also to the *q50* and *q90* high-tech firms. Differently, large firms are only positively affected by JAC externalities at 5 km and low-tech firms are not affected in any direction.

In conclusion, the empirical evidence emerging from our estimates does not provide a clear-cut answer to the issue of the relationship between agglomeration externalities and firm growth. They show that this phenomenon is quite complex, because the effect of agglomeration externalities strongly depend on the characteristics of spatial relationships, firms' size and their technological level. Therefore, we argue that simple and straightforward interpretations of the phenomenon would lead to misleading conclusions.

Having said that, however, we can draw the general indications that MAR externalities produce mostly a negative effect at small and medium distances and a positive effect at large distances, while, on the contrary, JAC externalities have mostly a positive effect at small and medium distances and a negative effect at large distances. This stylized fact suggests the existence of possible complementarities between the two kind of spatial externalities which may have important implications in terms of policies. It indeed suggests that, stimulating the occurrence of positive MAR externalities may, on the other hand, hinder the occurrence of positive JAC externalities and vice versa.

We included in the models the location coefficient calculated at NUTS3 level (*LOQ*) to refine our firm-level measures of spatial factors. Indeed, this location quotient is introduced in the regression as a further security check for the existence of MAR effects which are not captured by our firm-level measures. Our empirical results show that for small firms the coefficients are significant, but, again, very small and constant over the quantiles. For small firms, the introduction of this term into the regression allow us to rescale all the growth rates over the quantiles in order to correct for residual spatial correlation related to multiplant firms. Medium-large firms, instead, do not present significant coefficients.

With a similar argument we used a proxy of the diversity of environment at provincial level the concentration inverse of the Krugman specialization index. In this case, the effect is significant for small firm at *q25* and *q50*. Medium-large firms benefit from specialization at *q50* and *q90*.

A long literature is devoted to the positive effects on firm performances of industrial district as defined by ISTAT (Beccattini 1989). A firm active in an industrial district can benefit, for instance, find new workforce easily, workforce is specialized, suppliers are easier to reach because they have experience with other firms in the industrial districts, there exist public policies that regard specifically the industrial districts firms. These effects should be distinguished by spatial proximity of firms and agglomeration phenomena; hence, to capture these effects, we introduced a dummy variable identifying firms belonging to an industrial district. Results reveal that being located in a district produces a positive effect on growth of small firms at *q25* and *q50*. Medium-large firms are not affected by being in a district. In other words, larger firms do not benefit from the administrative aspects behind the definition of a district (e.g., the existence of subsidies for firms in a district), but may benefit by the pure market advantages coming from agglomeration.

As for the standard determinants of growth, we observe that the variable Age produces a negative effect on growth for all firms (see Table 4.3): as firms get older, they appear less prone to grabbing opportunities of growth. Another feature that quantile regression allows to capture is fact that the bigger the growth performance of firms, the stronger is the negative linkage. Indeed, coefficients range from −0.009 for small firms in *q10* to −0.05 at *q90*. Similarly, for medium-large firms these coefficients range from −0.02 for *q10* to −0.11 for *q90*. The effect is nonlinear as witnessed by the significance of the coefficient of age squared.

The variable size has a significant effect even if the heterogeneity of signs and magnitudes reveal that the size has a negative effect on growth both for small and medium-large firms. Interestingly, the largest coefficient is found for small firms at the 90th quantile (*q90*). In this case, the value is equal to −0.25 and significant, thus suggesting that small firms experience an increasing difficulty in growing as their size is bigger.

Liquidity constraints coefficient representing a key factor that can impede growth are introduced through the variable *cash flow* (an inverse proxy of liquidity constraint). The corresponding coefficients are positive and significant for all the groups of firms. Such factor is more important for medium-large firms compared to small firms across all quantiles.

4.6 Summary and Conclusions

In this chapter, we carried out an empirical analysis to study how localization economies shape the patterns of firm growth. Our investigation departs markedly from most of the recent literature on the subject, in that we adopt an alternative way of quantifying the effects of spatial externalities based on micro-data. In this respect, we suggested to use the Getis local K-function (Getis 1984; Getis and Franklin 1987) to define firm-level indicators that endogenize the emergence of geographical economies. In this way, we are able to tackle two methodological problems typically arising in empirical work when considering regional aggregated data: (a) the dependence of the results on the particular adopted geographical partition (into, e.g., counties or regions) and (b) the restrictive assumption of spatial homogeneity of the phenomenon within regions which does not allow to take into consideration the intra-regional variability.

Founding on the proposed methodology, we were able to assess empirically the prevalence of Marshall-Arrow-Romer externalities (MAR) on Jacobs externalities (JAC). As it is known, the former refers to knowledge spillovers between firms of the same industry, labor market pooling, transport saving cost and economies of scale arising from shared inputs. The latter are pure agglomeration economies arising from knowledge spillover external to the industry within which firm operates, diversity leading to economic growth and urbanization externalities.

Our exploration involves a large sample of small and medium Italian firms operating in the manufacturing sector over a period of eight years. The modeling is based on a quantile regression framework that better discriminates between the distinctive features of the growth rate distribution.

In summary, we obtained the following stylized facts:

- The action of the various externalities is a rather complex phenomenon, but there are important empirical evidences that small and medium-sized firms are affected in a different way by MAR and JAC externalities.
- Small firms, which in the recent past experienced slightly negative growth performance, are positively influenced by JAC diversity. This effect is more evident if the firms operate in low-technology sectors and the externalities are observed at short distances in space.
- Firms in low-technology sectors that performed well in terms of growth are more likely to exploit both MAR and JAC positive externalities.
- The effect associated with the two typologies of agglomeration economies varies with the distance threshold used to compute

the location indicators. For example, the growth opportunities for medium-large firms operating in low technology sectors are generally negatively affected by MAR externalities, but, conversely, are positively influenced by JAC externalities if observed at 50 kms.

These results may be of interest for policy makers and business practitioners in that they suggest some interesting implications that it is worth to briefly mention here.

First of all, the empirical evidence of different (and sometimes opposite) effects of geographical spillovers on firms depending on their size, on their different technological environment and on their recent growth history, suggest that a "*one-size fits-all*" approach to industrial policy is doomed to fail or even to produce results that move in the opposite direction with respect to the desired aims.

Secondly, managers and policy makers should be aware of the fact that the structural and strategic choices they implement can significantly mediate the sheer effects associated with geographical location. Indeed, some of these choices can mitigate the negative effects stemming from a higher competition in a given area. Other choices, conversely, allow the firm to absorb most of the knowledge spillovers spreading in the surrounding environment and in this way to exploit them as a growth factor.

References

Acs, Z., & Armington, C. (2004). Employment growth and entrepreneurial activity in cities. *Regional studies, 38*(8), 911–927.

Andersson, M., & Lööf, H. (2011). Agglomeration and Productivity: Evidence from Firm-Level Data. *The Annals of Regional Science, 46*, 601–620.

Antonietti, R., Cainelli, G., & Lupi, C. (2013). Vertical Disintegration and Spatial Co-localization: The Case of Kibs in the Metropolitan Region of Milan. *Economics Letters, 118*, 360–363.

Arbia, G. (1989). *Spatial Data Configuration in Statistical Analysis of Regional Economic and Related Problems*. Dordrecht: Kluwer Academic Publisher.

Arbia, G. (2001). Modelling the Geography of Economic Activities on a Continuous Space. *Papers in Regional Science, 80*, 411–424.

Arbia, G., Espa, G., Giuliani, D., & Mazzitelli, A. (2010). Detecting the Existence of Space–Time Clustering of Firms. *Regional Science and Urban Economics, 40*, 311–323.

Arbia, G., Espa, G., & Giuliani, D. (2012). Clusters of Firms in an Inhomogeneous Space: The High-Tech Industries in Milan. *Economic Modelling, 29*(1), 3–11.

Audretsch, D. B., & Dohse, D. (2007). Location: A Neglected Determinant of Firm Growth. *Review of World Economics, 143*(1), 79–107.

Autant-Bernard, C. (2001). The geography of knowledge spillovers and technological proximity. *Economics of Innovation and New Technology, 10*(4), 237–254.

Barbosa, N., & Eiriz, V. (2011). Regional Variation of Firm Size and Growth: The Portuguese Case. *Growth Change, 42*(2), 125–158.

Beaudry, C., & Schiffauerova, A. (2009). Who's Right, Marshall or Jacobs? The Localization Versus Urbanization Debate. *Research Policy, 38*(2), 318–337.

Beaudry, C., & Swann, P. (2009). Firm Growth in Industrial Clusters of the United Kingdom. *Small Business Economics, 32*(4), 409–424.

Beccattini, G. (1989). Sectors and/or Districts. In E. Goodman & J. Barnforth (Eds.), *Small Firms and Industrial Districts in Italy* (pp. 120–133). London: Routledge.

Becchetti, L., & Trovato, G. (2002). The determinants of growth for small and medium sized firms. The role of the availability of external finance. *Small business economics, 19*(4), 291–306.

Birch, D. L., & Medoff, J. (1994). Gazelles. In L. C. Solmon & A. R. Levenson (Eds.), *Labor markets, employment policy and job creation*. Boulder: Westview Press.

Bottazzi, G., Cefis, E., Dosi, G., & Secchi, A. (2007). Invariances and Diversities in the Patterns of Industrial Evolution: Some Evidence from Italian Manufacturing Industries. *Small Business Economics, 29*(1–2), 137–159.

Boots, B. N., & Getis, A. (1988). *Point pattern analysis* (Vol. 8). SAGE Publications, Incorporated.

Brown, W. M., & Rigby, D. L. (2010). *Marshallian Localization Economies: Where Do They Come From and to Whom Do They Flow?* Paper presented at the DIME Workshop 'Industrial Dynamics and Economic Geography', Utrecht, September.

Coad, A. (2007). A Closer Look at Serial Growth Rate Correlation. *Review of Industrial Organization, 31*(1), 69–82.

Coad, A., & Rao, R. (2008). Innovation and firm growth in high-tech sectors: A quantile regression approach. *Research policy, 37*(4), 633–648.

Contini, B., & Revelli, R. (1988). *Job Creation and Labour Mobility: The Vacancy Chain Model and Some Empirical Findings*. R&P Working Paper N.8.

Del Monte, A., & Papagni, E. (2003). R&D and the Growth of Firms: Empirical Analysis of a Panel of Italian Firms. *Research Policy, 32*, 1003–1014.

Diggle, P. J., & Ribeiro, P. J., Jr. (2007). *Model-Based Geostatistics*. New York: Springer.

Duranton, G., & Overman, H. G. (2005). Testing for Localisation Using Micro-geographic Data. *The Review of Economic Studies, 72*, 1077–1106.

Duschl, M., Schimke, A., Brenner, T., & Luxen, D. (2011). *Firm Growth and the Spatial Impact of Geolocated External Factors: Empirical Evidence for German Manufacturing Firms*. Working Paper series in Economics n.36. Retrieved from hdl.handle.net/10419/51558.

Ellison, G., & Glaeser, E. L. (1997). Geographic Concentration in U.S. Manufacturing Industries: A Dartboard Approach. *Journal of Political Economy, 105*, 889–927.

Espa, G., Arbia, G., & Giuliani, D. (2013). Conditional Versus Unconditional Industrial Agglomeration: Disentangling Spatial Dependence and Spatial Heterogeneity in the Analysis of ICT Firms' Distribution in Milan. *Journal of Geographical Systems, 15*(1), 31–50.

Feldman, M. P., & Audretsch, D. B. (1999). Innovation in Cities: Science-Based Diversity, Specialization and Localized Competition. *European Economic Review, 43*(2), 409–429.

Florence, P. S. (1939). *Report on the Location of Industry*. London: Political and Economic Planning.

Frenken, K., Cefis, E., & Stam, E. (2014). Industrial Dynamics and Clusters: A Survey. *Regional Studies, 8*, 1–18.

Frenken, K., Van Oort, F., & Verburg, T. (2007). Related variety, unrelated variety and regional economic growth. *Regional studies, 41*(5), 685–697.

Fujita, M., Krugman, P., & Venables, A. (1999). *The Spatial Economy–Cities, Regions and International Trade*. Cambridge, MA: MIT Press.

Getis, A. (1984). Interaction Modelling Using Second-Order Analysis. *Environment and Planning A, 16*, 173–183.

Getis, A., & Franklin, J. (1987). Second-Order Neighborhood Analysis of Mapped Point Patterns. *Ecology, 68*, 473–477.

Gibrat, R. (1931). *Les Ingalits Economiques*. Parigi: Sirey.
Gini, C. (1912). Variabilità e mutabilità. Reprinted in Memorie di metodologica statistica. E. Pizetti, & T. Salvemini (Eds.), Rome.
Gini, C. (1921). Measurement of Inequality of Incomes. *The Econometrics Journal, 31*(121), 124–126.
Glaeser, E., Kallal, H., Scheinkman, J., & Schleifer, A. (1992). Growth of Cities. *The Journal of Political Economics, 100*, 1126–1152.
Griliches, Z. (1992). R&D and productivity: the econometric evidence. *material from Scandinavian Journal of Economics, 94*, 251–268.
Hall, B. H. (1987). The Relationship Between Firm Size and Firm Growth in the US Manufacturing Sector. *The Journal of Industrial Economics, 35*(4), 583–606.
Haltiwanger, J., Jarmin, R. S., & Miranda, J. (2013). Who Creates Jobs? Small Versus Large Versus Young. *The Review of Economics and Statistics, 95*(2), 347–361.
Henderson, V. (2003). The urbanization process and economic growth: The so-what question. *Journal of Economic growth, 8*(1), 47–71.
Henderson, V., Kuncoro, A., & Turner, M. (1995). Industrial Development in Cities. *Journal of Political Economy, 103*(5), 1067–1090.
Hirschman, A. O. (1945). *National Power and the Structure of Foreign Trade*. Berkeley: University of California Press.
Jacobs, J. (1969). *The Economy of Cities*. New York: Random House.
Koenker, R., & Hallock, K. F. (2001). Quantile regression. *Journal of economic perspectives, 15*(4), 143–156.
Krugman, P. (1991). *Geography and Trade*. Cambridge: MIT Press.
Lotti, F., Santarelli, E., & Vivarelli, M. (2003). Does Gibrat's Law Hold Among Young, Small Firms? *Journal of Evolutionary Economics, 13*(3), 213–235.
Maine, E. M., Shapiro, D. M., & Vining, A. R. (2010). The Role of Clustering in the Growth of New Technology-Based Firms. *Small Business Economics, 34*, 127–146.
Marcon, E., & Puech, F. (2010). Measures of the Geographic Concentration of Industries: Improving Distance-Based Methods. *Journal of Economic Geography, 10*(5), 745–762.
Marshall, A. (1890). *Principles of Economics*. London: Macmillan.
McCann, P. (2001). Urban and regional economics. OUP Catalogue.
Neumark, D., Wall, B., & Zhang, J. (2011). Do small businesses create more jobs? New evidence for the United States from the National Establishment Time Series. *The Review of Economics and Statistics, 93*(1), 16–29.

Penttinen, A. (2006). Statistics for Marked Point Patterns. *The Yearbook of the Finnish Statistical Society, 2006*, 70–91.
Porter, M. E. (1990). *The Competitive Advantage of Nations*. London: Macmillan.
Raspe, O., & Van Oort, F. (2008). Firm Growth and Localized Knowledge Externalities. *Journal of Regional Analysis and Policy, 38*(2), 100–116.
Raspe, O., & Van Oort, F. (2011). Growth of New Firms and Spatially Bounded Knowledge Externalities. *The Annals of Regional Science, 46*, 495–518.
Rosenthal, S. S., & Strange, W. C. (2005). The geography of entrepreneurship in the New York metropolitan area. *Federal Reserve Bank of New York Economic Policy Review, 11*(2), 29–54.
Schabenberger, O., & Gotway, C. A. (2005). *Statistical Methods for Spatial Data Analysis*. Boca Raton: Chapman & Hall/CRC.
Staber, U. (2001). Spatial Proximity and Firm Survival in a Declining Industrial District: The Case of Knitwear Firms in Baden-Wurttemberg. *Regional Studies, 35*, 329–341.
de Vor, F., & de Groot, H. (2010). Agglomeration Externalities and Localized Employment Growth: The Performance of Industrial Sites in Amsterdam. *The Annals of Regional Science, 44*, 409–431.
Wennberg, K., & Lindqvist, G. (2010). The Effects of Clusters on the Survival and Performance of New Firms. *Small Business Economics, 34*(3), 221–241.

Part III

Inequality

5

Spatial Inequality: A Multidimensional Perspective

Giuseppe Pignataro

5.1 Introduction

Spatial inequality has received considerable attention from both scholars and politicians in the last two decades. It particularly coincides with the technological advance of developing countries like China, Russia, India, and Brazil, territories with geographical peculiarities characterized by high growth rates. Spatial and more specific regional inequalities may help to provide a completely different view of economic disparities and general social welfare indicators.

At least some of these questions remain unanswered or have received remarkably little systematic documentation in the literature. We should first understand the exact meaning of spatial inequality. To what extent spatial dimension should be relevant compared to the traditional inequality measurement? Why is it important in terms of policy response? How can geographical aspects influence the related measures of well-being?

G. Pignataro (✉)
University of Bologna, Bologna, Italy
e-mail: giuseppe.pignataro@unibo.it

S. Colombo (ed.), *Spatial Economics Volume II*,
https://doi.org/10.1007/978-3-030-40094-1_5

This chapter aims at studying such determinants, while proposing a conceptual perspective of theoretical and empirical contributions on spatial inequality and welfare in a jointly unified framework.

Spatial inequality is indeed a dimension of the overall disparity, but it contains additional multidimensional view. The idea of capturing the impact of the heterogeneous income distribution is typical of the standard literature of inequality measurement. Such aspects can be even more impressive by taking into account a spatial dimension as it helps to define the correct profile of inequality with unusual policy prescriptions.

The growing interest surrounding this issue has to do with the fact that spatial inequality involves different evaluations across geographical or administrative units, and such feature can be one component of overall income inequality across individuals. This topic may implicitly identify how much a rise in spatial inequality within a given country, other things being equal, does influence the overall national disparities. Suppose to get an accurate measure of the share of income inequality originated within a community of individuals located in a particular country or capture the average differences across societies. Moreover, gauging spatial difference may, for instance, be of interest in case of externalities in the geographical allocation of sources. Deriving the contributions of income sources implies, for example, to understand which spatial factor contributes to determining inequality in a local area. Such an effect can be even influenced by the internal migration flow that may shrink or enlarge the spatial gaps in terms of salary, opportunity, or general economic advantage profile. A clear answer to these points is far from being clear.

Our analysis, therefore, encloses different fields of the literature. The impact of measurement issue involves the use of some indices and their related properties able to disentangle the effect of inequality within and between territories (Shorrocks and Wan 2005). Second, the role of geographical characteristics is a source of spatial variation which emphasizes the necessity of georeferencing and digitizing maps, atlases, and census records, particularly in the historical perspective.

In the last decade, the discussion about measurement issues, besides theoretical implications, was useful to understand a proper combination of redistributive policies. We consider such aspects by looking at the inequality of opportunity literature. The idea is that not all elements that contribute to an unfair income distribution are illegitimate. The society needs to distinguish between characteristics rendering the inequality practically unfair and attributes through which inequality should be considered legitimate.

The spatial dimension should regulate the distributive procedures by which territories come to acquire especially advantageous positions in terms of income and other related variables. The topic is broader, and there are attempts to address the issue about what extent of inequality across the individuals and their different territories in the society can be captured using a correct index. Measuring the spatial income profiles is also required to discover whether the gap between the top rung of society and the bottom rung should be large or small taking into account their possible influences on economic performance in all areas. Therefore, we investigate some forms of decomposition inspired by Foster and Shneyerov (2000). They introduce the "path-independent" decomposable class of inequality indices, which is extremely useful to compute a correct measure of the overall inequality while taking into account the within and the between component that the spatial dimension necessarily requires. This combination even involves an evaluation of the geographical size in a multidimensional channel of growth and more in general economic performance. For instance, Michalopoulos et al. (2018) provide a recent analysis showing the effect of measuring inequality by looking at the geographical border and economic performances. They discover that a process of income redistribution that ensures income transfers in return for safe passage was advantageous to develop trade connections.

We finally examine the problem of public policies influencing economic geography through infrastructure or transfers to generate an equal spatial distribution of economic activities. The question would be: What is the impact of spatial analysis on equity grounds? Can regional policies be justified on this ground? This effect can be taken into account by the presence of externalities or spillovers with spatial industrial concentration, which induces lower costs of innovation. Hence, a trade-off exists between spatial equity in an industrial location and aggregate growth. This is the typical trade-off between efficiency and equity at regional level. Interestingly, Martin (1999) showed that concentrated economic geography is preferable due to the cost of innovation. However, the presence of trade-off is motivated by the role of the immobile workers in the impoverished region because, further away from the leading production site, they have to pay higher transaction costs. Potential public policy that influences the investment reducing the cost of innovation can obtain a more significant growth rate and even more spatial distribution of both income and economic activities. We show the conditions under which this result is possible capturing a new channel due to the typical competition and agglomeration effects that arises in the market.

The rest of the chapter is organized as follows. Section 5.2 provides a general overview of the spatial inequality based on different contributions in the literature. In Sect. 5.3, we instead propose a novel aspect of the measurement of spatial inequality of opportunity. Section 5.4 instead offers normative prescriptions showing the pros and cons of specific public interventions. Concluding remarks follow in Sect. 5.5.

5.2 Understanding the Concept of Spatial Inequality

The formal definition of spatial inequality attains to the measure of resources, services, or general outcomes that are specific of an area or location under investigation. It implicitly suggests an interdisciplinary role between economics and geography (see Krugman (1991)). Even better, it requires the use of tools that typically belongs to geographic analysis with the use of georeferenced data. The idea put forth in the recent literature of spatial inequality is to understand the role played by communities, neighborhoods, rural areas, and regions in the dispersion of a specific outcome distribution. For instance, some parts of a country can be considered highly developed with a more significant range of resources and general services compared to other areas.

The analysis within areas represents the identification of various groups of individuals with similar economic conditions. Kanbur and Zhang (2005) investigate, for instance, the rising of inequality between the coastal areas and the inland regions in China. The Chinese government reacts to such increasing disparities by process of redistribution directed to the western regions. This unequal distribution of sources is explained by a spatial pattern based on different aspects related, for instance, to race, culture, trade, connections, and so on. The problem is even more intense as they involve not only income disparities across regions, but even issues like discrimination among groups of citizens, for example rural farmers compared to urban residents or ethnic minorities or migrants or religious groups. This is the reason why the spatial dimension is abundantly treated in the literature of segregation (see Reardon and O'Sullivan (2004)). Moreover, differences in factor sources can even identify unequal disparities across groups that otherwise would be not possible to capture (Weil 2015). These factors may depend on how much the territories are rich in environmental, natural, architectural, and artistic characteristics. Several exercises can be developed to see whether or not differences in incomes across municipalities originate for different factors and which one is more important. Information about neighbors and the potential network, migration flows, quality of institutions, hospital services, roads, and railways may have enormous consequences for public policy interventions. The identification of the residence is not the only element useful to identify disparities among individuals (Kanbur and Venables 2005). The variation of the geographical location is crucial to separate the contribution of the spatial factors. Therefore, any additional information helping to identify the areas (districts, provinces, states) of individuals who live in disadvantaged conditions contributes to the measure of socioeconomic development across communities.

It is, however, fair to say that a severe drawback of this analysis is the requirement of information at the empirical level. It is challenging from an economic view to provide quantitative estimates in the absence of small-area data that characterize the local context to which individuals operate. Such scarcity of information is an element that we should take into account when we investigate any issue of spatial inequality looking at survey data. The result is somewhat weird. On one side, it can describe the kind of problems that may arise from the presence of heterogeneity at the local level and even put forth different policy prescriptions to reduce inequality. On the other side, we can hardly provide just a few economic contributions that have empirically shown the spatial dimension of inequality with georeferenced data (e.g., Michalopoulos et al. (2018)). The large part of contributions in this direction have studied particular issues like segregation, and they are mainly related to the field of geography (see Kanbur et al. (2006) and Östh et al. (2015, 2014)).

5.3 Spatial Inequality of Opportunity

An alternative option in the inequality perspective is the possibility to look at the inequality of opportunity (IOp, hereafter) issue (see Roemer (1998)). This branch of the literature suggests the precise distinction between factors through which individuals have no control, for example social or parental background, inherited wealth, genetic makeup, early childhood environment, and factors considered "total" responsibility of individuals, for example all measure of individual effort in a broad sense. People thus face unequal circumstances, but this inequality, due to unchosen factors, must be removed. Ex ante inequalities, and only those inequalities, should be eliminated or compensated for by public intervention. Justice requires the ideal of *leveling the playing field.* It implies that everyone's opportunities should be equal in an appropriate sense, and then, letting individual choices determine further outcomes.

5.3.1 The Basic Setting

Formally, this means that each individual outcome can be broadly explained by two characteristics. First, a vector of circumstances C which belongs to a finite set $\Omega = \left\{C_1, \ldots, C_j, \ldots, C_m\right\}$, for each type j, where $j \in \{1, \ldots, m\}$.[1] Second, a scalar variable of effort $E \in \Theta$. Outcome is generated by a function $f : \Omega \times \Theta \rightarrow \Re_+$ as the joint result

[1]It implies that individuals of each type t have identical circumstances in the vector C.

of individual decision E and social circumstances C:

$$y = f(C, E) \tag{5.1}$$

Note that efforts are endogenously determined and may thus partly depend on circumstances and other random characteristics denoted by η as,

$$E = g(C, \eta) \tag{5.2}$$

Therefore, the advantage model of Eq. (5.1) for each individual i is

$$y_i = f(\bar{C}, g(\bar{C}, \eta_i), v_i) \tag{5.3}$$

where v_i is a random-type component, while $\bar{C}$ identifies a vector of unique circumstances to which individual i belongs.

Interestingly, in the last decade, different papers have investigated the possibility to decompose and select the inequality originated from unequal circumstances (opportunity) to the one motivated by personal effort (responsibility) (see Pignataro (2012) for a general overview and Li Donni et al. (2014) for an application in the health context). However, only a few contributions have tried to look at a spatial methodology disentangling the impact of factors beyond the control of individuals.

5.3.2 Capturing the Spatial Pattern of Inequality

From our perspective, the focus would be to measure the effect of the spatial source of inequality due to the heterogeneity of residential locations. The idea indeed in this new frontier is to enclose the strict relationship that exists between the local community and the opportunities that IOp argument still does not consider. The variation among neighborhood areas can be defined as the main determinants of unfair inequality (circumstances outside the individual control) as made by de Barros et al. (2009). The literature developed in the last decade has considered some geographic aspects like birthplace or residence, unfortunately, limited to urban/rural codes or administrative units (see Ferreira et al. (2010, 2011) and Peragine and Serlenga (2008)). The use of these regressors does not allow for the heterogeneity at the local level. Consequently, it cannot capture peer aspects that influence income or educational performances of individuals.

A specific spatial pattern is necessary to provide individuals' past, and present information on the residential environment and the potential interaction between individuals at neighborhood dimension. Any variables able to encompass the opportunity sets from ages, parents or neighbors' education, roads, or general distance may help to gauge this new profile of unfair inequality. What matters for a spatial approach to inequality is the use of individual residential coordinates to construct a neighborhood network for each individual. The purpose is to provide for each agent a series of information based on a *k*-nearest neighbors approach as in Östh et al. (2015). The methodology consists of creating areas of neighbors of varying size using the individual location and then calculating the proportion of different groups of residents in each neighborhood.

The definition of the size of each neighbor's area is debatable. The literature on scalable egocentric blocks has adopted different techniques (see e.g., Chetty et al. (2015) and Reardon et al. (2008)), according to the different definition of neighborhoods. Galster (2001) argues that the neighborhood is a multidimensional phenomenon which has four actors: individuals or households, businesses, private property, and local institution. Part of this information is difficult to provide, and this attends to the problem of partial observability of circumstances treated later. The simplest possibility would be to identify the area as predetermined units and determine the spatial distribution across a set of fixed areal subdivisions such as census tracts or kernel-based density estimation. It is even possible to use the population density as a criterion to equalize the proportion of individual in sets with different size using bandwidths of kilometers. Alternatively, measuring the probability of meeting another person according to a spatial autocorrelation matrix in a set of people at the same distance level could be an interesting perspective. For instance, Östh (2014) proposes to find the *k*-nearest neighbor (using a variety of k-values) of each individual by computing the share of individuals belonging to a user-specified subgroup for each k.[2]

Independently of the criteria adopted to dimension the areas of analysis, it is always possible to decompose the overall inequality by population subgroups (Chakravarty 1990) identifying each type (circumstance) as the local area of individuals with similar pattern of characteristics. On the one side, the within-group inequality would capture the fair distribution of outcomes, that is, the difference that emerges within each area depends on characteristics within the individual control. On the other side, the between-group inequality would gauge the disparities in terms of individual opportunities.

5.3.3 Spatial Decomposition by Population Subgroups

Based on Checchi and Peragine (2010), it is possible to define two different outcome distributions helpful to distinguish the spatial pattern of inequality.[3]

First, a *smooth* distribution Y_C is created by replacing each individual outcome y_i in Y with its area-specific mean μ_t. The value I identifies the particular inequality index chosen so that $I\{Y_C\}$ eliminates the inequality within areas capturing *directly* the between component reflecting the inequality of opportunity. Second, a *standardized* distribution Y_E is computed by replacing each individual outcome y_i in Y as follows:

$$y_i \rightarrow \frac{\mu}{\mu_j} y_i \tag{5.4}$$

where μ_j is the mean of the subgroup t while μ is the mean of the entire distribution. The distribution Y_E is important as it ensures removing the inequality originated between areas. It measures only the inequality

[2]See Agovino et al. (2019) for the adoption of a Spatial Lag of X model for the determination of the spatial contiguity matrix.

[3]The model proposed here is a description of an *ex ante* approach where the within-inequality is measured for each opportunity set. The same analysis can be developed by looking at an *ex post* approach where the vector of circumstances enclosed individuals at the same degree of effort.

within similar locations and for this reason it can be interpreted as the inequality due to personal responsibility. The inequality of opportunity component in the standardized distribution can be obtained *residually* by the difference between $I\{Y\}$ and $I\{Y_E\}$. Calculating the IOp measure through these two distributions surely determine different results for different inequality indices. This is due to the dependence of the within component by the overall mean. Therefore, it is better to adopt a path-independent class of additive indice which is decomposable *by population subgroups*. This implies that it is always possible to derive a decomposition of the total inequality by distinguishing the within- and between-components (see Shorrocks (1984)). Indeed, the class of additive inequality indices reduces to a single inequality measure when the chosen reference income is the arithmetic mean, that is, the mean log deviation (MLD, hereafter), as demonstrated by Foster and Shneyerov (2000).[4]

$$MLD\{Y_C\} = MLD\{Y\} - MLD\{Y_E\} \tag{5.5}$$

the *direct* or *indirect* computation of the inequality at spatial level may perfectly coincides. Note that this is possible even in terms of public policy by looking at a measurement of equality of opportunity. Lasso de la Vega and Urrutia (2005) show the existence of path- independent class of multiplicative indices. In this class, when the arithmetic mean is the chosen reference income, the Atkinson coefficient A (Atkinson 1970) with $\epsilon = 1$[5] can be exploited due to its path-independent property and

[4]The formal definition of the Mean Log Deviation is as follows:

$$MLD = \frac{1}{N}\sum_{i=1}^{N} \ln \frac{\mu}{y_i}$$

where N is the number of individuals, y_i is the income of the individual i, and μ is the mean of the distribution.

[5]The Atkinson index for $\epsilon = 1$ is:

$$A = \frac{\left[\prod_{i=1}^{N} y_i\right]^{\frac{1}{N}}}{\mu} \tag{5.6}$$

while the between components is:

the conclusion are similar to the one proposed in Eq. (5.5) such that:

$$A\{Y_C\} = \frac{A\{Y\}}{A\{Y_E\}} \tag{5.10}$$

where the multiplicative effect is generally used to capture the marginal change produced by the opportunity and the responsibility components. The decomposition of Eqs. (5.5) and (5.10) shows that it is possible to obtain a direct and indirect impact of spatial inequality of opportunity by looking directly or indirectly to the difference between neighborhood areas.

Recently, Türk and Östh (2019) adopted a similar idea with interesting analysis on the spatial pattern. They used an egocentric neighborhood approach to capture the effect that local communities have on the opportunity sets of individuals. They look at educational and earning outcomes using Swedish longitudinal register data. In particular, they study the inequality and the school performance, respectively, in 2010 and 2011 following the individual of the 1985 cohort. They distinguish between *aspatial* and *spatial* information from the data. The formers are the typical

---

$$A_B = \frac{\prod_{j=1}^{m} (\mu_j)^{p_j}}{\mu} \tag{5.7}$$

where $p_j = N_j/N$ is the population share. Hence, we define the Atkinson's equality index within subgroup j as follows:

$$A_j = \frac{\left[\prod_{i=1}^{N_j} y_{ji}\right]^{\frac{1}{N_j}}}{\mu_j} \tag{5.8}$$

and the inner product is equal to

$$A_W = \frac{A}{A_B} = \frac{\prod_{j=1}^{m} (A_j \mu_j)^{p_j}}{\mu} \frac{\mu}{\prod_{j=1}^{m} (\mu_j)^{p_j}} = \prod_{j=1}^{m} A_j^{p_j} \tag{5.9}$$

variable used in the literature as parental background, that is, education and employment status, marital status, household income, migration, and so on. The novel aspect of their analysis consists of using peculiar spatial information which perfectly fits in terms of opportunity egalitarianism, in particular the share of (1) similar-age peers in the neighborhood, (2) visible minorities, and (3) equivalence household scales, according to the *k*-level differentiation discussed above. Moreover, they use an exposure index of potential adverse environments which surround the neighborhood computed under a different measure of poverty or general disparities. They even allow for the computation of the commuting measure based on the observed distance from the workplace.

Interestingly, Ordinary Least Square (OLS) estimation should be avoided when observations are included in larger hierarchical geographical units. OLS regressions underestimate standard errors when residuals at nearby locations are not identically and independently distributed. The violation of the *iid* assumption is typical when spatial inequality is measured at municipalities or georeferenced areas. The preferred methodology (as the one chosen by Türk and Östh 2019) thus consists of multilevel models. The advantage is the possibility to manage the spatial autocorrelation inferences across neighborhoods. The authors show that inequality of opportunity counts for more than 50% in the case of educational distribution, while the percentage is lower for earnings. Moreover, they demonstrate that spatial characteristics are more important in the definition of disparities. The difference between opportunity sets is more considerable for neighborhoods with visible minorities, and this figures out as the primary cause of inequality of opportunity inducing potential conclusion for targeting policy interventions.

5.3.4 Spatial Decomposition by Income Sources

The measurement issue of spatial IOp can even be discussed by looking at an alternative decomposition, called *income sources*. The idea here is to capture the impact of inequality through the measure of specific spatial income items. The literature has historically developed different methods to gauge total inequality concentrated in specific items. For instance, Shorrocks (1982) proposes one of the most interesting methodologies to face these types of decomposition. He demonstrates that an infinite number of decompositions is possible by income sources. This property is called the *natural* decomposition property, which is valid for all inequality indices. The traditional contributions on inequality measurement usually look at the Gini coefficient.[6] Instead, we propose a decomposition of the Atkinson index (Atkinson 1970) for all $\epsilon \in [0, 1]$ exploiting the well-known Shapley procedure (Shapley 1953) under the equality of opportunity principle.[7] Compared to the setting proposed in Sect. 5.3.1, we instead focus on the spatial variation of sources obtaining the total inequality as the weighted average of each factor components. For the sake of simplicity, we propose a simple exercise with two spatial factors that help to understand the sequence of analysis immediately.

We now define a society with N individuals. For the income vector $Y = \{y_1, \ldots, y_i, ..., y_N\}$ where $i \in \{1, \ldots, N\}$ and the partition of the population $\hat{N} = \{N_1, \ldots, N_j, \ldots, N_m\}$ where $j \in \{1, \ldots, m\}$. Note that in this new setting the label j does not identify the type of circumstances to which individuals belong, but instead identifies the sources of different income at spatial level. For example, we can distinguish between incomes above the individual's control as spatial endowments, lands, or even financial capitals, which are considered as circumstances, and labor household income, which is interpreted as responsibility factor. It's assumed that the total income Y is the sum of incomes from m-sources, that is,

$$Y = \sum_{j=1}^{m} y_{ij} \tag{5.11}$$

[6]See Fei et al. (1980), Lerman and Yitzhaki (1985), and Silber (1989).

[7]See Pignataro (2010) for a decomposition à la Shapley by population subgroups.

Let μ_j be the mean income for the j-th source, which can be written as:

$$\mu_j = \sum_{i=1}^{N_j} \frac{y_{i,j}}{N}$$

while the average income for all sources can be defined as follows:

$$\mu = \sum_{j=1}^{m} \sum_{i=1}^{N_j} \frac{y_{ij}}{N}$$

We are supposed to have only two income sources for the income Y. Define land resources as K, which represents our income component out of the individual's control, and labor earning as L, which is referred to as responsibility variable. They are used for producing the entire income distribution Y such that,

$$Y = f(K, L) \tag{5.12}$$

We express the Atkinson inequality measure *à la* Atkinson (1970) as follows:

$$A = A(y) = 1 - \frac{\left(\sum_{i=1}^{N} \frac{1}{N} y_i^{1-\epsilon} \right)^{\frac{1}{1-\epsilon}}}{\mu} \tag{5.13}$$

We can easily derive the contribution of each income source to unit Y applying the Shapley procedure to the Atkinson index of Eq. (5.13). When all sources are distributed evenly among all N individuals, that is, $K_i = k$ and $L_i = l$ for all $i \in \{1, \ldots, N\}$, income Y is equally distributed among individuals and $A = A(k, l) = 0$. This represents a simple example of a potential distribution of income sources:

Individuals / Incomesources	Ind.1	Ind.2	Ind.3
K	5	10	9
L	12	6	8

The average income of the distribution is equal to $\mu = 8.333333333$, while the average income for both capital and labor sources are, respectively, $\mu_K = 8 \quad \mu_L = 8.666666667$. Applying the Shapley decomposition, we divide the sequence of decomposition in four steps:

5.3.4.1 Measuring the Spatial Variation of Both Income Sources

In the first step, we represent the general case $A(K \neq k; L \neq l)$, which refers to the case where both income sources differ from their own mean. We may therefore write the overall Atkinson index of inequality A as:

$$A(K \neq k; L \neq l) = 1 - \frac{\left(\sum_{i=1}^{N} \frac{1}{N} y_i^{1-\epsilon}\right)^{\frac{1}{1-\epsilon}}}{\mu}$$

$$= 1 - \frac{\left[\frac{1}{6}\left(5^{\frac{1}{2}} + 10^{\frac{1}{2}} + 9^{\frac{1}{2}} + 12^{\frac{1}{2}} + 6^{\frac{1}{2}} + 8^{\frac{1}{2}}\right)\right]^2}{8}$$

$$= 1 - \frac{\left[\frac{1}{6}(2.23606 + 3.16227 + 3 + 3.46410 + 2.449489 + 2.82842)\right]^2}{8.33333}$$

$$= 1 - \frac{8.160867251}{8.33333} = 1 - 0.959304 = 0.0406$$

Following the decomposition of income sources, we can also express the Atkinson index taking into account the inequality derived for each income source. It follows that:

$$A = 1 - \frac{\left(\sum_{i=1}^{N} \frac{1}{N} y_i^{1-\epsilon}\right)^{\frac{1}{1-\epsilon}}}{\mu} = 1 - \frac{\left(\sum_{j=1}^{m} \sum_{i=1}^{N_j} \frac{1}{N_j} y_{ij}^{1-\epsilon}\right)^{\frac{1}{1-\epsilon}}}{\mu}$$

$$= \sum_{j=1}^{m} \frac{\mu_j}{\mu} A_j = \sum_{j=1}^{m} q_j A_j \tag{5.14}$$

where A_j is the inequality for the j-th source ,which is given by:

$$A_j = 1 - \frac{\left(\sum_{i=1}^{N_j} \frac{1}{N_j} y_{ij}^{1-\epsilon}\right)^{\frac{1}{1-\epsilon}}}{\mu_j} \tag{5.15}$$

applying expression (5.15) to both income source in our simulation, we can obtain:

$$A_K = 1 - \frac{\left(\frac{1}{3}(5^{\frac{1}{2}} + 10^{\frac{1}{2}} + 9^{\frac{1}{2}})\right)^2}{8}$$

$$= 1 - \frac{\left(\frac{1}{3}(2.23606 + 3.16227 + 3)\right)^2}{8} = 0.02039$$

$$A_L = 1 - \frac{\left(\frac{1}{3}(12^{\frac{1}{2}} + 6^{\frac{1}{2}} + 8^{\frac{1}{2}})\right)^2}{8.6666667}$$

$$= 1 - \frac{\left(\frac{1}{3}(3.46410 + 2.449489 + 2.82842)\right)^2}{8.6666667} = 0.02023$$

Therefore, the Atkinson index for this part of the distribution is:

$$A(K \neq k; L \neq l) = \sum_{j=1}^{m} \frac{\mu_j}{\mu} A_j = \frac{8\,(0.02039) + 8.66666\,(0.02023)}{8.33333}$$

$$= \frac{0.16312 + 0.175326666}{8.33333} = 0.0406$$

The following cases must be considered in the definition of the marginal contribution of both spatial determinants, respectively K and L.

5.3.4.2 Measuring the Spatial Variation on L-Source

In the second step, we represent the case in which $A(K = k; L \neq l)$. It refers to the inequality when capital income is equally distributed among individuals, while labor income differs from the average as:

$$A(K = k; L \neq l) = 1 - \frac{\left(\sum_{j=1}^{m} \sum_{i=1}^{N_j} \frac{1}{N_j} y_{ij}^{1-\epsilon} \right)^{\frac{1}{1-\epsilon}}}{\mu}$$

$$= 1 - \frac{\left[\frac{1}{3}(3.46410 + 2.449489 + 2.82842)\right]^2}{8.6666667} = 0.02023$$

5.3.4.3 Measuring the Spatial Variation on K-Source

Here, we define the situation in which labor income is equally distributed among individuals while this is not true in the case of capital income.

Therefore, the Atkinson index $A(K \neq k;\, L = l)$ can be expressed as:

$$A(K \neq k;\, L = l) = 1 - \frac{\left(\sum_{j=1}^{m}\sum_{i=1}^{N_j}\frac{1}{N_j}y_{ij}^{1-\epsilon}\right)^{\frac{1}{1-\epsilon}}}{\mu}$$

$$= 1 - \frac{\left[\frac{1}{3}(2.23606 + 3.16227 + 3)\right]^2}{8} = 0.02039$$

5.3.4.4 Capturing No Spatial Variation of Both Sources

Finally, when all income sources are equally distributed among individuals, we can have that $A(K = k;\, L = l) = 0$.

5.3.4.5 Total Marginal Contributions

We compute the marginal contribution to inequality for both capital and labor incomes:

$$\begin{aligned} C(K) &= \frac{1}{2}\{[A\,(K \neq k;\, L \neq l) - A\,(K = k;\, L \neq l)] \\ &\quad + [A(K \neq k;\, L = l) - A\,(K = k;\, L = l)]\} \\ &= \frac{1}{2}\,\{[0.0406 - 0.02023] + 0.02039\} \\ &= 0.02038 \end{aligned} \tag{5.16}$$

$$\begin{aligned} C(L) &= \frac{1}{2}\{[A\,(K \neq k;\, L \neq l) - A\,(K \neq k;\, L = l)] \\ &\quad + [A(K = k;\, L \neq l) - A\,(K = k;\, L = l)]\} \\ &= \frac{1}{2}\,\{[0.0406 - 0.02039] + 0.02023\} \\ &= 0.02022 \end{aligned} \tag{5.17}$$

The overall Atkinson index A is equal to 0.0406, according to Eq. (5.13). We demonstrate that the sum of the contributions of both land resources and labor earnings, respectively Eqs. (5.16) and (5.17), is equal to:

$$A = C(K) + C(L) = 0.02038 + 0.02022 = 0.0406$$

In this case, the spatial egalitarian interpretation suggests that actors, for example natural resources K, beyond the individual control identify the unfair distribution due to different opportunities, while factors, for example the level of labor earnings L, indicate the inequality which must be considered fair as originated within the communities' control. Therefore,

$$\textbf{opportunityinequality} : C(K) = 0.02038$$

$$\textbf{effortinequality} : C(L) = 0.02022$$

The decomposition and the consequent interpretation are compatible with more sources and alternative inequality indices.

5.3.5 Partial Circumstances and Causality

Before discussing the appropriate frame of policy prescriptions, it is useful to linger over some empirical concerns addressed in the literature of equality of opportunity. They should be corrected (or at least evaluated) to obtain a correct measure of income and welfare disparities.

We here point out the role of partial observability of circumstances and the causality of the estimate. The former is characterized by the difficulties to design data able to enclose all relevant circumstances concerning specific outcomes. Indeed, the possibility to include all opportunity traits is extremely difficult due to data limitations. We can easily imagine several unobservables which matter according to the real inequality of opportunity. The spatial dimension, therefore, enriches the framework due to the potential correlation among relevant characteristics attaining to the personal interaction of individuals. Although the interpretation of

Fleurbaey (2008) about a lower-bound estimation remains, the richness of information implies that the resulting IOp would be larger than the typical one without the accuracy of the spatial aspects. Moreover, as far as additional information at a local level contributes to describing the potential variation across individuals within and between types, then the identification of multiple circumstances ensures a larger accuracy in the estimation. This influences both parametric and nonparametric procedures used in the IOP estimation and the consequent use of the predicted values in the decomposition of inequality, as shown in the previous subsection.

Second, the argument about causality issue beyond the mere statistical association of the variables is instead in place, and the problem of identification can be even more severe than the traditional analysis. In particular, it is relatively challenging to accept that the spatial error does not feature any spatial autocorrelation. There are different approaches in this case that mainly involve the use of a set of instruments including, for instance, time lags and spatiotemporal lags of the related regressors and the more in general of the other covariates. A definite answer, however, cannot be provided as the complexities of the linkages between spatial characteristics indeed reduce the likelihood of identifying the impact of IOp accurately. It is a general problem of IOp literature and even more so when the spatial correlation matrix of neighborhood enriches the practical design of estimation. As long as we do not know whether and how likely unobserved variables or autocorrelations are determined, it may be difficult to separate the net effect of the spatial regressors due to their possible correlations. Further, the simultaneous determination of the networks at the local level should always lead to a discussion on the issue of endogeneity built on the idea of controlling for observable factors.

5.4 Policy Prescriptions on the Spatial Dimension

Spatial inequality generally implies the concentration of general affairs and business in a specific region compared to the others. Such economic activities seem to be essential characteristics of the development of a country and can be justified by efficiency reasons. Okun (1975) was the first to introduce the concept of the *leaky bucket,* such that "The money must be carried from the rich to the poor in a leaky bucket.... Some of it will disappear in transit, so the poor will not receive all the money that is taken from the rich." This argument was promoted in the historical debate by all those against any forms of redistribution.

Indeed, evaluating redistributive policies is always under the scrutiny of policymakers to take care of the necessity of the population. Any representative government of both developing and developed countries usually tries to counteract the unequal trend of the income profile based on equity ground. The problem of uneven patterns of local development involves all countries, even the one with a long tradition of no policy interventions and requires the analysis of the typical trade-off between equity and efficiency. It is, therefore, essential to analyze the potential effect of policies at the spatial level, for example regional one, and their political consequences. Spatial policies distort the landscape of economic activities since they may influence the location decisions of firms across regions.[8] The general idea is that a process of redistribution toward the poor areas should be profitable for the entire country (Jaffe et al. 1993). The causes of spatial disparities are generally related to the extent of capital mobility and labor agglomeration.

A higher level of inequality is observed in places with the presence of immobile agents with lower incentives to economic activity. The public intervention through pure redistribution and fiscal incentives directed to the territories induces firms to relocate in the poor areas. They can be in the form of progressive taxation or subsidies, helping or not to increase the efficiency of the economy. The results are not so obvious. Further, the introduction of economies of scale and transaction costs may help to justify at least in part that the concentration of activities in certain regions characterized better access to the large markets or more natural opportunity to innovate.[9] This partial concentration can create some

[8]Note that in this perspective even housing policies that influence the commuting of agents should be considered for the spatial effects of agents.

[9]The notion of the *neoclassical theory* of income disparities and trade suggests that a low level of productivity of a poorer region does not necessarily impede to gain from trade due to the

advantages at the national level looking at both inequality and welfare for the poorer regions.

The purpose of this section is, therefore, to understand better the dynamics of spatial inequality with an overview of different policies that can be locally implemented.

5.4.1 Externalities, Mobility, and Inequality

In the real world, much of the conclusion on the equity-efficiency ground depends on the role of externalities. In particular, technological externalities are the most cited elements to justify public intervention from a spatial viewpoint. The reason is that externalities influence physical space, increasing the productivity of areas due to the proximity effect. The vicinity of firms in an agglomerate reduces the transportation cost, and in particular it influences the value of innovation, facilitating the realization of a new production process, for example Silicon Valley. However, Matsuyama and Takahashi (1998) show that the high level of mobility may sometimes reduce the welfare of agents, causing the rise of inequality. Motivations are guided by the continuous agglomeration of people in urban areas which, above a certain threshold, increase the competition effect in the labor market, lowering their salaries. In turn, this has an impact on the poor regions, for example their production of goods declines due to the lack of specialized agents. Larger mobility of agents and their consequent concentration in certain regions are not welfare improving when congestion externalities prevail on the innovation process. The overall result can be harmful in a general equilibrium setting.

Part of the literature has studied the construction of infrastructure building, for example highways or railroads, as a possible solution to the unequal spatial distribution. Such policies decrease potential transaction costs in the country and, consequently, may induce manufacturing firms to relocate in more productive regions due to the innovation externalities. Therefore, a policy prescription devoted to the development of infras-

comparative advantage. It depends naturally on the decreasing/increasing return to scale of trade integration or potential liberalization of capital movements.

tructures may lead to a paradoxical result. The reduction of transaction cost should be accompanied by a fiscal incentive (not merely a subsidy for a unit of production) to induce firms investing in the poor regions. In this case, it is possible to exploit economies of scale due to the most extensive rise in trade and competition in the country. According to the geographical allocation of resources, this kind of combined interventions would improve welfare for all consumers (see Martin and Rogers (1995) for a theoretical analysis on this issue).

The spatial equity problem can be even observed within regions, not only across regions. In particular, empirical evidence shows that the higher the level of inequality among workers and capital owners, the larger is the problem of spatial variation that must be solved (see Piketty (2014)). Therefore, public policies aimed at correcting spatial disparities should take into account the role of capital owners. Even in this case, the results are not so simple. On the one side, significant mobility of individuals due to policy interventions drives up the profits of capitalists in the more impoverished regions due to the relocations of the largest companies in the richer ones. However, workers and consumers in those areas may lose part of their salaries as the market power increases in the hands of few sellers (see Scotchmer and Thisse (1992)). On the other side, the concentration process due to larger mobility across regions will also decrease inequality in the most prosperous areas. As the competition among firms increases, profits of such companies will fall, and this induces higher welfare for consumers at lower prices.[10] Spatial inequality definitively reduces in those areas.

Still, note that since the profits of capitalists increase in the more deprived areas, the spatial inequality even grows more when firms choose their location freely. More in general, whenever the transaction cost reduces (for any reasons), and more extensive mobility is ensured, then spatial inequality within areas may increase. This can be a significant

[10]Usually, more impoverished regions with a lower level of initial resources have higher returns on capital attracting money from abroad (think about the integrated European areas). Policy interventions toward the more deprived areas are more difficult to justify in a neoclassical perspective in case the competition effect is stronger without economies of scale.

argument in favor of a pure redistribution through progressive taxation at the local level with the purpose to converge the socioeconomic condition of the communities. The conclusion on this point should be that any policies that reduce the incentive to a relocation process may increase income disparities within and between regions. However, a rise of agents' mobility must always be supported by a pure redistribution within areas (particularly the poor ones) as the market power of companies increases.

5.4.2 Welfare Evaluation

The debate about the rise of inequality and the consequent trade-off between efficiency and equity reasons does not take into account the evaluation of individuals' welfare.

It is well known that the extent of technology spillovers increase the growth rate of a country. The net result in welfare terms intertwines both poor and rich regions at the same time. A large concentration in the wealthy regions rises the general welfare in the society because of more efficiency of production due to the agglomeration effect. Instead, individual welfares reduce in the more deprived area due to a large amount of spending on transaction costs on imports from the more prosperous regions. On this point, Martin and Ottaviano (1999) answer that more spatial concentration can be detrimental or beneficial to the welfare conditions of individuals. The prevalence of a positive or negative effect depends on the level of transaction costs across communities.

In case of limited transaction costs, indeed the positive agglomeration impact dominates. Welfare increases as the imports of products and services from the rich to the impoverished region play a marginal role. Geographical interconnections, therefore, become more efficient and more conducive to the growth of the country. Therefore, any policy interventions that can address the issue of infrastructure can be beneficial to the population. The public prescription will be effective if and only if it reduces the transportation costs of agents, products, and services influencing the mobility in general.

The net effect is even more vigorous, according to the initial endowment of the regions. The impact of growth produces as a consequence higher competition among firms, which in turn reduce their profits in the more prosperous areas. Poor areas have, by definition, a lower level of resources to exploit, which implies a more moderate reduction in the profits of companies there. However, the competition effect is even more beneficial for individuals due to lower prices and relatively low transportation costs.

We have seen in the previous paragraph some policies whose primary objective was to reduce cost and increase mobility among individuals. We have observed how policies like a pure redistribution toward the poorer or subsidies that induce companies to move to the more disadvantaged location do not always determine a reduction of inequality. Now we confirm that similar results are not so evident even for welfare evaluation. Whenever the technological spillovers are more effective with lower transaction costs, it is always better to concentrate the investments in the more productive regions due to the agglomeration effect. This helps in reducing spatial inequality and contributes to the increase of welfare in the poorer areas.

Conclusions suggest that the existence of localized spillovers and a different distribution of resources among regions are essential characteristics in the selection of the spatial policy program to implement.

5.4.3 Welfare and Spatial Inequality Measurement

We now propose an evaluation of social welfare based on the literature of inequality measurement.[11] The idea is to understand the relationship between inequality and welfare in society from a policy view. Understanding the dynamics of such evolution should help to address better public interventions described above. It is possible to observe the concrete pattern of welfare/inequality in a different direction. Here we choose a typical utilitarian welfare function, according to Atkinson (1970) described in the previous section. The advantage of this approach is to capture the

[11] See Pignataro (2009).

hypothetical level of income, called *equally distributed equivalent* income (ede, hereafter) y_e, that each individual should receive in order to keep the society to the same level of social welfare. Starting from an average utility function of N individuals in the society,

$$W = \frac{1}{N} \sum_{i=1}^{N} U_i(y_i) \tag{5.18}$$

where the function $U_i(y_i)$ refers to the utility function of each individual i. In particular, we can formally express the individual utility function based on the variation of inequality aversion ϵ such that,

$$U_i(y_i) = \frac{1}{1-\epsilon} y_i^{1-\epsilon} \quad if \ \epsilon > 0 \ \epsilon \neq 1 \tag{5.19}$$

$$U_i(y_i) = \log \ y_i \qquad \text{if} \ \ \epsilon = 1$$

In global perspective, we can select the condition for a general welfare of the society by looking at a proper redistribution among individuals,

$$W(y_1, \ldots, y_i, \ldots, y_N) = W(y_e, \ldots, y_e, \ldots, y_e) \tag{5.20}$$

and this is possible by searching for the hypothetical ede income defined above, able to ensure the same level of welfare among individuals. Therefore, from Eq. (5.19), we get:

$$U(y_e) = \frac{1}{1-\epsilon} {y_e}^{1-\epsilon} \tag{5.21}$$

and the expression of the social welfare function in the extensive form is:

$$W = \frac{1}{N} \sum_{i=1}^{N} \frac{y_i^{1-\epsilon}}{1-\epsilon} \tag{5.22}$$

A consequence of this approach is that it can be easily derived a functional form of the *ede* income y_e from Eqs. (5.21) and (5.22) as follows:

$$y_e = \left[\frac{1}{N}\sum_{i=1}^{N} {y_i}^{1-\epsilon}\right]^{\frac{1}{1-\epsilon}} \quad if\ \epsilon > 0\ \epsilon \neq 1$$

$$y_e = \left[\prod_{i=1}^{N} y_i\right]^{\frac{1}{N}} \quad \text{if } \epsilon = 1$$

However, the connection between welfare and inequality is summarized by the general expression of Atkinson index of inequality A of the entire distribution Y:

$$A = 1 - \frac{y_e}{\mu} = 1 - \frac{\left[\frac{1}{N}\sum_{i=1}^{N} \frac{y_i^{1-\epsilon}}{1-\epsilon}\right]^{\frac{1}{1-\epsilon}}}{\mu} \quad \text{if } \epsilon > 0\, \epsilon \neq 1 \tag{5.23}$$

$$A = 1 - \frac{y_e}{\mu} = 1 - \frac{\left[\prod_{i=1}^{N} y_i\right]^{\frac{1}{S}}}{\mu} \quad \text{if } \epsilon = 1 \tag{5.24}$$

5.4.4 Capturing the Spatial Dimension of Welfare

The same analysis can be developed by measuring welfare and inequality across regions. The proposal is the decomposition of the Atkinson index by taking into account differences in the income profiles of individuals belonging to richer and poorer regions.

$$W = \frac{1}{N}\sum_{j=1}^{m}\sum_{i=1}^{N} U_{ij}(y_{ij}) \tag{5.25}$$

The values of j and m precisely identify the subgroups as in Sect. 5.3.3. According to the population subgroup decomposition, we do not require any further restrictions on the functional form $U_{ij}(y_{ij})$. The procedure is similar to the one proposed by Atkinson (1970). This kind of utility function by population subgroups captures the income of individual i that belongs to group j. Hence, it follows that:

$$U_{ij}(y_p) = \frac{1}{1-\epsilon} y_{ij}^{1-\epsilon} \quad \text{if } \epsilon > 0 \ \epsilon \neq 1 \tag{5.26}$$

A similar result can be provided for the value of inequality aversion ϵ equal to 1. However, from Eqs. (5.25) and (5.26), the social welfare function assumed the following form:

$$W = \frac{1}{S} \sum_{j=1}^{m} \sum_{i=1}^{N} \tfrac{1}{1-\epsilon} y_{ij}^{1-\epsilon} \tag{5.27}$$

Let $(y_{e1}, \ldots, y_{ej}, \ldots, y_{em})$ define the *ede* income vector for subgroups $\{1, \ldots, j, \ldots, m\}$ such that:

$$\frac{1}{N} \sum_{j=1}^{m} \sum_{i=1}^{N} \tfrac{1}{1-\epsilon} y_{ij}^{1-\epsilon} = \tfrac{1}{N} \sum_{j=1}^{m} \sum_{i=1}^{N} \tfrac{1}{1-\epsilon} y_{ej}^{1-\epsilon} \tag{5.28}$$

Then, each *ede* income y_{ej} for subgroups $j \in \{1, \ldots, m\}$ is given by:

$$\sum_{i=1}^{N} \tfrac{1}{1-\epsilon} y_{ij}^{1-\epsilon} = N \tfrac{1}{1-\epsilon} y_{ej}^{1-\epsilon} \tag{5.29}$$

and implies that,

$$y_{ej} = \left[\frac{1}{N} \sum_{i=1}^{N} y_{ij}{}^{1-\epsilon} \right]^{\frac{1}{1-\epsilon}} \tag{5.30}$$

From Eqs. (5.27) and (5.30), a direct expression enclosing the *ede* income of the overall income profile as a function of the *ede* incomes in the subgroups is possible as:

$$\frac{1}{S}\sum_{j=1}^{m}\sum_{i=1}^{N}\frac{1}{1-\epsilon}y_{ij}^{1-\epsilon}=\frac{1}{m}\sum_{j=1}^{m}\sum_{i=1}^{N}\frac{1}{N}\frac{1}{1-\epsilon}y_{ij}{}^{1-\epsilon}$$
$$=\frac{1}{m}\sum_{j=1}^{m}\frac{1}{1-\epsilon}\left(y_{e_j}\right)^{1-\epsilon}=\frac{y_e^{1-\epsilon}}{1-\epsilon} \tag{5.31}$$

and consequently it follows that,

$$y_e=\left[\frac{1}{m}\sum_{j=1}^{m}\sum_{i=1}^{N}\frac{1}{N}y_{ij}{}^{1-\epsilon}\right]^{\frac{1}{1-\epsilon}} \tag{5.32}$$

The measurement of inequality, according to the Atkinson index proposed in Eq. (5.23), can be even expressed under the spatial evaluation of subgroups,

$$A=1-\frac{y_e}{\mu}=1-\frac{\left[\frac{1}{m}\sum_{j=1}^{m}\sum_{i=1}^{N}\frac{1}{N}y_{ij}{}^{1-\epsilon}\right]^{\frac{1}{1-\epsilon}}}{\mu} \tag{5.33}$$

This measure is compatible with the discussion of the previous section. It suggests the interconnection between inequality and welfare and the advantage of decomposing the inequality to capture the spatial dimension at subgroup or regional level.

5.5 Concluding Remarks

Theory and empirical evidence in the income inequality literature has reached a consensus about the important role that the evaluation of spatial pattern assumes in the measurement of inequality and welfare. The analysis of spatial inequality was observed from different views.

According to the definition of spatial disparities, we have focused on different decomposition methodologies at the local level, mainly related to inequality of opportunity. Formally, we proposed a novel framework of spatial inequality of opportunity by revising the traditional decompositions by population subgroups and income sources. We first look at emphasizing the effect of spatial variation within and between groups. Then we look at capturing the marginal contribution of each factor component with the help of Shapley (1953) procedure. The second part of the investigation is devoted to different policy proposals adopted in the last decade. The evaluation is made by taking into account the mobility of individuals, the technological externalities, and the transportation costs across regions. We have thus observed that the implementation of a single policy is not effective as several aspects should be taken into account in the redistribution process. For instance, we have suggested that favoring the construction of infrastructure building can paradoxically be harmful. It reduces the transaction costs, inducing companies to relocate in richer regions due to the agglomeration effect. This result implicitly suggests that the sustainability of population across areas requires a mix of targeting interventions associating pure redistribution to innovation policies. The traditional trade-off between equity and efficiency aspects breaks if a particular condition in terms of transportation cost and innovation mechanism realizes. We observe how the spatial dimension contributes to enrich the design of the public evaluation and how the relationship between inequality and welfare is important to identify the correct intervention. This is the reason why a spatial relationship between inequality and welfare is then finally described, according to Atkinson (1970).

Despite several recent empirical analyses investigating the issue of spatial inequality, which is the best procedure to decompose the income profile is far from being clear. The same problem exists for the mixture of public interventions according to the initial resources . Economic research on this front is in its infancy, and we call for further in-depth study of the issue.

References

Agovino, M., Garofalo, A., & Cerciello, M. (2019). Do local institutions affect labor market participation? The Italian case. *The B.E. Journal of Economic Analysis & Policy, 19*(2), 1–21.

Atkinson, A. B. (1970). On the measurement of inequality. *Journal of Economic Theory, 2*, 244–263.

Chakravarty, S. (1990). *Ethical social index numbers*. Berlin: Springer.

Checchi, D., & Peragine, V. (2010). Inequality of opportunity in Italy. *Journal of Economic Inequality, 8*, 429–450.

Chetty, R., Hendren, N., & Katz, L. F. (2015). The effects of exposure to better neighborhoods on children: New evidence from the moving to opportunity experiment. Technical Report, National Bureau of Economic Research.

de Barros, R., Ferreira, F., Vega, J., & Chanduvi, S. (2009). *Measuring inequality of opportunity in Latin America and the Caribbean*. Washington D.C.: The World Bank.

Fei, J., Ranis, G., & Kuo, W. (1980). Growth and the family distribution of income by factor components. *Quarterly Journal of Economics, 92*(1), 451–473.

Ferreira, F., Gignoux, J., & Aran, M. (2010). Inequality of economic opportunity in Turkey: An assessment using asset indicators and women's background variables. State Planning Organization of the Republic of Turkey and World Bank Welfare and Social Policy Analytical Work Program Working Paper (3).

Ferreira, F., Gignoux, J., & Aran, M. (2011). Measuring inequality of opportunity with imperfect data: The case of Turkey. *Journal of Economic Inequality, 9*(4), 651–680.

Fleurbaey, M. (2008). *Fairness, responsibility and welfare*. Oxford: Oxford University Press.

Foster, J., & Shneyerov, A. (2000). Path independent inequality measures. *Journal of Economic Theory, 91*, 199–222.

Galster, G. (2001). On the nature of neighborhood. *Urban Studies, 38*(12), 2111–2124.

Jaffe, A., Trajtenberg, M., Henderson, R. (1993). Geographic localization of knowledge spillovers as evidenced by patent citations. *Quaterly Journal of Economics, 108* (3), 577–598.

Kanbur, R., & Venables, A. (2005). Spatial inequality and development. In R. Kanbur & A. J. Venables (Eds.), *Spatial inequality and development*. Oxford: Oxford University Press.

Kanbur, R., Venables, A., & Wan, G. (2006). *Spatial disparities in human development: Perspectives from Asia*. Tokyo: United Nations Press.

Kanbur, R., & Zhang, X. (2005). Fifty years of regional inequality in China: A journey through central planning, reform and openness. In R. Kanbur, A. J. Venables, & G. Wan *Spatial disparities in human development: Perspectives from Asia*. Tokyo: United Nations University Press.

Krugman, P. (1991). Increasing returns and economic geography. *The Journal of Political Economy, 99*(3), 483–499.

Lasso de la Vega, C., & Urrutia, A. (2005). Path independent multiplicatively decomposable inequality measures. *Investigaciones. Economicas, 29*(2), 379–387.

Lerman, R., & Yitzhaki, S. (1985). Income inequality by income sources: A new approach and application to the United States. *The Review of Economics and Statistics, 67*(1), 151–156.

Li Donni, P., Peragine, V., & Pignataro, G. (2014). Ex-ante and ex-post measurement of equality of opportunity in health: A normative decomposition. *Health Economics, 23*(2), 182–198.

Martin, P. (1999). Public policies, regional inequalities and growth. *Journal of Public Economics, 73*, 85–105.

Martin, P., & Ottaviano, G. (1999). Growing locations: Industry location in a model of endogenous growth. *European Economic Review, 43*(2), 281–302.

Martin, P., & Rogers, C. (1995). Industrial location and public infrastructure. *Journal of International Economics, 39*, 335–351.

Matsuyama, K., & Takahashi, T. (1998). Self-defeating regional concentration. *The Review of Economic Studies, 65*(2), 211–234.

Michalopoulos, S., Naghavi, A., & Prarolo, G. (2018). Trade and geography in the spread of Islam. *Economic Journal, 128*, 3210–3241.

Okun, A. M. (1975). *Equality and efficiency, the big tradeoff*. Washington: The Brookings Institution.

Östh, J. (2014). Introducing the EquiPop software – an application for the calculation of k-nearest neighbour contexts/neighbourhoods. http://equipop.kultgeog.uu.se.

Östh, J., Clark, W., & Malmberg, B. (2015). Measuring the scale of segregation using k-nearest neighbor aggregates. *Geographical Analysis, 47*(1), 34–49.

Östh, J., Malmberg, B., & Andersson, E. (2014). Analysing egregation with individualized neighbourhoods defined by population size. In C. D. Lloyd, I. Shuttleworth, & D. Wong (Eds.), *Social-spatial segregation: Concepts, processes and outcomes* (pp. 135–161). Bristol: Policy Press.

Peragine, V., & Serlenga, L. (2008). Higher education and equality of opportunity in Italy. *Research on Economic Inequality, 16*(1), 67–97.

Pignataro, G. (2009). Decomposing equality of opportunity by income sources. *Economics Bulletin, 29*(2), 702–711.

Pignataro, G. (2010). Measuring equality of opportunity by Shapley value. *Economics Bulletin, 30*(1), 786–798.

Pignataro, G. (2012). Equality of opportunity: Policy and measurement paradigms. *Journal of Economic Surveys, 26*(5), 800–834.

Piketty, T. (2014). *Capital in the 21st century*. Cambridge: Harvard University Press.

Reardon, S. F., Matthews, S., O'Sullivan, D., Lee, B., Firebaugh, G., Farrell, C., et al. (2008). The geographic scale of metropolitan racial segregation. *Demography, 45*(3), 489–514.

Reardon, S. F., & O'Sullivan, D. (2004). Measures of spatial segregation. *Sociological Methodology, 34*, 121–62.

Roemer, J. E. (1998). *Equality of opportunity*. Cambridge: Harvard University Press.

Scotchmer, S., & Thisse, J. (1992). Space and competition: A puzzle. *Annals of Regional Science, 26*(3), 269–286.

Shapley, L. (1953). A value for n-person games. In H. W. Kuhn & A. W. Tucker (Eds.), *Contributions to the theory of games* (vol. 2). Princeton: Princeton University Press.

Shorrocks, A. (1982). Inequality decomposition by factor components. *Econometrica, 50*, 193–211

Shorrocks, A. (1984). Inequality decomposition by population subgroups. *Econometrica, 52*, 1369–1385.

Shorrocks, A., & Wan, G. (2005). Spatial decomposition of inequality. *Journal of Economic Geography, 5*, 59–81.

Silber, J. (1989). Factors components, population subgroups and the computation of the Gini Index of Inequality. *The Review of Economics and Statistics, LXXI*, 107–115.

Türk, U., & Östh, J. (2019). How much does geography contribute? Measuring inequality of opportunities using a bespoke neighbourhood approach. *Journal of Geographical Systems, 21*, 295–318.

Weil, Y. (2015). Spatial inequality. *Applied Geography, 61*, 1–116.

6

The Spatial Dimension of Inequality

Alessandra Michelangeli

6.1 Foreword

The past few decades have seen an important surge in economic growth, but in some countries this phenomenon has been accompanied by a daunting degree of inequality in various forms, such as widening income gaps and greater poverty in many regions of the world. Disparities in living standards between people located in different regions reflect the so-called spatial inequalities (Keeley 2015). When living standards are proxied by income, the study of spatial inequality translates into the analysis of the spatial distribution of income.

In the economic theory developed in the middle of the last century, regional inequality was seen as a transitory phenomenon. According to the neoclassical growth theory (Solow 1956; Borts and Stein 1964), regional disparities tend to disappear as a consequence of a process of convergence between regions. In the same period, Kuznets (1955, 1963) formulated

A. Michelangeli (✉)
DEMS, University of Milan-Bicocca, Milan, Italy
e-mail: alessandra.michelangeli@unimib.it

S. Colombo (ed.), *Spatial Economics Volume II*,
https://doi.org/10.1007/978-3-030-40094-1_6

the "inverted-U" hypothesis that describes income inequality at different stages of economic development. From a historical perspective, Kuznets hypothesis argues that inequality started to rise with the advent of industrialization. In the beginning, relatively few people benefited from investments in physical capital. After a first period of development, more and more households, until then mainly employed in the agricultural sector, moved to the industrial sector, in which income was less evenly distributed than in the former sector. At this stage of development, inequality fell. Overall, the Industrial Revolution transformed largely rural and agrarian societies into industrialized urban ones. As pointed out by Lessmann (2014), Williamson (1965) adopted the same historical perspective to explain the origin of spatial inequality. Williamson asserts that the industrialization process "was driven by the discovery and utilization of natural resources such as coal and iron" Lessmann (2014, p. 35). Hence, in the first stage of the Industrial Revolution, regions endowed with those resources grew faster than the other regions and spatial (regional) inequality rose. At a later stage of the industrialization process, workers from poorer regions moved towards the richer regions offering more employment opportunities. One of the consequences of these migration flows was a rise of wages in origin regions and a fall of wages in destination regions. Hence, regional inequality fell, and the relationship between economic development and spatial inequality can again be graphically represented by an inverted-U curve. More recently, Piketty (2014), focusing on the relationship between income inequality and growth in the United States over the last decades, finds the opposite relationship to that indicated by Kuznets, that is, a U-shape relationship between income inequality and economic growth. The large increase of inequality in recent decades has been mainly driven by the rise in the global competition for skills, skill-biased technical change and the rise of information technologies. These huge transformations have not been accompanied by an adequate educational investment for large segments of the US labor force (Piketty and Saez 2014). This explains the recent growing inequality in the country.

At a global scale, Lakner and Milanovic (2016) produce the "elephant chart" that depicts changes in income distribution across the world

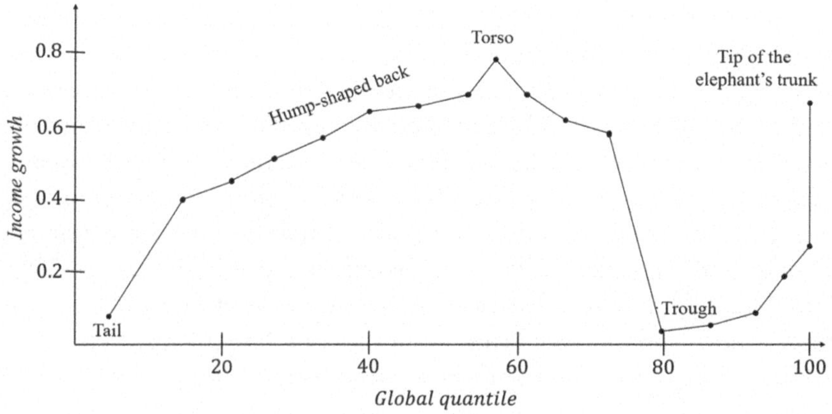

Fig. 6.1 The elephant chart (Lakner and Milanovic 2016). (Note: reproduced by the author)

between 1988 and 2008 (see Fig. 6.1). The elephant's tail indicates that the poorest people in the world are only slightly better off than in the past. The elephant's hump-shaped back shows the income growth of big countries, such as China and India, where millions of people have benefited from improvements in living standards. People having benefited more from economic growth in such countries are represented by the elephant's torso. The trough at the base of the elephant's trunk represents the income stagnation of poorer and middle classes mostly located in the advanced economies. The tip of the elephant's trunk represents the rise in income of the world's super-rich, mostly living in advanced countries. Overall, the elephant's chart suggests that globalization allowed poor countries to grow to the detriment of workers in rich countries.[1]

Beyond globalization, several studies identify other sources of income inequality in the world regions, such as the specific endowment of natural resources (Lessmann and Seidel 2017); agglomeration economies (Ciccone 2002); specific features of the workforce leading to productivity differences (Combes et al. 2008).

[1]The elephant chart, as well as its interpretation, has been at the center of an economic and political debate. See Ravaillon (2018) for a discussion on this issue.

As pointed out by Lessmann and Seidel (2017), addressing the issue of spatial inequality is justified both by equity reasons and for the development of the economy as a whole. Inequality between regions or between neighborhoods of a same city can generate negative externalities and fuel social discontent, eventually leading to social unrest. When inequality between regions is accompanied by political, ethnic, language or religion divisions, social cohesion and political stability may be threatened (Kanbur and Venables 2005). On the efficiency side, Benabou (1993) shows that high income disparities, polarized between rich and poor, can create ghettos and can even bring about the complete collapse of the city's productive capacity. Finally, from a social welfare perspective, income inequality across regions generates a loss in social welfare according to Atkinson's (1970) approach to inequality measurement. This approach relies on the hypothesis of inequality aversion, that is, it would be socially desirable having a homogeneous distribution of income across regions, rather than regions exhibiting huge income disparities. Under the assumption of inequality aversion, society is willing to renounce a share of income to obtain an equitable distribution of it across regions. The higher inequality aversion, the higher the share society is willing to renounce.

The goal of this chapter is to describe and explain the research about income spatial inequality addressing different issues. The first part of the study is devoted to the measures of spatial inequality. Several measures have been designed for the purpose of measuring spatial inequality of income. These measures may be broadly classified as follows:

1. Decomposable measures of inequality implicitly assuming a partition of the population into geographical regions. Actually, these measures can be used to assess whatever phenomenon in which the population may be divided into a set of mutually exclusive and completely exhaustive subgroups, for example, on the basis of gender or ethnicity. The common trait of such measures is that when they are applied to measure spatial inequality, they are sensitive to the way the territory is divided.
2. Measures based on the individual location which present the advantage of being independent of the type of areal unit one uses to compute

spatial inequality. On the other hand, measures based on individual location require the availability of georeferenced data either at the individual level or at very small administrative units. Geocoded information is not always available in national databases.

The main features of these two classes of measures are presented in Sects. 6.2 and 6.3, respectively.

The second part of this chapter focuses on regional inequality mainly in Europe, highlighting specific aspects of methodology used to assess spatial inequality (Sect. 6.3). The third part discusses the causal relationship between spatial inequality and economic activity. The last section concludes.

6.2 Measures of Spatial Inequality Based on Decomposition Techniques

As mentioned above, decomposable indexes used to measure spatial inequality assume that the territory is divided into a finite number of areas that contain subgroups of the statistical population under examination. Two components of aggregate inequality are usually calculated: a weighted average inequality value for a given territorial area—the so-called within component—that broadly captures inequality occurring within the areal unit; a between-group component that captures the inequality due to variations in average incomes between areas.

Following the notation used by Brambilla et al. (2015), let I be the total inequality; W is the within component; B is the between-group term. The latter coincides with the spatial component of inequality expressed in absolute terms. It can also be expressed in relative terms, as a share of total inequality, B/I. Both measures, in absolute and relative terms, increase as spatial disparities between territorial areas become more acute. It is worth mentioning that in the literature on neighborhood effects, the between component is a measure of income segregation (Dawkins 2007; Wheeler and La Jeunesse 2008). In this chapter, the between component is a measure of spatial inequality, unless otherwise specified.

Consider the following two extreme cases: first, all individuals living in the same area have equal income, then the within component is equal to zero and all difference in income is due to the spatial dimension measured by *B*. In the second opposite case, all areas exhibit the same average income and inequality is due only to the heterogeneous income distribution within areas. More generally, overall inequality may be thought to be the result of a certain degree of inequality within the territorial unit and between territorial units. Formally, overall inequality may be additively decomposable, as follows:

$$I = W + B. \tag{6.1}$$

Indices belonging to the Generalized Entropy Class (Theil 1967) are the only differentiable, symmetric and homogeneous inequality measures that can be additively decomposed in the within- and between-component (Bourguignon 1979; Cowell 1980; Shorrocks 1980). The indices belonging to this class may be formulated as follows:

$$E\,(\alpha) = \frac{1}{n\left(\alpha^2 - \alpha\right)} \sum_{i=1}^{n} \left[\left(\frac{y_i}{\overline{y}}\right)^{\alpha} - 1\right] \tag{6.2}$$

where $\alpha \in (-\infty; \infty)$ is the parameter that determines the specific form of the entropy index, as it is shown below; n is the total number of statistical units; y_i denotes the amount of income own by unit i; $\overline{y}$ is the average income.

When $\alpha = 0$, Eq. (6.2) becomes:

$$E(0) = \frac{1}{n} \sum_{i=1}^{n} \ln \frac{\overline{y}}{y_i}, \tag{6.3}$$

and it is called the mean logarithmic deviation or Theil's second measure.

When $\alpha = 1$, Eq. (6.2) becomes:

$$E(1) = \frac{1}{n} \sum_{i=1}^{n} \frac{y_i}{\overline{y}} \ln \frac{y_i}{\overline{y}}, \tag{6.4}$$

and it is called the Theil index.

Equations (6.3) and (6.4) are obtained by using a rule by de l'Hopital.[2] Notice that both indexes are not defined if there are zero incomes. The following index, called one-half of the squared coefficient of variation and obtained with $\alpha = 2$, can handle negative and zero incomes:

$$E(2) = \frac{1}{2n} \sum_{i=1}^{n} \left[\left(\frac{y_i}{\overline{y}} \right)^2 - 1 \right], \tag{6.5}$$

The indices of the Generalized Entropy Class differ in their sensitivity to changes in different parts of the income distribution. Indices with a value of α close to zero are more sensitive to income differences in the lower tail; the Theil index ($\alpha = 1$) is equally sensitive to changes across the whole distribution; indexes with a value higher than 1 are more sensitive to differences in the upper tail.

Let us consider one of these indices from the Generalized Entropy Class, for instance, the Theil index, to show the decomposability according to a spatial criterion. Suppose that a territorial area is partitioned in m subareas mutually exclusive and completely exhaustive. Let s_j be the share of total income of each subarea; let T_j be the Theil index of each subarea; let $\overline{y}_j$ be the average income of each subarea; let $\overline{y}$ be the average income of the whole population. Equation (6.4) may be rewritten as follows (Haughton and Khandker 2009):

$$E(1) = \sum_{j=1}^{m} s_j T_j + \sum_{j=1}^{m} s_j \ln \frac{\overline{y}_j}{\overline{y}}, \tag{6.6}$$

[2]For further details, see Bellù and Liberati (2006, p. 50).

The first term of Eq. (6.6) is the sum of the Theil indices calculated for the different subareas, weighted by the subarea share on total income. This term represents the within component, that is, the part of inequality attributed to income differences within the same subarea. The second term is the Theil index associated with a distribution in which each individual receives the average income of his subarea. This component then represents the between component of the overall inequality.

The Gini index, perhaps the inequality index most commonly used by political institutions and international organizations, is not additively decomposable according to Eq. (6.6), unless a specific condition is met, that is, the relative position of each statistical unit in the subgroup is exactly the same in the total income distribution. In all other cases, the Gini coefficient may be decomposed in a between component, in a within component and in a third term called interaction or stratification term, which is due to the overlapping of regional income distributions (Bhattacharya and Mahalanobis 1967; Pyatt 1976; Yitzhaki and Lerman 1991).

Shorrocks and Wan (2005) apply the main indexes from the Generalized Entropy Class—$E(0)$, $E(1)$, $E(2)$—and the Gini index to assess spatial inequality in a large number of countries. They show that the correlation among $E(0)$, $E(1)$, $E(2)$ is quite high, ranging from 0.83 to 0.98, suggesting that the results obtained using one of these indexes are very similar to those arising from the other two indexes. The correlation with the Gini index is instead lower (around 0.7), and this is most likely due to their different decomposability.

Shorrocks and Wan (2005) also address the problem of the dependence of the spatial inequality assessment on the way the territory is divided. This issue is discussed in the next session.

6.2.1 Spatial Inequality and the Modifiable Areal Unit Problem

Shorrocks and Wan (2005) argue that for a given population size, the between component, on average, tends to become larger as the number of regions in which the territory is divided increases. Novotný (2007) outlines this point. He argues that the between component, expressed both in absolute and relative terms, does not decrease but does not necessarily increase with the number of regions. For example, if inequality is measured between urban and rural areas—hence the territory under analysis is divided in only two "regions"—the between component is expected to be high. This suggests that also the manner of partition into regions matters. Novotný (2007) recommends following some basic principles in order to divide the spatial area being analyzed in an appropriate way. First, the division should be such that the subareas are contiguous and roughly comparable according to the area size. Second, "the essentially functional nature of a socio-geographical area should be taken into account" (Novotný 2007, p. 566). In particular, cities or metropolitan areas should not be separated by their surrounding peripheries.

Beyond the relationship between spatial inequality and the number of subareas, Novotný (2007) addresses the issue about the relationship between spatial inequality and population and area size of subunits in the case in which the Theil index Eq. (6.6) is used to assess inequality. In his paper, the Theil index is applied to assess inequality in 46 countries observed over a very long period, from 1820 to 2003. It turns out that the rank order correlation between spatial inequality indicators—B and B/I—and the area size turns out to be not statistically significant. A weak positive correlation exists instead between spatial inequality expressed in absolute terms—B—and population considered as a measure of the region size. Moreover, the value of the Theil index turns out to be dependent on the number of regions for which it is calculated.

The sensitivity of the results to the choice of spatial scale is a special case of the Modifiable Areal Unit Problem (MAUP) that arises when the spatial analysis is applied to the same data, but different aggregation schemes are used. The assessment of spatial inequality changes when the scale of the aggregation units changes (Openshaw 1984; Wong 2009). The MAUP can take two forms: the *scale effect* and the *zone effect.* The scale effect implies that the analysis using data aggregated, for example, by census tract will provide different results than the same analysis carried out on data aggregated by municipality. The zone effect arises when the scale of analysis is fixed but the shape of the aggregation units changes.

For example, the assessment of spatial inequality using data aggregated into one-mile grid cells will differ from the assessment based on one-mile hexagon cells.

It is worth emphasizing that the MAUP affects all phenomena having a spatial characterization, hence this problem has been addressed in different fields, in particular in the literature of income segregation. The next session briefly presents the approach developed by this strand of literature to handle with MAUP. Then I will show how this approach has been recently adopted to measure spatial inequality.

6.3 Measures of Spatial Inequality Based on Individual Location

In the last decades, several studies on income segregation have developed measures that do not depend on the type of areal unit one uses to assess segregation. These measures are individually based, that is, they consider the local environment surrounding each person. There are basically two approaches to construct individually based measures. The first approach constructs the local environment of each individual by expanding a variable-width buffer around each individual location. The fact that the radius is allowed to vary reflects different geographical scales. For example, Reardon et al. (2008) define the local environment of each individual using four radii ranging from 500 meters to 4 kilometers. They correspond to local environments ranging from a neighborhood pedestrian in size to those that are considerably larger, similar in some cases to large high-school attendance zones. The concentric local environments aggregate the k-nearest neighbors that are used to calculate different scale-dependent measures of segregation. Once such measures of segregation are calculated, they are used to compute a *spatial segregation profile*, which is a curve that depicts the level of segregation at a range of spatial scales. Reardon et al. (2008) apply this methodology to assess residential segregation in of the 40 largest metropolitan areas of the United States.

The second approach, developed by Östh et al. (2015), uses the population size, instead of the radius, for measuring neighborhood scale.

The authors argue that the key variable to define the size of a city is its population. In the same vein, segregation measures should be "based on individualized neighborhoods with the same population count to compare segregation levels across urban areas and across countries" (Östh et al. 2015, p. 45).

In a recent work, Andreoli and Peluso (2018) use the radius approach to assess spatial inequality. They propose a new spatial index of inequality based on the income heterogeneity within the local environment of each individual. To show their methodology, some basic notation is first introduced. Individuals are indexed by i, with $i = 1, \ldots n$. They are endowed with an income y_i. The radius of the local environment is denoted by d, while d_i denotes the set of individuals located within the local environment of individual i. The average income of the local environment of individual i is $\mu_{id} = \frac{1}{n_{id}} \sum_{j \epsilon d_i} y_j$, where n_{id} is the number of individuals located in the i's local environment. The index is a function of the average deviation of income from the i's income, divided by the average income in the local environment. Deviations from the average income are considered in absolute value. Formally:

$$\Delta_i = \frac{1}{\mu_{id}} \sum_{j \epsilon d_i} \frac{|y_j - y_i|}{n_{id}} \tag{6.7}$$

The inequality index, denoted by NI, is defined as follows:

$$NI = \frac{1}{2} \sum_{i=1}^{n} \frac{1}{n} \Delta_i \tag{6.8}$$

The index combines the average variabilities observed in the environment of all individuals. The average Δ_i is divided by 2 in order to rescale the index between 0 and 1. A value of the index equal to 0 indicates the absence of inequality since all incomes are equal. A value equal to 1 implies that in each individual neighborhood one individual has all the income. Hereafter, the inequality index defined by Eq. (6.8) will be indifferently called the NI inequality index or the Local Inequality index.

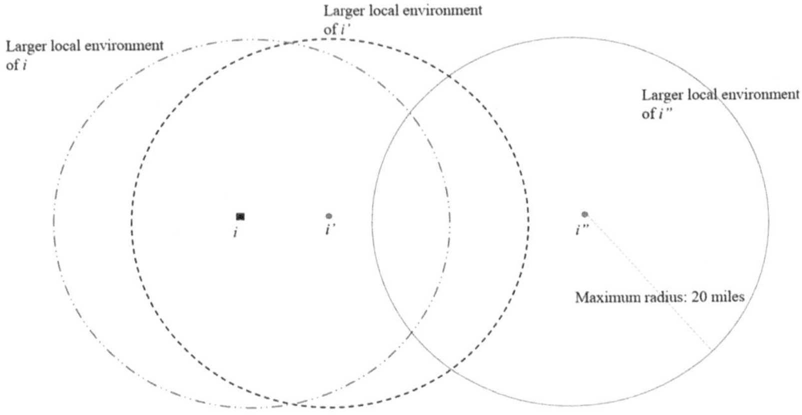

Fig. 6.2 Individual local environment. (Note: Spatial location of three individuals. The largest local environment is depicted for each individual. Individuals i and i' are each located in at least the largest local environment of the other, while individual i'' is outside the local environments of the other two)

The *NI* inequality index is used to derive a *local inequality curve* that depicts the level of inequality at a range of spatial scales. This methodology is applied to assess inequality in American metropolitan areas over the last 35 years. The radius ranges from 0.2 miles to 20 miles, similarly to what was done by Reardon et al. (2008). The main results are twofold: first, local inequality has substantially increased over the period 1980–2014; second, inequality patterns are highly heterogeneous across American cities.

Notice that Δ_i is a measure of the average variability of incomes depurated from the average amount of income in the local environment of individual i. Let us consider the following example with three individuals, i, i' and i''. Individuals i and i' are distant one from the other 0.1 miles, while i'' is distant from i and i' more than 20 miles. The location of the three individuals is represented in Fig. 6.2. As the maximum radius in Andreoli and Peluso's (2018) application is 20 miles, the income of i'' does not affect either the value of Δ_i or the value of $\Delta_{i'}$.

Now, suppose that the income of i'' doubles or becomes ten times bigger. The value of $\Delta_{i''}$ remains unchanged as well as the value of the

NI inequality index. This means that the *NI* inequality index does not capture the wider gap in income between the first two individuals—i, i' and i''. Andreoli and Peluso (2018) address this point by proposing a further inequality index that corresponds to the Gini coefficient calculated over the average incomes observed in the local environments of i, i' and i''. In equivalent terms, the second inequality index they propose is the Gini coefficient applied to the distribution of average incomes $(\mu_{id}, \mu_{i'd}, \mu_{i''d})$.

The Gini coefficient increases when the income of i'' or becomes ten times bigger.

In their paper, American cities are assessed on the basis of both the Neighborhood Index and the Gini Index specified above. The results clearly identify four groups of cities:

1. Cities with a low value of the Local Inequality Index and a low value of the Gini index (Cities LL). These cities are called even cities (see figure 3 in the original paper) since the local inequality individually based is low and income is quite evenly distributed across all the local environments.
2. Cities with a low value of the Local Inequality Index and a high value of the Gini index (Cities LH). These cities are called polarized cities since the biggest disparities are between neighborhoods while the distribution of income within each neighborhood is quite low. Detroit and Washington show such a pattern of inequality.
3. Cities with a high value of the Local Inequality Index and a low value of the Gini index (Cities HL). These cities are called mixed cities since neighborhoods exhibit a quite similar average income while the main source of income heterogeneity is within neighborhood. Among the 50 largest metropolitan areas, San Francisco and Miami belong to this group.
4. Cities with a high value of the Local Inequality Index and a high value of the Gini index (Cities HH). These cities are called unstable cities since inequality is high both at the local level as well as between neighborhoods. Los Angeles, New York and Chicago show such a

pattern of inequality. The authors argue that other factors other than income, such as ethnicity, play a role in widening income disparities.

It is worth mentioning that the local inequality index (6.8) discussed so far, as well as the inequality measures presented in Sect. 6.2.1 are purely descriptive. In a further paper, Andreoli and Peluso (2019) extend their approach by transposing their measure of spatial inequality on the inferential ground. More specifically, they provide unbiased estimators of the *NI* index and its standard error. In this way, they are able to make statements about inequality in American cities beyond the confines of the sample used.

In the next section, we review the literature about spatial inequality focusing on specific issues arising from the empirical analysis.

6.4 Spatial Inequality in Europe and Empirical Methods

This section focuses on regional inequality mainly in Europe highlighting specific aspects of methodology used to assess spatial inequality.

Several studies support the evidence of convergence between European countries in relatively recent years. For instance, Ezcurra et al. (2007) show the presence of a process of regional convergence in terms of inequality within the European Union between 1993 and 1998. Moreover, they find that income inequality across households decreased in 40% of the regions considered. Most of these regions are the less-developed of the EU and are mainly located in the less-developed countries. This reduction in inequality especially in the less-developed countries is interpreted as a positive result of the structural funds on personal-income distribution. Ezcurra et al. (2007) also show that the measure of inequality considered in their analysis, that is, the Gini index, varies considerably across regions and that it is spatially nonstationary. The lowest value is 0.1961 for Thüringen while the highest value is twice the lowest and it is observed for Açores. The existence of spatial autocorrelation in the regional distribution of inequality is verified on the basis of the Moran's

I and Geary's c global tests that correlate the value of a variable with the value of the same variable in neighbor regions (Cliff and Ord 1973, 1981; Haining 1990). The Moran's I is related to the Peason's correlation coefficient since it represents the deviations of the values of a variable by its mean. In formal terms:

$$I = \frac{N}{\sum_{i=1}^{N}\sum_{j=1}^{N} w_{i,j}} \frac{\sum_{i=1}^{N}\sum_{j=1}^{N} w_{i,j}\left(y_i - \overline{y}_i\right)\left(y_j - \overline{y}_j\right)}{\sum_{i=1}^{N}\left(y_i - \overline{y}_i\right)} \tag{6.9}$$

where N is the number of regions indexed by i and j; y is the Gini index; $\overline{y}$ is the Gini average value; $w_{i,j}$ is an element of a weights matrix $\boldsymbol{W}$ of $N \times N$ size. The calculated Moran's I varies between -1 (negative autocorrelation) and 1 (positive autocorrelation). A positive (negative) coefficient corresponds to a value of Moran's I that is larger (lower) than its theoretical mean equal to $\frac{-1}{N-1}$.

The Geary's c measures the difference between values of the variable at nearby locations. It is defined as

$$c = \frac{(N-1)}{\sum_{i=1}^{N}\sum_{j=1}^{N} w_{i,j}} \frac{\sum_{i=1}^{N}\sum_{j=1}^{N} w_{i,j}\left(y_i - y_j\right)^2}{2W\sum_{i=1}^{N}\left(y_i - \overline{y}_i\right)^2} \tag{6.10}$$

where W is the sum of all $w_{i,j}$. The value of Geary's c varies between 0 (positive autocorrelation) and some unspecified value close to 2 (strong negative autocorrelation).

The results of Ezcurra et al. (2007) provide a very strong evidence of spatial dependence. The distribution of the Gini index is not random across regions but tends to be clustered, with regions having relatively high (low) value of the Gini index and neighbor regions having high (low) values as well. The highest Gini coefficient values are observed in regions of Ireland, the UK, and some of the southern European countries. The lowest values are found in central and Northern European countries.

The analysis carried out by Hoffmeister (2009) considers the European Union divided according to different criteria. More specifically, the EU area is divided on three geographical levels and the decomposition of the inequality measure used in the analysis is made accordingly as I will show below. The main aim of the study is to evaluate the effectiveness of social policies in Europe. The first geographical level is such that European countries are divided in two groups: the first group includes the original 15 countries in the EU prior to 1 May 2004 (EU15); the second group includes the ten countries that joined the EU in 2004 (AC10).[3] These two parts of Europe exhibit a huge income gap. The second level is the country, in which the national government is responsible for social policy in the EU and plays a key role in the redistribution of income across individuals within the country. The third level is subnational and corresponds to the Eurostat Nomenclature of Territorial Units for Statistics (NUTS) classification level.[4] Each region, on average, covers between 3 and 7 million of people. Such regions are the main recipients of resources from the EU's and Member States' regional policies. The index used for the analysis is the mean logarithmic deviation defined by (1.3). The decomposition is repeated three times on the different geographic levels described above. The results reveal that European countries converged during the second half of the 1990s at all investigated geographic levels, then between EU15 and AC10; throughout the countries, and throughout individuals within countries. From his findings, Hoffmeister (2009) draws the conclusion that social policies promoting balanced spatial development may have played a role in this process of convergence.

More recently, Mussini (2017) shows that income inequality between EU regions overall decreased from 2007 to 2011. The analysis is based on the Gini index, used to measure inequality in absolute and relative terms. The Gini index of absolute inequality is broken down into three components explaining the role played by population change, re-ranking, and changes in absolute income disparities between regions.

Widening the boundaries of the supranational entity from the EU to OECD countries, Arnold and Blöchliger (2016) find that inequality has been decreasing between countries over the period 1995–2013. Within-country disparities have instead widened. The measures used to assess inequality are the coefficient of variation, the Gini coefficient and the

[3] The ten countries that joined EU in 2004 are: the Czech Republic, Cyprus, Estonia, Hungary, Latvia, Lithuania, Malta, Slovakia, Slovenia, and Poland.

[4] The NUTS classification is a hierarchical system for dividing up the economic territory of the EU.

range. The coefficient of variation and Gini coefficient exhibit a similar pattern of decreasing inequality over time due to the catching up of less developed regions. The range provides another type of information. It shows an increasing pattern up to 2004, indicating that the gap between the most equal (lowest Gini coefficient) regions and the most unequal (highest Gini coefficient) has widened from 1995 to 2004, then started to reduce and thereafter started to decline.

The amount of inequality between regions and the level of GDP within a country are negatively related, indicating that countries in the sample lie on the downward-sloping side of the Kuznets (1955) curve. The same finding is found by Novotný (2007) for EU. In the next section, the relationship between spatial inequality and economic activity is further investigated.

6.5 The Causal Relationship Between Spatial Inequality and Economic Activity

Several studies investigate the relationship between regional inequality and economic growth without addressing the problem of simultaneity of these two variables. Most of them show the magnitude and the sign of the correlation without identifying the causal relationship between inequality and economic growth. A recent paper by Lessmann and Seidel (2017) addresses this issue, analyzing the causal impact of spatial inequality on economic activity in a large number of countries. Their methodology is inspired by Easterly (2007) and Henderson et al. (2017) and consists in adopting an instrumental variable approach. The instruments are purely exogenous natural factors of development, such as geography, climate and resource endowments, which contribute to determine the physical setting of a location and the output production independently of man-made factors. These instruments are called first-nature determinants of development (Krugman 1993) and they differ from other factors that are man-made and are endogenous to economic activity, geography and spatial inequality. Man-made factors, called second-hand factors, contribute to determine markets size effects, factor mobility and infrastructure.

According the New Economic Geography,[5] the exogenous first-nature factors are the original cause of agglomeration of economic activity in a specific area. The effects of first-nature factors may be amplified or mitigated by man-made factors.

Economic activity at the regional level is proxied by nightlights, as in Henderson et al. (2017). Inequality is measured by the Gini index formulated as follows:

$$G_j = 1 + \frac{1}{n_j} - \frac{2}{y_j n_j^2} \sum_{i=1}^{n_j} (n_j + 1 - i)\, y_{ij}, \tag{6.11}$$

where y_{ij} is the nightlight in cell i in country j; n_j is the number of grid cells attributed to country j. The authors adopt a weighted formula of the Gini index, in which the weights are the amounts of land mass inside each grid cell. This implies that grid cells with huge water areas contribute less in determining inequality than cells with bigger amounts of land.

Equation (6.11) is also used to calculate the Gini coefficient considering predicted incomes from first-nature geography. Predictions are from linear regression and a machine learning algorithm (random forest). The latter is a more flexible tool than the former since accounts for potential nonlinearity between physical geography and the outcome variable. Moreover, it admits interdependent relationship between first-nature variables, that is, each explanatory variable may affect the others. This is not the case for the ordinary least squares model. The predicted values of the Gini coefficient enter as explanatory variable in the auxiliary regression of the two-stage equation model, as explained below.

The empirical strategy consists in estimating a two-stage equation model. In the first equation, first-nature characteristics are the predictors of spatial inequality, in addition to other variables. More precisely, the log spatial inequality observed in country j is regressed on:

[5]Venables (2005) provides the following definition of the New Economic Geography: "*The New Economic geography provides an integrated and micro-founded approach to spatial economics. It emphasizes the role of clustering forces in generating an uneven distribution of economic activity and income across space. The approach has been applied to the economics of cities, the emergence of regional disparities, and the origins of international inequalities.*"

- An instrumental variable, denoted by *GIV*, based on predicted incomes from the first-nature geography
- A set of first-nature factors averaged on the country level and denoted by *GEO*
- A set of control variables, *X*, used in some of the specifications; a world region fixed effect, denoted by γ

$$\log\left(\mathrm{G}_j\right) = \beta_0 + \beta_1 GIV_j + \beta_2 GEO_j + \beta_i \sum_i X_{ij} + \gamma + \varepsilon_j, \tag{6.12}$$

The predicted values, $\hat{G}$, of spatial inequality are used in the second-stage regression in which the dependent variable is the log light density *Y* in country *j*[6] :

$$\log\left(\mathrm{Y}_j\right) = \widetilde{\beta}_0 + \widetilde{\beta}_1 \hat{G}_j + \widetilde{\beta}_2 GEO_j + \widetilde{\beta}_i \sum_i X_{ij} + \gamma + \eta_j, \tag{6.13}$$

The authors point out that predicted spatial inequality, $\hat{G}_j$, based on the first-nature characteristics, is a strictly exogenous variable since it does not depend on second-nature man-made factors. Then one can be confident that the exclusion restriction is satisfied.

The empirical model is applied to investigate the causal relationship between economic activity and spatial inequality in 184 countries over the period 2008–2012. The analysis is cross-section because of very low variability of geographic variables. Data are averaged over the 5 years to avoid bias due to extreme weather events or other local shocks. The data used by Lessmann and Seidel (2017) are gridded in order to neglect any administrative boundaries that are subject to political influences.

[6]Equations (6.2) and (6.3) correspond to equations (3) and (4), respectively, in the original paper.

The results show a highly significant negative relationship between spatial inequality and economic activity. This means that the higher the spatial inequalities, the lower the economic activity in the country. A 0.01 unit increase in the Gini coefficient determines a reduction in economic activity ranging between 1.7% and 3.8%, depending on specification and prediction method.

Lessmann and Seidel (2017) implicitly provide the direction for further research. Indeed, the authors claim that the paper does not causally identify those factors moderating the negative relationship between spatial inequality and economic activity. They suggest that infrastructure as well as equalization payments may counteract the disadvantages arising from poor first-nature geographic characteristics. A detailed causal investigation on economic activity still remains to be done.

6.6 Concluding Comments

Research on spatial economics has generally provided several important insights to the understanding of inequality patterns across regions. For instance, it has been able to quantify the importance of spatial inequality in determining overall income differentiation. Other sources of inequality are gender, age, ethnicity or education. As noted by Kanbur (2006), if one or more of these sources are not randomly distributed across space, the between-group component does not properly reflect the significance of space as a determinant of inequality. This concern provides the direction for further research. The analysis of spatial inequality could be associated with the analysis of traits mentioned above that contribute to socioeconomic stratification. The result would be a deeper comprehension of regional inequality and its determinants (Novotný 2007). A full and complete knowledge of regional disparities is essential for policy makers to identify appropriate policy actions to reduce spatial inequality. Such policies would be able to deal with the relative importance of different drivers of regional disparities.

References

Andreoli, F., & Peluso, E. (2018). *So Close Yet So Unequal: Neighborhood Inequality in American Cities*. ECINEQ Working Paper N. 477.

Andreoli, F., & Peluso, E. (2019). *Inference for the Local Inequality Index*. mimeo.

Arnold, F., & Blöchliger, H. (2016). *Regional GDP in OECD Countries: How Has Inequality Developed Over Time?* OECD Economics Department Working Papers No. 1329.

Atkinson, A. (1970). On the Measurement of Inequality. *Journal of Economic Theory, 3*, 244–263.

Bellù, L. G., & Liberati, P. (2006). Describing Income Inequality. Theil Index and Entropy Class Indexes. EASYPol, Module 051.

Benabou, R. (1993). Working of a City: Location, Education, and Production. *Quarterly Journal of Economics, 108*, 619–652.

Bhattacharya, N., & Mahalanobis, B. (1967). Regional Disparities in Household Consumption in India. *Journal of the American Statistical Association, 62*, 143–161.

Borts, G. H., & Stein, J. L. (1964). *Economic Growth in a Free Market*. New York: Columbia University Press.

Bourguignon, F. (1979). Decomposable Inequality Measures. *Econometrica, 47*, 901–920.

Brambilla, M., Michelangeli, A., & Peluso, E. (2015). Cities, Equity and Quality of Life. In A. Michelangeli (Ed.), *Quality of Life in Cities: Equity, Sustainable Development and Happiness from a Policy Perspective* (pp. 91–109). Routledge.

Ciccone, A. (2002). Agglomeration Effects in Europe. *European Economic Review, 46*(2), 213–227.

Cliff, A., & Ord, J. (1973). *Spatial Autocorrelation*. London: Pion.

Cliff, A., & Ord, J. (1981). *Spatial Process: Models and Applications*. London: Pion.

Combes, P., Duranton, G., & Gobillon, L. (2008). Spatial Wage Disparities: Sorting Matters! *Journal of Urban Economics, 63*(2), 723–742.

Cowell, F. (1980). On the Structure of Additive Inequality Measures. *Review of Economic Studies, 7*, 521–531.

Dawkins, C. J. (2007). Space and the Measurement of Income Segregation. *Journal of Regional Science, 47*, 255–272.

Easterly, W. (2007). Inequality Does Cause Underdevelopment: Insights from a New Instrument. *Journal of Development Economics, 84*(2), 755–776.

Ezcurra, R., Pascual, P., & Rapún, M. (2007). The Spatial Distribution of Income Inequality in the European Union. *Environment and Plannin A, 39*(4), 869–890.

Haining, R. (1990). *Spatial Data Analysis in the Social and Environmental Sciences*. Cambridge: Cambridge University Press.

Haughton, J. H., & Khandker, S. R. (2009). *Handbook on Poverty and Inequality*. Washington, DC: World Bank Publications.

Henderson, J. V., Squires, T., Storeygard, A., & Weil, D. (2017). The Global Distribution of Economic Activity: Nature, History, and the Role of Trade. *The Quarterly Journal of Economics, 133*(1), 357–406.

Hoffmeister, O. (2009). The Spatial Structure of Income Inequality in the Enlarged EU. *Review of Income and Wealth, 55*(1), 101–127.

Kanbur, R. (2006). The Policy Significance of Inequality Decompositions. *The Journal of Economic Inequality, 4*(3), 367–374.

Kanbur, R., & Venables, A. (2005). *Rising Spatial Disparities and Development*. Number 3 in United Nations University Policy Brief. Helsinki.

Keeley, B. (2015). *Income Inequality: The Gap between Rich and Poor*. Paris: OECD Insights, OECD Publishing.

Krugman, P., 1993. First Nature, Second Nature, and Metropolitan Location. Journal of Regional Science 33 (2), 129–144.

Kuznets, S. (1955). Economic Growth and Income Inequality. *American Economic Review, 45*, 1–28.

Kuznets, S. (1963). Quantitative Aspects of the Economic Growth of Nations: VIII, Distribution of Income by Size. *Economic Development and Cultural Change, 2*, 1–80.

Lakner, C., & Milanovic, B. (2016). Global Income Distribution: From the Fall of the Berlin Wall to the Great Recession. *The World Bank Economic Review, 30*(2), 203–232.

Lessmann, C. (2014). Spatial Inequality and Development – Is There an Inverted-U Relationship? *Journal of Development Economics, 106*, 35–51.

Lessmann, C., & Seidel, A. (2017). Regional Inequality, Convergence and Its Determinants – A View from Outer Space. *European Economic Review, 92*, 110–132.

Mussini, M. (2017). Decomposing Changes in Inequaliy and Welfare Between EU Regions: The Roles of Population Change, Re-Ranking and Income Growth. *Social Indicators Research, 130*, 455–478.

Novotný, J. (2007). On the Measurement of Regional Inequality: Does Spatial Dimension of Income Inequality Matters? *Annals of Regional Science, 41*, 563–580.

Openshaw, S. (1984). *The Modifiable Areal Unit Problem. Concepts and Techniques in Modern Geography #38*. Norwick: Geo Books.
Östh, J., Clark, W. A., & Malmberg, B. (2015). Measuring the Scale of Segregation Using K-Nearest Neighbor Aggregates. *Geographical Analysis, 47*(1), 34–49.
Piketty, T. (2014). *Capital in the Twent-First Century*. Harvard University Press.
Piketty, T., & Saez, E. (2014). Inequality in the Long Run. *Science, 344*, 838–843.
Pyatt, G. (1976). On the Interpretation and Disaggregation of Gini Coefficient. *Economic Journal, 86*, 243–254.
Ravaillon, M. (2018). Inequality and Globalization: A Review Essay. *Journal of Economic Literature, 56*(2), 620–642.
Reardon, S. F., Matthews, S. A., O'Sullivan, D., Lee, B. A., Firebaugh, G., Farrell, C. R., & Bischoff, K. (2008). The Geographic Scale of Metropolitan Racial Segregation. *Demography, 45*(3), 489–514.
Shorrocks, A. F. (1980). The Class of Additively Decomposable Inequality Measures. *Econometrica, 48*, 613–625.
Shorrocks, A., & Wan, G. (2005). Spatial Decomposition of Inequality. *Journal of Economic Geography, 5*(1), 59–81.
Solow, R. M. (1956). A Contribution to the Theory of Economic Growth. *The Quarterly Journal of Economics, 70*(1), 65–94.
Theil, H. (1967). *Economics and Information Theory*. Amsterdam: North-Holland.
Venables, A. J. (2005). New Economic Geography. In *Palgrave Dictionary of Economics*. London: Palgrave Macmillan.
Wheeler, C. H., & La Jeunesse, E. A. (2008). Trends in Neighbourhood Income Inequality in the U.S.: 1980–2000. *Journal of Regional Science, 48*(5), 879–891.
Williamson, J. G. (1965). Regional Inequality and the Process of National Development: A Description of Patterns. *Economic Development and Cultural Change, 13*(4), 3–45.
Wong, D. (2009). The Modifiable Areal Unit Problem (MAUP). In A. S. Fotheringham & P. Rogerson (Eds.), *The SAGE Handbook of Spatial Analysis* (pp. 105–124). Los Angeles: SAGE.
Yitzhaki, S., & Lerman, R. (1991). Income Stratification and Income Inequality. *Review of Income and Wealth, 37*(3), 313–329.

Part IV

Transportation and International Trade

7

Export Activity and Firms' Financial Constraints

Emanuele Forlani

7.1 Introduction

The sunk costs associated with the export activity are a fundamental characteristic of the current literature in international trade and industrial organization. Both empirical and theoretical evidences underline the role of fixed cost. Firms that overcome these costs become exporter. Therefore, it becomes crucial to understand if and how firms are able to face fixed costs associated to exports.

Investments' structure contemplates a temporal discrepancy between present cost and expected future profits. In the case of exporting (sunk) costs are certain and immediately paid, while revenues are uncertain and postponed in the future. Imperfect capital markets (e.g., information asymmetries) may decrease the probability to start the export activity. Lenders and borrowers may not own the same information set. Thus, potential lenders are not able to evaluate the investments' value, given

E. Forlani (✉)
Department of Political Science, University of Pavia, Pavia, Italy
e-mail: emanuele.forlani@unibo.it

S. Colombo (ed.), *Spatial Economics Volume II*,
https://doi.org/10.1007/978-3-030-40094-1_7

the uncertainty about future profits, and firms cannot gather enough resources to overcome fixed costs. For example, Das et al. (2007) estimate, for a sample of Mexican firms, an average fixed investment of $400,000 for potential exporters.

This chapter aims at analyzing the role of internal financing on export activity for credit-constrained firms. In the first instance, financially constrained firms are those firms for which internal source of financing cost less than external sources. If it is the case, investments (as exports) are sensitive to the availability of internal resources. This does not imply that the "non-constrained" firms do not use internal funds to implement/increase investments: also "healthy" firms show a positive correlation between investments and internal financial resources (Kaplan and Zingales 1997).

The key point is to understand how much the internal (financial) resources are relevant for the export activity of credit-constrained firms (compared to unconstrained ones). Therefore, the chapter addresses also the question of which type of firms are more likely to face financial constraints.[1]

Using a representative sample of Italian firms, we analyze if financially constrained firms increase their entry probability in the export market, once they own a larger amount of internal financial resources. Since that a credit-constrained firm finds less costly internal resources, we expect a positive effect of the firm's cash flows on the process of internationalization for these firms.[2]

The chapter covers two important issues. First, it is necessary to define a methodology to identify a priori the extent of a firm's credit constraints. Employing a detailed information on asset and liabilities, a firm's credit status is defined as financial reliability in the long and in the short run. This approach consists in evaluating the riskiness of firm from the point of view of a potential lender (bank) using ratio indices. The methodology puts light on the mechanism behind credit constraints, and it allows to

[1]Constrained firms are "constrained" to use their own liquidity for investments because not reliable from the lenders' point of view.

[2]Present chapter is not focusing on trade credits.

understand how the relationship between firms' and banks may affect the investments' choice for the former.[3]

In such a framework, it is possible to offer additional insights for the economic policy analysis. It would be feasible to evaluate the implementation of a more stringent credit requirements, if these requirements rely, among other things, on balance sheet indices.[4]

The present chapter can be ideally placed in the between of two streams of literature: the first one concerns the investments' sensitivity to cash flows as measure of credit constrains, and the second one regards the relationship between exporting and credit constraints. In the former group, since Fazzari et al. (1988), there existed a large body of literature that analyzes the sensitivity of investments to internal resources.[5] Similarly, the entry in the export market is considered as an investment, and consequently entry decision can be sensitive to the level of internal financing.

The second stream of research focuses on the relationship between export and financial health. Such stream may be classified into three subgroups of analysis. The first one analyzes how credit availability affects the export's decisions (Campa and Shaver 2002; Chaney 2016; Manova 2013; Muùls 2015); the second describes whether the export activity eases credit constraints (Manole and Spatareanu 2009); the third observes how financial health changes before and after entry into the export market (Greenaway et al. 2007; Bellone et al. 2010; Wagner 2014 for literature review).

From a theoretical point of view, Chaney (2016) introduces liquidity constraints into a model of international trade with heterogeneous firms (Melitz 2003), so that liquidity becomes a second source of heterogeneity

[3]The methodology allows to describe what happens whether banks' financial requirements become more stringent.

[4]It is important to mention that Basel III agreement uses also balance sheet ratio to monitor the riskiness of banking activity. Basel III is a source of concern for Italian SMEs, which rely on local capital market. For example, short-term debt is one of the indicators used in the monitoring activity. Most of the time, short-term debts are used by firms to finance current operations of production process (Onida 2003).

[5]See Hubbard (1998) and Bond and Van Reenen (2005) for a literature review.

across firm.[6] In an empirical framework, the role of credit constraints has been demonstrated crucial to explain some features of international markets. Manova (2013) shows that credit constraints determine both the zeros in bilateral trade flows, and the variations in the number of exported products as well as the number of destination markets. Berman and Héricourt (2010) find evidence that credit access is an important factor in determining the entry into the export market for firms in developing countries; however, they also show that exporting does not improve firms' financial health ex post.

Despite the increasing literature, the main conclusion remains contrasting. Greenaway et al. (2007), using a dataset for British firms, find that new exporters do not show a larger pool of financial resources than domestic firms before the entry, but long-term exporters own more liquidity than domestic firms.[7] Differently, Bellone et al. (2010), using French data, empirically show that new exporters have an ex ante financial advantage compared to domestic firms, but not an ex post effect.

Similarly to Bellone et al. (2010), in the present chapter we define an index of credit constraints using information on asset and liabilities; however, we use thresholds for balance sheet indices to define a clear-cut rule for a firm's financial reliability. These thresholds are commonly defined as rule of thumb in business economics. As we illustrate in the next sections, we assess credit constraints analyzing the firms from the point of view of a potential lender (bank).

Two papers are close to the present chapter, in terms of both data and research questions. Firstly, Minetti and Zhou (2011) show that the probability of exporting and the level of foreign sales are lower for credit-constrained firms. They evaluate credit rationing using firms' responses to survey questions about their credit status. Differently from them, we assess credit status exploiting the information in the balance sheet data rather than using survey question.

[6] In a Ricardian comparative advantage framework, the basic prediction is that either all or no firms export in each sector. Beck (2002, 2003) finds evidence of links between trade, financial development and credit access.

[7] New exporters generally display low liquidity and high leverage (compared to continuous exporters), probably due to the sunk costs which need to be met to enter export markets.

The second one is by Caggese and Cunat (2013), where they develop a dynamic industry model where financing frictions affect the entry decision in the home market as well as the riskiness of firms' activity. Calibrating the model, they predict that financing friction reduce the likelihood of a given firm to become an exporter, but overall they have an ambiguous effect on the number of firms starting to export. In addition, they find that financing constraints distort selection in the export reducing the aggregate gains due to trade liberalization. Using a similar dataset to Minetti Zhou (2011), their empirical analysis confirms the calibration findings.

The analysis is composed of two parts. In the first one, we develop the methodology to construct an index that allows to identify a priori the firm's financial status. We consider a firm's financial reliability both in a long-term and in a short-term perspective. In the second part, we empirically show that the amount of internal resources affects the entry probability into the export market for those firms identified as highly credit constrained (or without long-term reliability).

From a methodological point of view, we suggest a different strategy for testing the hypothesis of liquidity constraints and export. We classify firms in four groups. The firm clustering can be viewed also as a credit score: depending on firm classification a firm's financial score changes and consequently also its financial reliability. We directly estimate the impact of liquidity across group of firms. Indirectly, we are also able to understand the effect of more stringent criteria, if changes in criteria changes firms' classification.[8]

Finally, we control for potential endogeneity in the clustering process (exogenous to the entry in the export market). As Minetti and Zhou (2011), we use the same instrument set, but we proceed in a more rigorous way; since that we estimate a nonlinear model (probit) we prefer to follow a two-stage residual inclusion approach (2SRI, Terza et al. (2008)) rather than a more standard two-stage predictor inclusion.

[8]Therefore, if banks define criteria, we offer additional insights in the relationship between banks, and firms' investment activity.

The chapter provides two main results. First, we find that the entry in the export market is affected by the level of internal liquidity: for the more constrained firms, or firms which are not reliable in the long run (from lenders perspectives), exporting is sensitive to cash flows availability. The entry probability for constrained firms raise, compared to unconstrained firms, as the level of liquidity increases. The value of marginal effects remains constant across the different specifications; when we correct for the endogeneity bias in the clustering process, the magnitude of marginal effect increases.

Second, we find that an expansion in additional markets is affected by internal liquidity. However, the effect is not sensitive to firm's financial status. Using a different subsample of firms (only continuous exporters), we find that the entry in new markets is positively correlated with the internal level of liquidity, for every group of firms. Finally, the export activity in close market (EU15) does not depend on internal cash, while exporting in more distant market depend on it.

The results are robust to different thresholds used to identify credit-constrained firms, as well as to financial indices employed to evaluate the level of financial reliability. Independently from the definition of credit constraints we use, the main massage does not change.

The rest of chapter is structured as follows. In Sect. 7.2, we present the data, describing the relevant characteristics and descriptive statistics. In Sect. 7.3, we introduce the motivations for the methodology proposed, and the strategy for identifying the credit-constrained firms. In Sect. 7.4, we present the empirical specifications and we discuss the results. Finally, Sect. 7.5 deals with the endogeneity of clustering process, and Sect. 7.6 concludes.

7.2 Data

The main data source is the "Indagine sulle Imprese Manifatturiere," a survey conducted by the Italian bank Capitalia.[9] Each survey was collected every three years. In the present chapter, we are going to consider the eighth and the ninth wave of the survey, which cover respectively the period 1998–2000 and 2001–2003. Each wave collects data for manufacturing firms with more than 10 employees. A survey includes the universe of large firms, and a stratified sample of firms with less than 500 employees.[10] Each survey includes of 4680 firms, and the surveys can be matched among them every two waves (as in our case eighth and ninth).

An important feature of the survey is that it represents quite well the heterogeneity in the Italian manufacturing sector. Moreover, it allows to focus our analysis on medium- and small-sized firms: the median firm in the sample has 25 employees. The survey investigates different firms' activities such as trade, R&D, and financial activities. The data are relative to year 2000 (eighth wave) or 2003 (ninth wave). It means that it is possible to observe only two time periods, even if the survey covers a three-year period.[11]

The second main data source is the balance sheet dataset associated to surveys. The balance sheet dataset is collected on yearly basis, and it provides information on firms' item as fixed assets or revenues.[12] Most importantly, it collects detailed data on firms' financial activities such as short- and long-term debts, assets, and equity.

Given that, survey data are collected every three years, there exists a problem of matching survey information with the balance sheet data (defined on yearly basis). A researcher cannot associate a survey data

---

[9]The survey was formerly conducted by MedioCredito Centrale (controlled at the time of the survey by Capitalia). In 2007, Capitalia has merged with *Banca Unicredito*.

[10]The sample is stratified by gross product per employee, size, industry, and location.

[11]For example, in the case of export the questionnaire asks: "Did the firm export at least part of its products in year 2001/2003?" In case of export activity, it implies that we are not able to identify in which exact year a firm starts to export. According to the survey, export may occur in the three year of analysis. In the ninth survey, a firm can export in 2001, or in 2002 or in 2003 (or in all the three years).

[12]The variables' deflators are sector-specific and they come from EU-Klems.

(export status) with the balance sheet data for a specific year. To deal with it, we calculate the average value of balance sheet items on a three-year basis (i.e., average for periods 1998–2000, and 2001–2003). Then, averaged data (from balance sheet) are merged with the corresponding survey.

Finally, the match between the eighth and the ninth wave allows us to follow 2263 firms. Table 7.1 reports the descriptive statistics for the matched observations (firms are classified according with a two-digit ATECO 2002 industrial classification), while Table 7.8 (Appendix) presents the description of data used in the analysis.[13] Finally, we integrate our dataset with "*Struttura funzionale e territoriale del sistema bancario italiano, 1936–1974*" (SFT) from Bank of Italy, that includes our instrumental variables (Sect. 7.5).

7.3 Methodology

Our main hypothesis is that the availability of financial resources affects the entry in the export market, through sunk costs.[14] Fixed investment is paid at the begin of export activity, while profits are uncertain and realized in the future. In this framework, asymmetric information and capital market friction may create a wedge in the cost of financing between internal and external sources. Therefore, the entry probability (in the export market) can be sensitive to the level of internal liquidity for credit rationed firms, for whom external funds are relatively more expensive.

In order to analyze export sensitivity, we proceed similarly to *Euler equation's models* testing the effect of credit constraints on investments' level (Bond and Van Reenen 2005).[15] In these class models, financially constrained firms pay higher prices for external source of financing (issue

[13] For more details on data source, see Minetti and Zhou (2011).

[14] We can interpret these sunk costs as investments in which a firm incurs to enter in the foreign markets (development of a new product, organize distribution, etc.).

[15] The theory of investments and credit constraints has been applied to different field of research analysis (Konings et al. 2003; Love 2003; Forbes 2007).

Table 7.1 Averages by sectors

ATECO Code	Firms	Share	Turnover	Workers	Added value (in th of Euros)	KL	Remuneration per employee (in th of Euros)
DA	208	0.092	27,392.40	105.25	5911.77	100.65	28.56
DB	259	0.114	22,292.19	104.45	5793.51	52.63	41.74
DC	107	0.047	9854.59	44.69	2072.94	28.71	28.17
DD	81	0.036	9691.90	49.83	3036.87	51.29	25.75
DE	116	0.051	17,250.65	95.22	5407.32	50.90	29.30
DG	103	0.045	77,858.44	198.01	15,301.92	70.17	43.44
DH	123	0.054	13,806.88	77.83	4556.11	134.47	84.49
DI	137	0.06	22,791.32	117.61	8646.43	80.99	29.86
DJ	370	0.163	17,606.64	73.46	3988.59	51.15	30.68
DK	345	0.152	24,302.69	136.15	7972.32	311.90	72.95
DL	197	0.087	34,150.63	181.73	12,634.82	53.06	45.16
DM	65	0.029	97,607.76	318.92	22,979.71	58.27	33.54
DN	154	0.068	10,846.89	55.06	2864.09	39.68	28.86
Total	2263	100	25,576.24	112.68	6986.13	101.69	42.54

Data source: Capitalia Survey and balance sheet dataset. The observations used consider firms reported on both balance sheets (from 1998 to 2000 and from 2001 to 2003 for the 2263 matched firms). The first and last centile of observations are eliminated from the mean calculation to avoid outliers. The averages are calculated from 1996 to 2003 new equity, or debt).[16] Therefore, internal liquidity affects the rate of inter-temporal substitution between investment today and investment tomorrow; the more constrained the firm is, the larger (and positive) is the impact of cash availability on the investment level.

For the empirical estimation, it is crucial to identify a priori firms' credit status, because the relationship between liquidity and investment varies in function of firms' characteristics. Therefore, we analyze the role of liquidity for exporting, by clustering firms according to their level of financial reliability.

The direct estimate of liquidity for the entry choice is biased. For example, if we estimate the impact of cash stock (*CS*) on the entry probability (*Enter*) for firm *i* as follows,

$$\Pr(\text{Enter}|X, CS)_i = \alpha X_i + \beta CS_i + \epsilon_i \tag{7.1}$$

where X_i is a set of control variables. We have no a priori on β coefficient. If constrained and unconstrained firms are not differentiated in the empirical model, the effect of internal liquidity can be biased. We may identify three different potential situations. First, a not-constrained firm enters into the export market even with a low level of liquidity, because the sources of external financing are not too costly. Second, a healthy firm can also self-finance its own export activity (Kaplan and Zingales 1997): in this case, we observe a positive correlation between liquidity and the entry probability. Finally, a credit-constrained firm must rely on internally generated resources: also, in this case, we expect that entry is sensitive (positively) to internal liquidity.

Therefore, it is crucial to identify a priori firms' financial status to estimate β in Eq. 7.1 across different types of firms (class of financial status). For this reason, we cluster firms in four groups according to their

[16] In the presence of perfect capital markets, financial variables should have no impact on the investment decisions of firms. If an investment is profitable, internal and external financing are supposed to be perfect substitutes with frictionless capital markets.

level of financial status, and for each group we assess the role of internal liquidity in the internationalization's process.[17]

In the existing literature, many indices have been used to assess the financial health of a firm, as liquidity ratio or leverage ratio (Greenaway et al. 2007). However, as Bellone et al. (2010) underline, these indices do not capture the differences between short-term and long-term financial stability. Conversely, we define credit status from long- and short-term perspectives. To do that, we exploit information in the balance sheet to assess the degree of credit constraints.

Similarly to external investors, using balance sheet data, we can assess a firm' financial reliability calculating financial ratios. In business economics, such ratios are often employed to determine the "goodness" of an investment.[18] More recently, financial ratios are used by banks (among other procedures) to assess the riskiness of granted loans; according to the principles imposed by Basel III agreement (Bank for International Settlements 2006), banks have to manage the risk of credit by using objective criteria.

This approach allows to define an exogenous clustering process (exogenous to investment choice); the financial reliability is assessed by criteria external to firm's decision process.[19] To simplify the clustering process, we consider two indices, for which conventional thresholds exist. The two ratios consider respectively a firm's financial reliability in the long run and in the short run.[20]

- The *Equity Ratio* (ER hereafter) is used to assess long-term financial reliability. It is defined as the ratio between the total amount of internal resources (equity plus profits and reserves) and the total amount of capital invested (total assets). *ER* measures the proportion of the total

[17]In the previous literature, the common practice is to plug into the main equation an indicator for credit rationing, and then interact it with a measure of internal liquidity (Bellone et al. 2010; Minetti and Zhou 2011). A continuous index for credit constraints is not able to capture potential not-monotonicity for the relationship between credit status, liquidity, and entry decision.

[18]For more specific discussion of this subject, see Brealey and Myers (1999).

[19]In the robustness check analysis, we test the exogeneity of our clustering process.

[20]Table 7.9 reports the ratios' means and the standard deviations.

assets that are financed by internal funds: it evaluates to what extent a firm is self-financing its economic activities. A ratio lower than *0.33* suggests a situation of sub-optimality, because a firm has a low capacity to self-financing; at least one-third of firm's assets have be covered by internal resources in order to reach a financial stable situation in the long run (Brealey and Myers 1999).

- The *Quick Ratio* (QR hereafter) assesses short-term financial reliability, and it is a rough indicator of cash's availability; *QR* measures a company's ability to meet its short-term obligations with its most liquid assets. It is defined as the ratio of instantaneous liquidity or cash assets (cash, bank, and current account) to short-term debts (interests, furniture, wages etc.). The optimal value is fixed as greater than 1: if *QR* meets this criterion, a firm owns enough resources to face the daily cost of production process. The ratio indicates a firm's chances of paying off short-term debts without the need for additional external funds.

A firm's financial health improves when the ratios increase. Nonetheless, we test if the indices are reliable indicators for a firm's financial health. Therefore, we exploit information on credit rationing, provided by the survey data. Each survey (the eighth and the ninth survey) report firms' response to the following questions.

(a) "In 2000 (or 2003), would the firm have liked to obtain more credit at the market interest rate ?" In case of a positive answer, the following question is asked:
(b) "In 2000 (or 2003), did the firm demand more credit than it actually obtained?"

According to question (a) and (b), we create two dummy variables, *Des* and *Ask*, respectively. *Des* is equal to 1 if a firm replies yes to question (a), otherwise 0; similarly *Ask* is equal to 1 if a firm replies yes to question (b), otherwise 0. We use such information to understand if *ER* and *QR* can approximate a firm's credit constraints.[21]

We expect that for high values of ER and *QR* correspond a lower probability to answer yes to questions (a) and (b). We estimate

$$Y_i = \alpha_0 + \alpha_1 \delta \text{Index}_i + \gamma \overline{X_i} + \epsilon_i, \tag{7.2}$$

where *Y* represents the binary information *Des* and *Ask*. δ*Index* takes value of 1 if ER or QR criteria are meet, and $\overline{X_i}$ is a vector of control variables. We expect a negative sign for α_1. We estimate Eq. 7.2 for firms that appear in both surveys (eighth and ninth).[22] Table 7.2 reports the results for the Probit estimation of Eq. 7.2, where *Des* is the dependent variable (dummy).[23,24]

The coefficients suggest that the degree of self-reported credit status is statistically correlated with the two ratios. As expected, the coefficients' sign for the two dummies is negative, so that a firm is less likely to self-report as credit constrained when a threshold is satisfied. The magnitude (of coefficients) does not change with the inclusion of control variables.

Results suggests that the ratios (and thresholds) are correlated with firms' ability to raise funding. Using *QR* and *ER* thresholds, we cluster firms in four different groups, according to the concept of short-term and long-term financial reliability. In our framework, the most constrained firms do not satisfy the conditions for both short-term and long-term financial reliabilities, that is, both *QR* and *ER* thresholds are not satisfied, respectively.

Firms in cluster *0* are defined as the most constrained firms, because they report an *ER* lower than *0.33*, and *QR* smaller than *1*. Table 7.3 illustrates how clusters are constructed. Then, we define with *Cluster*, an

---

[21]These two dummies are used by Minetti and Zhou (2011) to directly assess a firm's credit rationing.

[22]The dependent variable (credit status from survey) refers to year 2003, and it is explained by the correspondent financial ratios (year 2003).

[23]Results are unchanged if ER and QR are included as continuous variables.

[24]Given that *Des* implies question related to variable *Ask*, we do not report results for also for the second dummy. The inclusion of *Ask* as dependent variable does not change the conclusions. Additional tables are available upon request.

Table 7.2 Credit request and financial indices

	Des $_{i03}$	Des $_{i03}$	Des $_{i03}$	Des $_{i03}$
δER_{i03}	−0.288***	−0.271***	−0.239**	−0.235**
	[0.084]	[0.088]	[0.094]	[0.092]
δQR_{i03}	−0.460***	−0.496***	−0.509***	−0.503***
	[0.080]	[0.081]	[0.096]	[0.098]
Banks $_{i03}$			0.034**	0.034**
			[0.014]	[0.014]
Share $_{i03}$			0.006***	0.006***
			[0.001]	[0.001]
Expo $_{i03}$				−0.002
				[0.102]
NDest $_{i03}$				−0.01
				[0.010]
Log(Age) $_{i03}$		0.122	0.113	0.121
		[0.082]	[0.102]	[0.102]
Log(Y) $_{i03}$		−0.126***	−0.155***	−0.151***
		[0.021]	[0.034]	[0.038]
Cons.	−0.572**	−0.247	0.489	0.444
	[0.246]	[0.294]	[0.490]	[0.477]
Obs.	1598	1598	1598	1598
Pseudo R^2	0.067	0.079	0.095	0.095

Probit estimation. Robust standard errors are clustered by regions and are reported in squared brackets. Sector and area dummies are included. The regressors are contemporaneous to the dependent variables, that is, relative to 2003. δER and δQR are, respectively, equity ratio and quick ratio. Data description in Table 7.8. All balance sheet data are defined as averages for years 2001–2003. Significance level: * is the p-value < 0.1, ** is the p-value < 0.05, and *** is the p-value < 0.01

indicator variable that takes value 0,1,2, or 3 according to firm's financial reliability.

The cluster should identify (exogenously) whether a firm is constrained or not; it is likely that a firm in group 0 or 1 faces difficulties to finance investments with external resources, because not reliable in the long

Table 7.3 Cluster definition

Cluster	0	1	2	3
Description	$\delta ER=0; \delta QR=0$ Neither short-term (QR<1) nor long-term reliability (ER<0.33)	$\delta ER=0; \delta QR=1$ No long-term reliability (QR>1; ER<0.33)	$\delta ER=1; \delta QR=0$ No short-term reliability (QR<1; ER>0.33)	$\delta ER=1; \delta QR=1$ Both ratios satisfied(QR>1; ER>0.33)

term.[25] We can also think to clusters in Table 7.3 as a financial score. The lower is the score, the lower is the financial reliability of a firm.[26]

7.4 Empirical Specification

In this section, we describe the empirical model to test if financially constrained firms largely rely on internally generated cash to overcome sunk costs associated to exports.

Comparing the eighth and the ninth wave, we estimate a discrete choice model (probit) for continuous nonexporting firms and new exporters. We observe 644 firms in 12 different manufacturing sectors: among them 122 firms are reported as new exporter in 2003 (i.e., reported domestic in the eighth survey, and exporter in the ninth survey).[27] The empirical model follows the nonstructural approach of Roberts and Tybout (1997) or Bernard and Jensen (1999), namely

$$\text{Entry}_{i03} = \begin{cases} 1\,if\ G\left(\alpha_0 CS_i + \sum_{c=0}^{3}\alpha_c X_c * CS_i + \mathbf{Z}(n)_i + \gamma + \epsilon_i\right) > 0 \\ 0 \text{ otherwise} \end{cases} \tag{7.3}$$

where Entry_{i03} is the firm i export status in the ninth survey. Variable Entry_{i03} takes a value of 1 if a firm starts to export between the eighth and the ninth survey, otherwise it takes value of 0. X_c, with $c=0,1,2,3$ is a

---

[25] We specify two alternative clustering process; the main source of concern is the different capital intensity across sectors, so that a low value of ER or *QR* may not have the same implication for different firms. We can define alternative thresholds using sectoral distribution of the indices. ER and QR thresholds are satisfied if the indices are above the 25th or the median for the corresponding sector. In addition, we can use the sectoral distribution of liquidity and leverage ratio. Finally, we can use variations across the two surveys of ER and QR indices. Main conclusions do not change. Results available upon request.

[26] As explained in Sect. 7.2, we take the averages of ER and QR within each survey period. Therefore, clustering process refers to a period of three years (i.e., clusters refer to the three-year period 2001–2003). If a firm belongs to cluster 0, it means that the average ratios of ER and QR are below the thresholds.

[27] More precisely, we consider as exporters, a firm that report to sell abroad at least the 2% of their total revenues, in order to minimize the risk of temporary exporting activity.

set of dummies that specify cluster membership; for example, if $X_0 = 1$, a firm belongs to cluster *0*. Our terms of interest are the coefficient of cash stock (α_0) for log of cash stock *Log(CS)*, and the interactions between liquidity and clusters (α_c).[28]

The α's coefficients capture the effect of liquidity on the entry probability, so that a positive sign indicates that the export probability rises when the level of internally generated cash increases. The interaction term is introduced to identity if cash stock has different effect depending on firms' financial status.

Equation 7.3 also includes a vector of control variables ($\boldsymbol{Z}(n)$), while ε is the *i.i.d.* error term. The control variables are retrieved from the Capitalia surveys, or from the associated balance sheet dataset. The former group includes information about the number of banks (*Banks*), R&D indicator (dummy variable), or product innovation/upgrading dummy (*UpProd* or *NewProd*). Balance sheet controls include capital intensity (*KL*), labor productivity (*LabProd*), and additional financial ratios as *LiqRatio* and *LevRatio* (see Greenaway et al. 2007). The balance sheet controls are defined as averages for the three-year period 2001–2003 (subscript *03*). Vector γ includes sector and area dummies (North East, North West, Center, South and Islands). Finally, we cluster the standard error across regions, given that Italian economy is highly regionalized.[29]

In Table 7.4, we directly report the marginal effects (average marginal effect) obtained by estimating Eq. 7.3. Coefficients can be interpreted as the elasticities of cash with respect to entry probability. Each column represents a different regression, and financial score are defined according to Table 7.3. The average level of cash stock has no effect on the entry probability; instead, the interaction of cash with the dummy X_0 (and X_1) has a positive and significant coefficient. In column (1), the effect of cash cancels out across different groups. In the other specifications (from Col.(2) to Col.(7)), an increase by 10% in the level of cash stock raises the

---

[28]Unlike the Euler equation for investment (Fazzari et al. 1988), we do not scale the level of cash with tangible assets; the fixed costs of exporting are assumed to be equal across firms. The results and conclusions do not change if we introduce a scaled measure of cash stock (*CSKB*). Results available upon request.

[29]See Table 7.8, for a detailed data description.

Table 7.4 Baseline results

	(1)	(2)	(3)	(4)	(5)	(6)	(7)
	Exp_{i03}	Exp_{i03}	Exp_{i03}	Exp_{i03}	Exp_{i03}	Exp_{i03}	Exp_{i03}
$Log(CS)_{i03}$	0.02	0.023	0.026	0.023	0.023	0.023	0.027
	[0.019]	[0.016]	[0.022]	[0.015]	[0.019]	[0.019]	[0.021]
X_0 *$Log(CS)_{i03}$		0.017***	0.015***	0.013***	0.017***	0.017***	0.010**
		[0.004]	[0.004]	[0.004]	[0.004]	[0.004]	[0.005]
X_1 *$Log(CS)_{i03}$		0.016***	0.016***	0.014**	0.016***	0.016***	0.011**
		[0.006]	[0.005]	[0.005]	[0.005]	[0.005]	[0.005]
X_2 *$Log(CS)_{i03}$		0.010*	0.010*	0.008	0.010*	0.010*	0.008
		[0.005]	[0.006]	[0.005]	[0.006]	[0.006]	[0.006]
$Banks_{i03}$			0.006				−0.004
			[0.030]				[0.026]
$ShareMainBank_{i03}$			0.007				0.008
			[0.006]				[0.006]
LiqRatio $_{i03}$				−0.072			−0.111
				[0.057]			[0.076]
LevRatio $_{i03}$				0.032			0.032
				[0.026]			[0.036]
R&D $_{i03}$					0.045	0.058*	0.031
					[0.032]	[0.033]	[0.030]
NewProd $_{i03}$					0.016		0.034*
					[0.018]		[0.020]
UpProd $_{i03}$						−0.032	−0.027
						[0.027]	[0.024]
Log(KL) $_{i03}$	0.038***	0.029***	0.025**	0.021*	0.026***	0.029***	0.011
	[0.009]	[0.011]	[0.011]	[0.012]	[0.010]	[0.009]	[0.010]
LabProd $_{i03}$	0.000	0.000	0.000	0.000	0.000	0.000	0.000
	[0.000]	[0.000]	[0.000]	[0.000]	[0.000]	[0.000]	[0.000]
Obs.	641	640	562	640	519	520	445
Pseudo R^2	0.071	0.115	0.125	0.118	0.117	0.131	0.143
$X^2(4)$	0	0	0	0	0	0	0

Marginal effect reported for probit estimation. Robust standard errors are clustered by regions and are reported in squared brackets. Sector and area dummies are included. X_0, X_1, and X_2 are dummies that take value of 1 if a firm is in cluster 0, 1, and 2, respectively. All balance sheet data are defined as averages for year 2001–2003. The χ^2 reports the p-value of joint test of significance for $Log(CS)_{i03}$ and three interacted variables; the statistics is distributed as a χ^2 with degrees of freedom in parenthesis: H_0 four coefficients are jointly not different from zero. Significance level: * is the p-value < 0.1, ** is the p-value < 0.05, and *** is the p-value < 0.01

entry probability by almost 0.2% for credit-constrained firms belonging to group *0* (i.e., firms without long- and short-term financial reliability). Similarly, an increase by 10% in the level of cash stock for firms in cluster *1* raise their entry probability by 0.1\%.

The coefficient of *Log(CS)* is the average marginal effect for all the firms, while interacted terms report the extra gains for firms in groups *0*, *1*, and *2* compared to group *3*. Then, a 10% increase in cash raises the entry probability for constrained firms (in Cluster *0*) by an additional 0.2% compared to the entry probability of not-constrained firms.[30] The results are statistically more robust for firms in cluster *0* than in cluster *1*. It suggests that long-term financial reliability plays a central role in the access to external credit. Finally, coefficients in Table 7.4 are constant across specifications maintaining the same magnitude and sign.

Estimation results suggest that credit access is an important factor to determine the first entry in the export market. If a firm is not reliable from a financial point of view (lack of long-term stability), it has to pay higher price for external financing, and consequently it has to increasingly rely on internal funds. In such a framework, a credit-rationed firm experiences difficulties to overcome sunk cost associated to trade and the entry probability raises with the level of internal liquidity.

7.4.1 Expansion to New Markets

We demonstrated in the previous section that the entry probability of credit-constrained firms is affected by internal liquidity. Now, we want to understand if trade activity of established exporters is affected by cash stock, and financial reliability too. Therefore, we exploit information about regions served by exporting firm.[31]

We perform three exercises, and in all of them we consider continuous exporters (firms that export in both surveys). We analyze the effect of

[30] In all the specifications cluster *3* is omitted (for reasons of multicollinearity), so that marginal effects must be interpreted in comparison with the group of the less-constrained firms. If we omit cluster 0 instead of 3, the signs of the coefficients become negative.

[31] Regions are Europe 15, East Europe, Russia, Asia, China, North America, South America and Oceania.

liquidity on the decision to reach new foreign markets. Compared to previous exercises, sample has changed given that new exporters and domestic firms are excluded.[32] In the first two exercises, we estimate a probit model (like Eq. 7.3).

1. We estimate the export status in each region in function of cash stock (and interacted values): in this case, the dependent variable is a dummy equal to 1 if a firm exports in a region in 2003; otherwise the dummy takes value of 0.
2. In the second exercise, we estimate if cash affects the entry probability in additional markets: here the dependent dummy variable takes value of 1 if a firm adds new regions among its destination markets in 2003 (compared to 2000); otherwise the dummy is equal to 0.

Table 7.5 presents estimations' results for the first exercise (control variables are not reported for the sake of space). Each column represents an equation for each destination market.[33] Dependent variable takes value of 1 if a continuous exporter (in eighth and ninth surveys) is exporting in a given region in the period 2001–2003, otherwise 0.

Cash stock coefficient turns to be positive and significant for all destination markets, with the exclusion of EU15 (column 1), while the interacted terms are not statistically significant. Given sample composition, we are just providing correlations among exporting and liquidity, that is, exporters own (on average) a higher liquidity (Greenaway et al. 2007) for each market they serve. Alternatively, a higher in liquidity is associated to a higher probability to serve a foreign market (EU15 excluded).

[32]Given that our aim is to understand whether the choice to serve an additional market involves an additional sunk cost, we focus only on the expansion of the extensive margin of trade (number of markets). Quitters, entrants and continuous domestic firms are excluded from the regression, in order to eliminate any type of noise that biases the estimation. The inclusion of new entrants, quitters or domestic firms would have introduced firms' choices different from our main dichotomous choice, that is, exporting in a new market or not.

[33]We exclude South America and Oceania both for reasons of space and lack of variability in the dependent variable.

Table 7.5 Expansion to new markets

	(1)	(2)	(3)	(4)	(5)	(6)
	$EU15_{i03}$	$RestEU_{i03}$	$RussiaEU_{i03}$	$Asia_{i03}$	$China_{i03}$	$NorthA_{i03}$
$Log(CS)_{i03}$	0.004	0.052***	0.028***	0.053***	0.020***	0.046***
	[0.007]	[0.010]	[0.009]	[0.008]	[0.005]	[0.012]
X_0 *$Log(CS)_{i03}$	−0.003	0.001	0.006	0.004	−0.001	0.007
	[0.002]	[0.004]	[0.004]	[0.003]	[0.003]	[0.004]
X_1 *$Log(CS)_{i03}$	0.000	−0.002	0.001	0.002	0.001	0.001
	[0.003]	[0.004]	[0.004]	[0.004]	[0.003]	[0.004]
X_2 *$Log(CS)_{i03}$	0.003	−0.006	0.001	0.003	0.000	0.012*
	[0.005]	[0.006]	[0.007]	[0.008]	[0.002]	[0.007]
Obs.	1353	1353	1353	1353	1353	1353
Pseudo R^2	0.037	0.04	0.041	0.046	0.083	0.062
$X^2(4)$	0.231	0.000	0. 000	0. 000	0. 000	0. 000

Marginal effect reported for probit estimation. Robust standard errors are clustered by regions and are reported in squared brackets. Sector and area dummies are included. Each column represents a regression for a specific area. X_0, X_1, and X_2 are dummies that take value of 1 if a firm is in cluster 0, 1, and 2, respectively. All balance sheet data are defined as averages for year 2001–2003. The χ^2 reports the *p*-value of joint test of significance for $Log(CS)_{i03}$ and three interacted variables; the statistics is distributed as a χ^2 with degrees of freedom in parenthesis: H_0 four coefficients are jointly not different from zero. Significance level: * is the *p*-value < 0.1, ** is the *p*-value < 0.05, and *** is the *p*-value < 0.01. Controls variable non-reported

In the second exercise, the binary-dependent variable describes if an exporter enters in new markets between 2000 and 2003. Also in this case, cash stock coefficient *Log(CS)* is positive and significant for all the specifications, while interacted term is not. Again, we observe a positive correlation between export activity and liquidity independently from firms' credit status: an expansion in the extensive margin of trade is associated to higher internal liquidity. It is interesting to note that *R&D* activity plays an important role to expand regions of destinations rather than to start exporting. Both *R&D* dummy and new product dummy (*NewProd*) suggest a positive relationship between firms' innovation and exporting (Van Beveren and Vandenbussche 2010). Therefore, the development of new products seems important to enter in different destination markets.[34]

[34]Table with the second exercise is not reported for space constraints. Table is available upon request.

In the last exercise, we estimate the effect of financial variables on the number of new destination markets. We define the dependent variable as a discrete number of new regions served among established exporters (ΔDest_{i03}). Dependent variable takes value 1, 2, 3, or 4, depending on the number of new added markets.[35] Given the nature of the dependent variable (ordered and discrete) we are going to estimate an ordered logit model; compared to Eq. 7.3, the ordered logit model maintains the same vector of independent variables. This last exercise confirms the previous results. First, higher liquidity is associated to a larger number of new regions, independently from credit status; second, innovation activity facilitates the entry in more than one new market.[36]

We can conclude that the availability of internal resources is particularly relevant for credit-constrained firms that aim to start export activity *ex-novo*. Internally generated cash are important to increase the extensive margin of export of established exports, but this effect does not vary in function of firms' financial reliability. The key role of liquidity for new entrants suggests that credit-constrained firms must pay higher cost for external source of financing.[37]

7.5 Endogenous Selection of Financial Score

Even if we assume that our clustering process is exogenous (it is exogenous because we are evaluating firms from the external point of view of an investor),[38] firms' selection in groups may be endogenous to the entry in the export market. The endogeneity can be generated by two sources:

---

[35]We consider only firm that decide to serve additional markets in 2003 compared to 2000. We exclude exporters that do not expand export activity in the next period: it would have included a first stage of self-selection (i.e., first, a firm decides to export, and, second, it decides how many markets to serve).

[36]Table with the third exercise is not reported for space constraints. Table is available upon request.

[37]These firms may offer few collaterals, and have no experience of international markets, or sunk cost associated to export are higher for the new entrants than for established export.

[38]The use of averages for financial variables should reduce the concerns of endogenous clustering (Kaplan and Zingales 1997).

1. The first source is the omitted variable bias. Whether or not a firm is constrained is likely to be correlated with unobserved firm's characteristics, even if we include control variables (i.e., from Eq. 7.3, *X(i)* is correlated with some unobserved characteristics).
2. The second type of problem is that credit constraint level and entry decision may be jointly determined; for example, a firm may worsen its financial situation (reduction in *ER*) because it is using external financing to start export activity. Firms in lower clusters self-select in the export market through anticipated investments. Therefore, financial ratios are endogenous to export status.[39]

In order to deal with endogeneity, we use an instrumental variable approach. We are going to define an instrument that may explain firm's ability to obtain financing (or to not be credit constrained), but uncorrelated with export status. Similarly to Minetti and Zhou (2011), we are going information reported in "*Struttura funzionale e territoriale del sistema bancario italiano, 1936–1974*" (SFT).[40]

In the beginning of 1930s, the Italian regulatory authorities were concerned about financial and banking instability: they thought that an excess of competition has favored this instability. As a result, in 1936 the *Comitato Interministeriale per il Credito e il Risparmio* (CICR) enacted strict norms for the entry of banks into local credit markets. As a consequence, from 1938 each credit institution could only open branches in an area of competence (one or multiple provinces) determined on the basis of its presence in 1936. Banks were also required to shut down branches outside their area of competence. Guiso et al. (2004) demonstrated empirically that the1936 regulation had a profound impact on the local supply of banking services and credit (creation and location of new branches) and, hence, on firms' ability to obtain credit.

In this report, SFT are reported several information on Italian banking system in 1936:

---

[39]Indeed, data shows that ex ante new exporters are more likely to show high leverage ratios.

[40]SFT contains historical data on the regional structure of the Italian banking system, such as the number of financial institutions by type and province. It also contains information on the implementation of the financial reform in 1936.

1. the number of savings by Italian provinces (*SavBank*);
2. the number of cooperative banks by Italian province (*CooBank*);
3. number of overall credit institute by region (NUTS 2) per 1000 inhabitants (*RegBank*);
4. the average number of banks per province by Italian regions (*PrBan*). We use this information as instrumental variables.

We exploit the variability in the types of banks across provinces in 1936 to predict current level of credit clustering (i.e., the firm's probability to stay in one of the four clusters). While, territorial distribution of banks in 1936 is unlikely to affect firms' export decision between 1998 and 2003, it is very likely that the share of different bank types affects credit availability for the Italian firms today.[41]

Given that the clustering process is a discrete (and not-ordinal) variable, we are going to estimate a multinomial probit in order to capture the sorting effect (assuming independence of irrelevant alternatives, I.I.A.). Therefore, both the first and the second stage are not linear models, and traditional (linear) instrumental variable approach may not seem adequate. As Terza et al. (2008), we address this issue using the two-stage residual inclusion (2SRI). The 2SRI estimator has the same first stage of a 2-Stage Least Square (2SLS), but in the second stage the endogenous variables are not replaced by their predicted values but by residuals from the first stage are included in addition to endogenous regressors.[42] Following the 2SRI technique, the main equation in our empirical model is as follows:

$$\text{Entry}_{i03} = \begin{cases} 1\, if\ G\left(\alpha_0 CS_i + \sum_{c=0}^{3} \alpha_c X_c * CS_i + \boldsymbol{Z}(n)_i + \eta_n \boldsymbol{Res}\ (\mathbf{X_c})_i + \gamma + \epsilon_i\right) > 0 \\ 0 \ \text{otherwise} \end{cases} \tag{7.4}$$

[41] According to Guiso et al. (2004), the territorial distribution of banks (by type) that occurred in 1936 was relatively random. It is unlikely that structural characteristics of the provinces (constant over time) are correlated with location and creation of branches.

[42] Terza et al. (2008) support the use of 2SRI, showing that 2SRI is generally statistically consistent in the broader class of nonlinear model, whereas 2SLS is not (they provide an example where the first stage is estimated with a multinomial probit and the second stage is a probit).

Table 7.6 First stage (multinomial logit)

	(1)	(2)	(3)	(4)	(5)	(6)
	$CL0_{i03}$	$CL1_{i03}$	$CL2_{i03}$	$CL0_{i03}$	$CL1_{i03}$	$CL2_{i03}$
SavBank	−0.027***	−0.038***	−0.045**	−0.028***	−0.032	−0.034*
	[0.010]	[0.014]	[0.019]	[0.007]	[0.022]	[0.018]
CooBank	−0.001	0.032***	0.035*	−0.004	0.024*	0.034**
	[0.007]	[0.012]	[0.021]	[0.006]	[0.013]	[0.017]
RegBank	−0.011	0.07	−0.357***	0.240***	0.225***	−0.225**
	[0.056]	[0.053]	[0.087]	[0.092]	[0.078]	[0.095]
PrBan	−0.001	−0.025**	−0.040**	−0.008***	−0.016	−0.035**
	[0.002]	[0.011]	[0.020]	[0.002]	[0.012]	[0.017]
$LiqRatio_{i00}$				−9.609***	−4.513***	−4.887***
				[0.891]	[0.849]	[1.149]
$LevRatio_{i00}$				−0.066	0.257	−0.304
				[0.358]	[0.353]	[0.537]
Obs.	644	644	644	490	490	490

Multinomial probit. Exogenous variables are omitted. Entrants and domestic firms are considered in the sample. Robust standard errors are clustered by region and are reported in squared brackets. Sector and area are dummies included. Baseline choice, cluster 3. CL stays for cluster. Significance level: * is the p-value < 0.1, ** is the p-value < 0.05, and *** is the p-value < 0.01. Controls variable non-reported

where *Res* $(\mathbf{X_c})_i$ is a vector of residual from multinomial first stage estimation. Given that, in our first stage, we estimate a multinomial probit, we obtain four vectors of residuals, one for each category. To calculate residuals' vectors, we use the formula for generalized residual for discrete choice models (Vella 1993).

Table 7.6 reports first-stage estimations (we omit exogenous variables). We present the results for the instrumentation of *Cluster* (as in Table 7.3) considering group *3* as baseline choice. In the first three columns, we use as instruments only credit data for Italian provinces in 1936 (as excluded instruments); in the last three columns we introduce the lagged values of *LevRatio* and *LiqRatio* as additional instruments (i.e., lagged averages for period 1998–2000). In this case, we also instrument *LevRatio* and *LiqRatio* in 2001–2003 with their lagged values (but we do not report first stage for these two additional variables). The coefficients show that instruments are correlated with endogenous sorting.[43] In particular,

[43]The first stage results hold also for alternative clustering process. Results available upon request.

larger is the presence of saving banks (*SavBank*) in 1936, and the lower is the probability for a firm (in a given province) to be credit constrained (belonging to group 0)

Given that, our instruments seem to have very high explanatory power, we include in the second-stage residuals, for alternatives *0*, *1*, and *2* Eq. 7.4. We estimate the model it with probit (again cluster 3 is omitted for multicollinearity). Finally, to retrieve robust standard errors, we bootstrap the entire two-stage procedure stratifying the sample by regions (Terza 2008; Wooldridge 2008). Table 7.7 presents the second-stage results (marginal effect reported).

The estimations confirm the previous intuitions. The coefficients' sign does not change compared estimations from Table 7.4. The cash stock and interacted terms are jointly significant (X^2 I° test). For all the specifications, an increase of liquidity raises the entry probability for constrained firms (group 0). More precisely, if cash stock raises by 10%, the entry probability of rationed firms increases by 0.11% (column 1).[44] Finally, the additional controls (both exogenous and endogenous) have a negligible impact on the entry probability.

Some final comments concern 2SRI approach. In large part of the specifications, the joint significance of the residuals (*Res(x)*) is rejected (X^2 II° test): under the null, the coefficients are jointly equal to zero. It suggests that our clustering process is potentially exogenous to the entry decision.

We test if instruments have some explicative power on the main dependent variable (export decision). So, we include instruments from first stage in the second stage (Eq. 7.4). We report in Table 7.7 the *p*-value of overidentification test (LR test).[45] The *LR test* for overidentification

[44]We obtain similar results for alternative clustering process. Interaction between group 1 and cash is significant with alternative clustering procedures.

[45]In order to test overidentification, we perform a likelihood ratio test. First, we calculate the log likelihood of second stage of Eq. 7.4 (*L*1). Then, we estimate Eq. 7.4, by including also instruments of first stage (i.e., *SavBank*, *CooBank*, *RegBank*, and *PrBan*), and we calculate again the log-likelihood (*L*2). The likelihood ratio test is defined by 2*(*L*2–l*L*1), and it is distributed as a X^2 with degrees of freedom equal to the difference between the parameters in the first and the second model (i.e., 4). Under the null, the new variables (instruments) are not jointly significant so that instruments do not explain additional variability of main dependent variable.

Table 7.7 Entry in the export market (second stage)

	(1)	(2)	(3)
	Exp_{i03}	Exp_{i03}	Exp_{i03}
Log(CS) $_{i03}$	0.083	0.141	0.206
	[0.105]	[0.126]	[0.140]
X_0 Log(CS) $_{i03}$	0.112***	0.112***	0.110***
	[0.028]	[0.029]	[0.027]
X_1 Log(CS) $_{i03}$	0.041	0.049	0.023
	[0.027]	[0.033]	[0.039]
X_2 *Log(CS) $_{i03}$	0.031	0.036	0.023
	[0.034]	[0.041]	[0.048]
Log(KL) $_{i03}$	−0.026	0.039	−0.041
	[0.195]	[0.189]	[0.210]
LabProd $_{i03}$	0.002	−0.002	−0.004
	[0.006]	[0.006]	[0.005]
Banks $_{i03}$		0.128	
		[0.352]	
Share $_{i03}$		0.057	
		[0.067]	
LiqRatio $_{i03}$			1.101
			[1.393]
LevRatio $_{i03}$			0.127
			[0.346]
$Res(0)_i$	−1.153	0.268	−0.745***
	[0.924]	[0.400]	[0.232]

(Continued)

Table 7.7 (continued)

	(1)	(2)	(3)
$Res(1)_i$	0.293	0.126	0.389
	[0.349]	[0.252]	[0.246]
$Res(2)_i$	−0.011	−0.01	−0.052
	[0.161]	[0.163]	[0.161]
$Res(LQ)_i$			0.19
			[0.601]
$Res(LV)_i$			−0.915
			[1.701]
Obs.	642	642	490
Pseudo R^2	0.129	0.126	0.194
X^2 I°	0	0	0
X^2 II°	0.531	0.821	0.001
LR Test	0.067	0.189	0.642

Marginal effect reported for probit estimation. Robust bootstrapped standard errors (200 replications stratified by regions). Sector and area dummies are included. X_0, X_1, and X_2 are dummies that take value of 1 if a firm is in cluster 0, 1, and 2, respectively. All balance sheet data are defined as averages for year 2001–2003. Significance level: * is the *p*-value < 0.1, ** is the *p*-value < 0.05, and *** is the *p*-value < 0.01. The X^2 I° reports the *p*-value of joint significance test for $Log(CS)_{i03}$, and three interacted variables. The statistics is distributed as a X^2: in the null the four coefficients are jointly not different from zero. The X^2 II° reports the *p*-value of joint significance test for residuals *Res(x)*. *LR test* reports the *p*-value for the likelihood ratio test: under the null, the instruments of first stage have no additional explicative power in the second stage suggests that instruments have not additional explanatory power in large part of regressions. Moreover, the test provide evidence that the instruments satisfy the exclusion restriction. This result reinforces also the idea that the sorting process is relatively exogenous.

As last exercise, we implement the 2SRI approach also to analyze expansions of export activity in new regions; we evaluate the effect of financial variables on the export status for a given region, on the binary decision of expanding in new markets. In both cases, we compare firms that report export activity in both surveys.

The results for the second stage show that the coefficients' signs and statistical significance do not change, when we deal with endogeneity (results remain unchanged compared to Table 7.5). Similarly, to previous analysis, cash stock is positive correlated with exporting. Residuals from first stage are not jointly significant, and the *LR Test* suggests that instruments have no additional explicative power.[46]

7.6 Conclusion

Exporting is an activity that entails several costs, and most of them are sunk costs associated with the first entry in the export. In real world, the new exporter faces a well-defined entry costs against an uncertain future profit. If we assume the existence of asymmetric information and imperfect capital markets, not all potential exporters begin export activity. Throughout the chapter, we discuss the impact of financial resources on the probability of entry into the export market, particularly for credit-constrained firms.

In the current chapter, we analyze two important issues. On the one hand, we develop a methodology for identifying a priori the level of a firm's financial health, borrowing insights from the literature on investments' sensitivity on cash flows, and using ratios from business economics. On the other hand, we empirically evaluate whether the level

[46]Table available upon request.

of internal resources affects both first entry in the export market and the extensive margin of trade.

We find that the internal resources are an important factor for firms' internationalization. The level of cash stock is crucial for new entrants which are identified as credit constrained. Moreover, we find that internal liquidity is positively correlated with the extensive margin of trade: an expansion in new destination market is associated to higher liquidity. Findings are robust also to endogeneity concerns.

However, further work is needed to understand the mechanisms through which liquidity affects the internationalization process of medium- and small-sized firms, with a more detailed dataset about export and asset/liabilities.

A.1 Appendix

Table A.1 Data description

Name	Description	Details	Source
Log(Y)	Log of sales	Operating revenues	Balance sheet
Log(KL)	Log of capital intensity	Ratio of fixed assets to labor force	Balance sheet
Log(Age)	Log of age	Difference between year of reference and year of foundation	Balance sheet
LabProd	Labor productivity	Value added per worker	Balance sheet
ER	Equity ratio	Sect. 7.3	Balance sheet
QR	Quick ratio	Sect. 7.3	Balance sheet
Log(CS)	Log of cash stock (broad measure of liquidity)	CS=Profits+DA+TFR+liquid assets	Balance sheet
CSKB	Cash stock divided by capital value at begin of period t	*CSKB=CS/KB*	Balance sheet
Inv	Investment in tangible fixed assets	$Inv_{it} = K_{it} - (1 - \delta)K_{it-1}$ with $\delta = 0.1$	Balance sheet
DA	Value of depreciation and amortization		Balance sheet
TFR	Trattemento Fine Rapporto	Worker leave indemnity	Balance sheet
KB	Fixed asset at begin of period t	$KB_{it} = K_{it} - Inv_{it} + DA_{it}$	Balance sheet
LevRatio	Leverage ratio	Ratio of firm's short-term debt to current assets	Balance sheet
LiqRatio	Liquidity ratio	Ratio of firm's current assets minus its short-term debt to total assets	Balance sheet
Banks	Number of banks	Number of banks used by a firm	Survey
Share	Share of principal bank	Share of debt owned by principal bank in percentage point	Survey

(Continued)

Table A.1 (Continued)

Name	Description	Details	Source
R&D	R&D activity dummy	Dummy equal to 1 if firm invests in R&D activity	Survey
NewProd	Product innovation dummy	Dummy variable equal to 1 if a firm invest in product innovation	Survey
UpProd	Quality upgrading dummy	Dummy variable equal to 1 if a firm invest product upgrading	Survey
Expo	Export status	Dummy variable equal to 1 if a firm export at least the 2% of revenues	Survey
Ndest	Number of regions covered by export	Europe 15, East Europe, Russia, Asia, China, North America, South America, Oceania	Survey
Cluster	Four cluster groups	Clusters defined by ER>0.3 and QR>1	Own calculation
Cluster(Med)	Four cluster groups	Clusters defined by ER and QR greater sector median	Own calculation
Cluster(P25)	Four cluster groups	Clusters defined by ER and QR greater sector 25th percentile	Own calculation
Cluster(StMed)	Four cluster groups	Clusters defined by LevRatio and LiqRatio greater than sector median	Own calculation
Variation ER	Four cluster groups-based *ER*	Clusters defined by ER variation across two survey periods: Worsen, Bad Improve, Good	Own calculation

Table A.2 Descriptive statistics

Variable	Mean	S.D	Obs.	Min	Max	Domestic	Exporter	Cont.Dom	New Export
Log(Y)	8.92	1.33	2553	3.97	15.69	8.23	9.01	8.19	8.49
Log(KL)	3.53	0.97	2553	0.85	12.18	3.48	3.49	3.44	3.59
Age	27.26	18.79	2553	4	313	24.88	27.74	24.21	28.93
LabProd	96.54	999.82	2553	−114.78	41,191.38	52.61	133.21	51.83	54.43
δER	0.32	0.47	2553	0	1	0.33	0.32	0.35	0.14
δER	0.38	0.49	2553	0	1	0.44	0.38	0.46	0.21
North-West	0.37	0.48	2553	0	1	0.33	0.4	0.32	0.38
North-East	0.29	0.46	2553	0	1	0.26	0.31	0.25	0.33
Center	0.2	0.4	2553	0	1	0.21	0.18	0.22	0.13
South	0.13	0.34	2553	0	1	0.19	0.11	0.2	0.15
QR	1.06	0.83	2553	0.02	18.36	1.17	1.05	1.2	0.82
ER	0.26	0.2	2553	−4.06	0.9	0.25	0.27	0.26	0.18
Log(CS)	8.39	1.38	2550	3.09	14.55	7.74	8.46	7.71	7.87
CSKB	858.93	42,459.52	2491	−6.64	2,119,159	3359.67	8.71	3887.95	7.11
LevRatio	0.49	0.94	2553	0	39.63	0.41	0.49	0.4	0.49
LiqRatio	0.14	0.22	2553	−3.76	0.85	0.11	0.16	0.12	0.04
IKB	0.14	0.33	2490	−0.95	7.51	0.17	0.13	0.16	0.11
Log(Debt)	5.08	2.68	2553	0	13	4.1	5.18	4.02	4.69
Banks	5.01	3.13	2006	1	25	4.2	5.38	4.1	4.75
Share	34	26.72	1811	0	100	35.54	33.23	36.28	39.66
R&D	0.42	0.49	2013	0	1	0.22	0.52	0.2	0.36
Ask	0.37	0.48	333	0	1	0.33	0.39	0.34	0.39
Des	0.17	0.37	1981	0	1	0.19	0.15	0.19	0.28
UpProd	0.57	0.5	2553	0	1	0.7	0.71	0.7	0.68
NewProd	0.43	0.5	2553	0	1	0.32	0.53	0.31	0.39

(Continued)

Table A.2 (Continued)

Variable	Mean	S.D	Obs.	Min	Max	Domestic	Exporter	Cont.Dom	New Export
Expo	0.68	0.47	2015	0	1	0	1	0.05	1
NewExpo	0.13	0.34	644	0	1	0	1	0	1
Ndest	1.55	2.05	2553	0	9	0	2.86	0	1.45
Expo(EU15)	0.48	0.5	2553	0	1	0	0.89	0	0.77
Expo(EU-Rest)	0.15	0.36	2553	0	1	0	0.29	0	0.12
Expo(Russia)	0.18	0.38	2553	0	1	0	0.33	0	0.19
Expo(Asia)	0.16	0.37	2553	0	1	0	0.3	0	0.07
Expo(China)	0.05	0.22	2553	0	1	0	0.09	0	0.01
Expo(NorthA.)	0.2	0.4	2553	0	1	0	0.37	0	0.14

Data source: Capitalia Survey and balance sheet dataset. We consider 2263 firms which are present both in the eighth and the ninth survey. First five columns include statistics at aggregate level. S.D.: Standard deviation. Exporter: Exporters in 2003. Domestic: nonexporting firm in 2003. New-Export: Exporting firm in 2003, but domestic in 2000. Cont.Dom.: nonexporting firm in 2000 and 2003

References

Bank for International Settlements. (2006). International Convergence of Capital Measurement and Capital Standards: A Revised Framework – Comprehensive Version.

Beck, T. (2002). Financial Development and International Trade. Is There a Link? *Journal of International Economics, 57*(1), 107–131.

Beck, T. (2003). Financial Dependence and International Trade. *The Review of International Economics, 11*(2), 296–316.

Bellone, F., Musso, P., Nesta, L., & Schiavo, S. (2010). Financial Constraints and Firm Export Behavior. *The World Economy, 33*(3), 347–373.

Berman, N., & Héricourt, J. (2010). Financial Factors and the Margins of Trade: Evidence from Cross-Country Firm-Level Data. *Journal of Development Economics, 93*(2), 206–217.

Bernard, A. B., & Jensen, B. J. (1999). Exceptional Exporter Performance: Cause, Effect or Both? *Journal of International Economics, 47*(1), 1–25.

Bond, S., & Van Reenen, J. (2005). Microeconometric Models of Investments and Employments. In J. J. Heckman & E. E. Leamer (Eds.), *Handbook of Econometrics. Vol. 6*. Amsterdam: Elsevier.

Brealey, R., & Myers, S. (1999). *Principles of Corporate Finance*. Boston: McGraw-Hill.

Caggese, A., & Cunat, V. (2013). Financing Constraints, Export Decisions and Aggregate Productivity. *Review of Economic Dynamics, 16*(1), 177–193.

Campa, J. M., & Shaver, J. M. (2002). *Exporting and Capital Investment: On the Strategic Behavior of Exporters*. IESE Research Papers D/469. IESE Business School.

Chaney, T. (2016). Liquidity Constrained Exporters. *Journal of Economic Dynamics and Control, 76*, 141–154.

Das, S., Robert, M. J., & Tybout, R. (2007). Market Entry Costs, Producer Heterogeneity, and Export Dynamics. *Econometrica, 75*(3), 837–873.

Fazzari, S. M., Hubbard, M. G., & Petersen, B. C. (1988). Financing Constraints and Corporate Investment. *Brookings Papers on Economic Activity, 19*(1), 141–206.

Forbes, K. (2007). One Cost of the Chilean Capital Controls: Increased Financial Constraints for Smaller Traded Firms. *Journal of International Economics, 71*(2), 294–323.

Greenaway, D., Guariglia, A., & Kneller, R. (2007). Financial Factors and Exporting Decisions. *Journal of International Economics, 73*(2), 377–395.

Guiso, L., Sapienza, P., & Zingales, L. (2004). Does Local Financial Development Matter? *The Quarterly Journal of Economics, 119*(3), 929–969.
Hubbard, G. (1998). Capital Market Imperfections and Investments. *Journal of Economic Literature, 35*, 193–225.
Kaplan, S. N., & Zingales, L. (1997). Do Investment-Cash Flow Sensitivities Provide Useful Measures of Financing Constraints. *The Quarterly Journal of Economics, 112*(1), 169–215.
Konings, J., Rizov, M., & Vandenbussche, H. (2003). Investment Constraints in Transition Countries. *Economics Letters, 78*, 253–258.
Love, I. (2003). Financial Development and Financing Constraints: International Evidence from the Structural Investment Model. *Review of Financial Studies, 16*(3), 765–791.
Manole, V., & Spatareanu, M. (2009). Exporting, Capital Investment and Financial Constraints. *Review of World Economics, 146*(1), 23–37.
Manova, K. (2013). Credit Constraints, Heterogeneous Firms and International Trade. *The Review of Economic Studies, 80*(2), 711–744.
Melitz, M. (2003). The Impact of Trade on Intra-industry Reallocations and Aggregate Industry Productivity. *Econometrica, 71*(6), 1695–1725.
Minetti, R., & Zhou, S. C. (2011). Credit Constraints and Firm Export: Microeconomic Evidence from Italy. *Journal of International Economics, 83*(2), 109–125.
Muùls, M. (2015). Exporters, Importers and Credit Constraints. *Journal of International Economics, 95*(2), 333–343.
Onida, F. (2003). *Growth, Competitiveness and Firm Size: Factors Shaping the Role of Italian Productive System in the World Arena*. KITeS Working Papers n.144.
Roberts, M. J., & Tybout, J. R. (1997). The Decision to Export to Colombia: An Empirical Model of Entry with Sunk Costs. *American Economic Review, 87*(4), 545–564.
Terza, J. V., Basu, A., & Rathouz, P. J. (2008). Two-Stage Residual Inclusion Estimation: Addressing Endogeneity in Health Econometric Modeling. *Journal of Health Economics, 27*(3), 531–543.
Van Beveren, I., & Vandenbussche, H. (2010). Product and Process Innovation and Firms' Decision to Export. *Journal of Economic Policy Reforms, 13*(1), 3–24.
Vella, F. (1993). A Simple Estimator for Simultaneous Models with Censored Endogenous Regressors. *International Economic Review, 34*(2), 441–457.
Wagner, J. (2014). Credit Constraints and Exports: A Survey of Empirical Studies Using Firm-Level Data. *Industrial and Corporate Change, 23*(6), 1477–1492.

Part V

Location and Employment

8

Geographical Boundaries of External and Internal Agglomeration Economies

Katiuscia Lavoratori and Lucia Piscitello

8.1 Introduction

The literature on location choices of multinational enterprises (MNEs) highlight that the search for agglomeration economies is a key determinant of the process (for a review, see Iammarino and McCann 2013). Specifically, MNEs seek geographic proximity with other companies (e.g. Chang and Park 2005; Arauzo-Carod et al. 2010; Nielsen et al. 2017), mainly to access information and knowledge externalities, by co-agglomerating with subsidiaries of other MNEs and with local companies from which they can benefit in terms of information, knowledge and

K. Lavoratori (✉)
Warwick Business School, University of Warwick, Coventry, UK
e-mail: Katiuscia.lavoratori@wbs.ac.uk

L. Piscitello
Henley Business School, University of Reading, Reading, UK

DIG-Politecnico di Milano, Milan, Italy
e-mail: lucia.piscitello@henley.ac.uk

S. Colombo (ed.), *Spatial Economics Volume II*,
https://doi.org/10.1007/978-3-030-40094-1_8

innovation (Mariotti et al. 2010). More recently, however, increasing attention has been paid to geographic proximity among different activities of the same parent company, i.e. to the intra-firm co-location, or internal agglomeration (Alcácer and Delgado 2016; Castellani and Lavoratori 2019b; Woo et al. 2019). In fact, since MNEs are by definition multi-unit firms, they need to coordinate the various units, and to monitor and control geographically dispersed activities to reach efficiency and gain in terms of competitive advantages (Howells and Bessant 2012; Buciuni and Finotto 2016).

Using 447 greenfield investments made by foreign multinational companies in Italy (during the period 1998–2012) at NUTS-3 level (the Italian province), the present chapter investigates the factors driving these new location decisions, with a special focus on external and internal agglomeration forces, and their spatial decay effects. Our conditional logit estimates confirm that both external and internal agglomeration economies play a role in driving foreign location choices in the province and that not controlling for internal agglomeration forces leads to overestimation of the effect of external ones. Moreover, augmenting the model with the spatial lags of both internal and external agglomeration economies, we find that internal agglomeration economies require a closer geographical proximity among the firm's operations and their effects do not cross the geographical boundaries of the province. Additionally, we find that Marshallian (specialisation) agglomerations require a stronger geographical proximity among units, whereas the benefits of diversity (Jacobsian) economies significantly extend beyond the province's geographical boundaries.

The reminder of the chapter is organized as follows. The next section illustrates our theoretical background on external and internal agglomeration factors driving the location decision of foreign MNEs, and on the role of the spatial decay effect. Section 8.3 describes the data. Section 8.4 presents our empirical strategy and Sect. 8.5 illustrates and discusses our empirical findings. Section 8.6 concludes with some suggestions for future research.

8.2 Theoretical Background

8.2.1 External Agglomeration Economies

The concept of agglomeration economies encompasses many interpretations and forms, and has been the subject of numerous empirical analyses (e.g. Ellison et al. 2010; Combes and Gobillon 2015). A traditional dichotomous classification distinguishes between Marshallian and Jacobsian economies (Glaeser et al. 1992). The former refers to the pioneering contribution of Marshall (1920) and its subsequent formalisation as the MAR (Marshall-Arrow-Romer) model. These economies are *external* to the enterprise, but internal to the industry, and concern the local formation of a specialised labour market, input-output linkages between customers and suppliers and the emergence of industry-specific knowledge spillovers. The Jacobsian economies (Jacobs 1969) are *external* to both the enterprise and the industry, as they derive from the variety of local activities in a specific area due to urbanisation processes. Indeed, diversity fosters wide-ranging, highly fungible knowledge spillovers, in addition to the circulation of ideas and innovation and their recombination across sectors. A complementary classification extensively adopted in the literature distinguishes between *sharing, matching* and *learning* effects (Duranton and Puga 2004; Boschma and Frenken 2011). *Sharing* effects include the advantages of sharing local indivisible assets and infrastructures, the sharing of business risks, the variety of inputs and industrial specialisation. *Matching* refers to the quality and quantity of matching between enterprises and workers in the labour market, while *Learning* effects concern the generation, diffusion and accumulation of knowledge.[1]

Concerning location choices of MNEs, an extensive range of theoretical and empirical literature assess the positive role of local agglomeration forces (e.g. Head et al. 1995; Mariotti and Piscitello 1995; Driffield and

[1]However, the evidence about the significance and the role of the different sources of agglomeration economies are still controversial and conflicting results have often been often obtained (e.g. Rosenthal and Strange 2004; Beaudry and Schiffauerova 2009; De Groot et al. 2009; Melo et al. 2009).

Munday 2000; He 2002; Barrios et al. 2006; Bobonis and Shatz 2007). Recent studies have shown that the agglomerative behaviour of MNEs does not merely mimic the agglomeration of economic activities in the host country, but follows a distinct model that leads to more spatial concentration of their activities in privileged areas (Mariotti et al. 2010; Alfaro and Chen 2014). Indeed, the MNEs' location decision process is strongly bounded in rationality as they suffer from a limited familiarity with the spatial environment, namely with those factors that ultimately influence the effectiveness of the location choice, such as the access to production factors, networks of suppliers, infrastructure and services, and local institutions. In order to reduce information costs and sunk costs connected to wrong location choices, MNEs often adopt a risk-averse approach by locating their subsidiaries in regional clusters and, especially, in metropolitan areas (Mariotti and Piscitello 1995; Henisz and Delios 2001). In fact, clusters generally have an international reputation of industrial excellence, securing the widest access to Marshallian economies, and metropolitan areas are the locus of Jacobsian economies, offering access to infrastructure hubs, human capital and other tangible and intangible resources (Glaeser et al. 1992; McCann and Acs 2011). Additionally, metropolitan areas also allow access to so-called 'archipelago economies' (Veltz 2000; Rodríguez-Pose and Zademach 2006), that is the benefits produced by global interconnectivity and by inclusion in the networks of economic, political and institutional power. As such, they perform the role of gateways for MNEs entering into a foreign country (Drennan 1992; Short et al. 2000; Taylor 2004).

This process of spatial over-concentration in the host country is further reinforced by MNEs' adoption of an imitative behaviour of their peers (e.g. Lieberman and Asaba 2006), likewise motivated by the need to reduce information costs and uncertainty. Indeed, MNEs integrate the observation of their predecessors' spatial behaviour into their decision-making process as important information about the quality of the regions in the host country: as a result, information spillovers and observational learning give rise to locational cascades, which foster the agglomeration of new entries with MNEs that have already made a location choice, wherever this is perceived as a successful operation (Caplin and Leahy 1998; Mariotti et al. 2010; Vicente and Suire 2007).

8.2.2 Internal Agglomeration Economies

Firms' location decisions are also influenced by their need to generate and preserve special linkages among activities (Woo et al. 2019). In fact, a "multinational firm's external organization should not be constituted to the detriment of its organizational coherence; it should, on the contrary, be completed by the implementation of relations of proximity internal to the firm, which we refer to as 'internal proximity'" (Blanc and Sierra 1999: 188). Inevitably, this presents a trade-off between the geographical dispersion of the firm's operations in search for the best external factors vs. the concentration of their facilities in the same place to preserve internal linkages and the related benefits (Blanc and Sierra 1999; Mariani 2002).

Traditional approaches in regional sciences and economic geography have distinguished between internal agglomeration economies related to horizontal integration (or internal economies of scale), lateral integration (or internal economies of scope) and vertical integration (Parr 2002). All these internal economies can be achieved through the *expansion* of the activities at the level of the single plant. Indeed, such an expansion can reduce transport costs and production costs due to the maximized use of physical space, land and (also indivisible) assets or production technologies that require processes to be physically close (Lavoratori et al. 2019). Thus, internal economies may be achieved through the geographic proximity of distinct units of the same firm, thanks to the possibility of sharing physical assets (plant and machinery), specialised people, teams, logistic and support services (Alcácer and Delgado 2016) and economies of scale and scope in other activities, such as procurement and branding (Rawley and Seamans 2015). Pursuing other lines of analysis, a small yet growing body of literature at the intersection between economic geography and management offers evidence on further drivers of internal agglomeration. Organisation and managerial costs can increase with the increase in the geographical dispersion of activities (Coase 1937). Coordination, monitoring and control of activities is a key aspect for competitive advantage of the company (Howells and Bessant 2012). Thus, intra-firm co-location can be a mechanism of coordination and control of complex and geographically dispersed organisational structures, more important for less experienced firms in operating internationally, and firms who rely relatively less on codified knowledge, because tacit knowledge and information transfer can be facilitated through co-location (Castellani and Lavoratori 2019b). Such a relationship between distance-based costs and agglomeration has been acknowledged also by the economic geography literature (e.g. McCann and Shefer 2004; Wood and Parr 2005). Several studies provide empirical evidence for the idea that distance-sensitive costs of monitoring/control and coordination may lead enterprises to seek greater geographical proximity between their units, particularly between their headquarters and subsidiaries (Kalnins and Lafontaine 2004, 2013; Berger and DeYoung 2006; Henderson and Ono 2008; Giroud 2013; Lu and Wedig 2013), as well as between units that carry out complementary activities, such as R&D and manufacturing (Mariani 2002; Ketokivi and Ali-Yrkkö 2009; Gray et al. 2015).

Other studies about intra-firm spillovers also highlight the beneficial effects of proximity and co-location as factors that facilitate the sharing of experience, information and tacit knowledge between different functional units of the enterprise that can be more difficult and costlier when the distance increases (Liberti and Mian 2009), with a positive impact on the latter's productivity, also thanks to the two-way exchange of local knowledge and experience (Rawley and Seamans 2015). This can be more relevant in engineering intensive industry (Ivarsson et al. 2016), or in relation to key development functions that represent a crucial source of ideas for maintaining innovative capabilities (Buciuni and Finotto 2016). Benefits from intra-firm co-location can also be different in relation to agglomeration typologies. In supply-side agglomeration settings (e.g. manufacturing), mechanisms of 'internal technology-based knowledge sharing' may prevail, while in demand-side settings (e.g. services or retail) 'internal operating resource sharing' mechanisms are more likely to be exploited (Woo et al. 2019).

Theoretical and empirical literature on internal agglomerations is still growing. Some studies are focused on specific industries (e.g. the biopharma in Alcácer and Delgado 2016), a limited geographical area such as a set of global cities (e.g. Belderbos et al. 2016; Castellani and Lavoratori 2019a), or on the location choice of R&D activities worldwide (Castellani and Lavoratori 2019b). Other studies investigate the spatial organization of global value chains and the location of new investments by MNEs, by developing multi-sector analyses referred to a level of geographical aggregation that seems too high for a correct detection of intra-firm co-location (e.g. the European regions in Defever 2012; or the Economic Areas in US in Alcácer and Delgado 2016).

8.2.3 Spatial Decay Effect of External and Internal Agglomeration Economies

The rapid decay of agglomeration effects is a consolidated evidence in the regional science field (Duranton and Puga 2004; Rosenthal and Strange 2004; Cantwell and Piscitello 2005). Combes and Gobillon (2015) highlight that agglomeration effects arise within 100 kilometres, but the threshold can be lower. Indeed, a survey conducted by Drucker (2012) shows that in 60% of studies on agglomeration economies effects, this threshold is 20 kilometres or less; in over 80% of studies the threshold is less than 80 kilometres. However, the role of geographical proximity can vary across industries and type of agglomeration. Rosenthal and Strange (2003) find that specialisation economies strongly decline with an increase in distance among economic units, whereas diversification economies show a less clear pattern. Andersson et al. (2019) investigate the role of agglomeration economies within the cities of Stockholm, Gothenburg and Malmö. They uncover that the effect of specialisation economies arises in one squared kilometre around the company, but diversification externalities operate at a greater scale. Thus, these agglomeration forces may operate simultaneously, but at different geographical scales. A study based on the United Kingdom shows that diversification externalities play a role at a higher level of geographical aggregation—the city, whereas specialisation externalities operate at a smaller level in a closer neighbourhood to the firm, within the city (Lavoratori and Castellani, 2020), presenting a stronger spatial decay effect.

Moreover, this spatial decay effect of specialisation economies is even stronger in the case of creative and knowledge-intensive sectors where face-to-face interactions, sharing of ideas and information are crucial (van Soest et al. 2006; Andersson et al. 2019).

Although there is a well-developed literature on spatial decay effects regarding external agglomeration economies, there is a lack of studies that investigate these effects on internal agglomeration economies.

Previous studies have investigated the role of internal agglomeration economies (internal proximity or intra-firm co-location) at different levels of spatial aggregation: on the one hand, a high level of geographical aggregation, such as the US economic area and the EU NUTS-2 (Alcácer and Delgado 2016; Defever 2012); on the other, recent studies have adopted a more fine-grained approach, at city and NUTS-3 level (Castellani and Lavoratori 2019a, b; Belderbos et al. 2016; Lavoratori et al. 2019). All these studies find a positive effect of intra-firm co-location on domestic and foreign location decisions. It is not hard to believe that more aggregated levels of analysis can hide factors that operate at smaller geographical scales.

Indeed, Adams and Jaffe (1996) investigate the role of proximity with R&D labs on the productivity of manufacturing plants of firms operating in the chemical industry, looking at the transfer of knowledge across facilities within a firm and spillovers across firms. They show that the effects of parent firm R&D on plant-level productivity decline with an increase in geographical and technological distance between R&D labs and production plants. Lavoratori et al. (2019) investigate the role of co-location with other (manufacturing and knowledge-intensive business services (KIBS)) units of the same parent company, on the latter's location choice. Specifically, introducing the analysis of a spatial decay effect of internal agglomeration economies, they find that the probability of locating a new investment in a given province is positively influenced by the presence of the same parent company's manufacturing activities. When the firm's prior presence in the province concerns KIBS activities (e.g. computer and related activities, business activities like legal, accounting, tax, business and management consultancy, and management activities relating to holding companies), mechanisms of temporary proximity can substitute the need for permanent geographical proximity, because the exchange of knowledge and information between manufacturing and KIBS activities can be exploited through professional mobility and dedicated temporary interorganisational mechanisms (periodic meetings, project teams, etc.). Moreover, the probability of choosing a given province for a new manufacturing investment does not increase with the presence of other activities of the same parent company in contiguous provinces, thus confirming a strong spatial decay effect of internal agglomeration economies.

8.3 Data and Descriptive Statistics

Our research aims to empirically test the role played by agglomeration economies in the location choices by foreign MNEs at the sub-national level, disentangling the role of internal and external agglomeration forces. To this end, it was necessary to define a suitable empirical strategy. The analysis relies on data on greenfield investments made by foreign MNEs in Italy throughout 1998–2012, from the REPRINT database (for more details, see Mariotti et al. 2015). The database reports information about the location of new investments in manufacturing, along with the sector and home country of the parent companies. Moreover, the database contains the information on the other activities of the same parent companies, already located in Italy before the focal new investment. Specifically, we know the location and the activity of these prior investments (manufacturing vs. other activities, such as sales and marketing, maintenance and servicing, technical support, logistics and transportation), and we use this information as a stock for computing the firm's internal agglomeration measure.

We focus on the location choice of 447 new investments in manufacturing, undertaken by 384 MNEs during the period considered. Our geographical unit of analysis is the Italian province, corresponding to the NUTS-3 level of the Eurostat classification. Eurostat has established the Nomenclature of Units for Territorial Statistics (NUTS) as a hierarchy of geographical levels, for each European country. The current NUTS classification subdivides the economic European territory into 97 regions at NUTS-1 level, 270 regions at NUTS-2 level and 1294 regions at NUTS-3 level. NUTS-3 areas correspond to a population between 150,000 and

800,000 people (Eurostat 2011). Italy is divided into 110 provinces, with an average extension of 2746 square kilometres and an average distance capital-to-capital of provinces of 40 kilometres.

The investments considered interest 81 out of the 110 provinces. Table 8.1 reports the geographical distribution of the investments. The top 10 provinces receive 46% of investments made in the period of analysis; these are localized in the northern and central part of Italy (e.g. Milan, Turin, Varese, Bergamo and Rome). Figure 8.1 graphically shows this spatial distribution.

The data also reveal that in 14% of cases (namely 63 cases out of 447), companies have other activities in manufacturing co-located in the same province in Italy, while the same parent companies have investments in other activities in 11.6% of cases.

8.4 Empirical Strategy and Variables

8.4.1 The Model

We develop a location choice model estimating a conditional logit model (McFadden 1974). Namely, the conditional logit (CL) models the profitability of choosing a location within a set of alternatives, and each location is associated with a profit. Thus, the model assumes that the firm chooses the location, in our case the province, that maximizes this profit. More formally:

$$\pi_{ifrst} = \sum \beta \text{Internal}_{frst-1} + \sum \delta \text{External}_{lst-1} + \gamma_r + \varepsilon_{ifrst}$$

However, the profit associated with each location is not directly observed, but we observe the characteristics of all possible alternative choices; in other words, the profit is a function of observed characteristics (Z_{fr}) and the error term ε_{fl}. Specifically, the probability that a location r

Table 8.1 Geographical distribution of manufacturing greenfield investments, by province

Province	No. FDIs	Percent	Province	No. FDIs	Percent
Milan	52	11.63	Belluno	3	0.67
Turin	44	9.84	Cuneo	3	0.67
Varese	19	4.25	Frosinone	3	0.67
Monza-Brianza	18	4.03	Pescara	3	0.67
Bergamo	15	3.36	Terni	3	0.67
Rome	15	3.36	Asti	2	0.45
Padova	12	2.68	Avellino	2	0.45
Brescia	11	2.46	Catania	2	0.45
Verona	10	2.24	Cremona	2	0.45
Vicenza	10	2.24	Foggia	2	0.45
Alessandria	9	2.01	Isernia	2	0.45
Lecco	9	2.01	Macerata	2	0.45
Pavia	9	2.01	Matera	2	0.45
Modena	8	1.79	Messina	2	0.45
Trento	8	1.79	Pesaro-Urbino	2	0.45
Bologna	7	1.57	Pordenone	2	0.45
Bolzano/Bozen	7	1.57	Salerno	2	0.45
Florence	7	1.57	Siracusa	2	0.45
Forl-Cesena	6	1.34	Sondrio	2	0.45
Livorno	6	1.34	Taranto	2	0.45
Lucca	6	1.34	Teramo	2	0.45
Pisa	6	1.34	Ascoli Piceno	1	0.22
Potenza	6	1.34	Benevento	1	0.22
Ancona	5	1.12	Caltanissetta	1	0.22
Biella	5	1.12	Campobasso	1	0.22
Genova	5	1.12	Chieti	1	0.22
Parma	5	1.12	Como	1	0.22
Ravenna	5	1.12	Cosenza	1	0.22
Udine	5	1.12	Enna	1	0.22
Venice	5	1.12	Imperia	1	0.22
Ferrara	4	0.89	La Spezia	1	0.22
Gorizia	4	0.89	Massa-Carrara	1	0.22
L'Aquila	4	0.89	Nuoro	1	0.22
Latina	4	0.89	Palermo	1	0.22
Lodi	4	0.89	Perugia	1	0.22
Mantova	4	0.89	Rimini	1	0.22
Naples	4	0.89	Siena	1	0.22
Novara	4	0.89	Vercelli	1	0.22
Piacenza	4	0.89	Viterbo	1	0.22
Reggio nell'Emilia	4	0.89	Total	447	100
Treviso	4	0.89			
Bari	3	0.67			

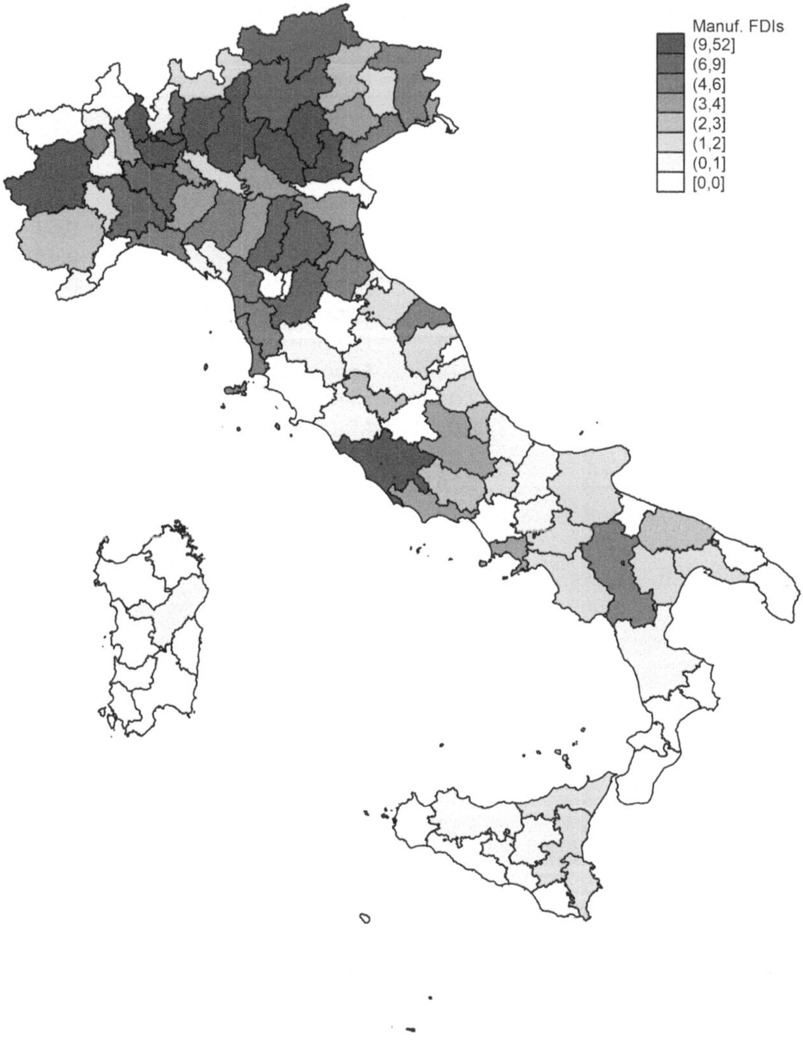

Fig. 8.1 Spatial distribution of manufacturing greenfield investments, by province. (Source: Authors' elaboration from REPRINT database)

results in the highest profitability for a new investment decision can be formally expressed by the following expression:

$$P_{fr}^{CL} = \frac{\exp\left(\beta Z_{fr}\right)}{\sum_{l=1}^{L} \exp\left(\beta Z_{fl}\right)}, \forall l \neq r \; (l = 1, \ldots, L)$$

The function is estimated using maximum likelihood techniques, and the results will be illustrated and discussed in the following sections.

8.4.2 The Variables

8.4.2.1 Dependent Variable: Location Choice of New Manufacturing Greenfield Investment

Our dependent variable is the location of a new greenfield investment i (in manufacturing activity) undertaken by firm f in sector s, in location r, at time t. The variable assumes value 1 for the location chosen, and zero for the other possible alternative locations. The 110 Italian provinces compose our location choice set.

8.4.2.2 External Agglomeration Economies

Specialization Economies. We measure the degree of industrial specialisation (Marshallian economies) in province r as the share of firms that operate in sector s (three-digit NACE Rev. 1.1) in province r in 2001 on the share of firms operating in sector s in Italy. More formally,

$$\text{Specialisation}_{rs} = \frac{N_{rs} / \sum_{s} N_{rs}}{\sum_{r} N_{rs} / \sum_{r} \sum_{s} N_{rs}}$$

where N_{rs} is the number of local firms operating in sector s in province r, provided by ISTAT (the Italian National Institute for Statistics).

Diversification Economies. We measure the degree of industrial diversification (Jacobsian economies) in each province r using the entropy index (Batty 1976):

$$\text{Diversification}_r = \left(\sum_s X_{rs} \log \frac{1}{X_{rs}} \right)$$

where $x_{rs} = N_{rs}/\Sigma_s N_{rs}$ *and* N_{rs} is the number of firms operating in sector s in province r in 2001, provided by ISTAT.

8.4.2.3 Internal Agglomeration Economies

Internal agglomeration captures the presence of other activities of the same focal firm f in province r at time t-1, either in manufacturing or in other non-manufacturing activities. Specifically:

(1) *Other_Manufacturing* is a dummy variable that equals one if other manufacturing activities of the same parent company are located in the province, and zero otherwise.
(2) *Other_Non-Manufacturing* is a dummy that equals one if other activities (non-manufacturing) of the same parent company are located in the same province, and zero otherwise.

Both these measures are computed using REPRINT data.

8.4.2.4 Spatial Lags of External and Internal Agglomeration Economies

In order to empirically test the spatial decay effect of both external and internal agglomeration economies, we generate the spatial lags of our variables. We adopted a spatial contiguity-based matrix in a first order of contiguity. A spatial matrix is a data structure that allows for geographical relationships (and dependences) among locations. Since we are interested in boundaries, we created a continuity-based matrix

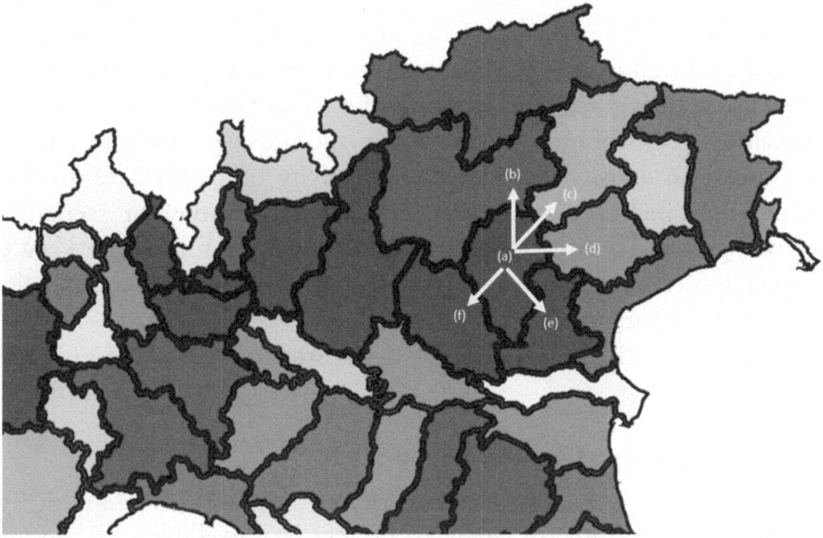

Fig. 8.2 Queen-based spatial contiguity matrix. (Source: Authors' elaboration)

looking at border-to-border proximity. Each value in the matrix is a binary measure: two provinces are neighbours if they share a common boundary (in this case the value is equal to 1), using the queen-contiguity technique.[2] This technique allows to consider spatial relations in several directions between the focal province and the surrounding provinces, such as vertical, horizontal and orthogonal. Figure 8.2 graphically presents this spatial pattern.

In the case of external agglomeration economies, we compute specialisation and diversification indexes in the contiguous provinces of each

[2]There are two approaches for computing a spatial weight matrix, namely (1) weights based on distance and (2) weights based on boundaries (contiguity). In the former, the weights (w_{ij}) are based on the distance between two geographical units i and j (between their centroids), using the inverse of squared distance, k-nearest neighbours, negative exponential or threshold distance techniques. In the latter, the contiguity relationship between two spatial units can be obtained following two main criteria: the rook contiguity, whether two units share a common border; and the queen technique whether two units share a common border or a point-length border (vertex). The rook is a more stringent definition of contiguity, and the choice depends on the purpose of the analysis and the phenomenon under investigation, as well as the irregularity in the spatial unit polygons.

focal province. Instead, in the case of internal agglomeration economies, we account for the presence of the parent company's activities in the provinces contiguous to the focal province, both in manufacturing and non-manufacturing activities (Lavoratori et al. 2019).

Finally, we control for a set of location-specific characteristics, such as the population density, the global connectivity of a province, whether the province includes primary (i.e. Milan and Rome) or secondary (i.e. Bologna and Turin) global cities. Namely, we follow the GaWC classification (Globalisation and World Cities Research Network, Taylor 2005). We also include Province fixed effects.

Tables 8.2 and 8.3 report descriptive statistics and correlation matrix.

8.5 Econometric Results

Results of our econometric analyses are reported in Tables 8.4. Specifically, Model (1) reports estimates from the location model with the only inclusion of location fixed effects (provinces) that control for any characteristics of the province, external agglomerations and (also unobservable) endowments that can affect a firm's location choices. In model (2) we estimate the location model introducing proxies for the external agglomeration economies, without location fixed effects. In model (3) we add the proxies for MNEs' internal agglomeration, i.e. the presence in the same province of other activities of the focal firm, with province fixed effects. In models (4) and (5) we jointly estimate both the external and the internal agglomeration economies, including other location factors. Finally, in model (6) we include spatial lags both for external and internal agglomeration forces.[3]

The estimates obtained in model (1), in which the province fixed effects measure external location factors, suggest that the latter (including external agglomeration economies) and the location endowment are strong drivers for the location of a new establishment. Thus, in

[3]As the same parent company may have several new investments during the considered period, in order to consider this multi-presence we cluster the standard errors by MNE. The coefficients are calculated as odds ratio to facilitate interpretations and comparisons.

Table 8.2 Descriptive statistics

Variable	*N*	Mean	SD	Min	Max
Choice	49170	0.0090909	0.0949128	0	1
Specialisation Economies	49170	0.0085547	1.00851	−0.8004187	45.23284
Diversification Economies	49170	1.69E-09	1.000001	−6.358377	1.604913
Other Manufacturing	49170	0.0172056	0.1300382	0	1
Other Non-Manufacturing	49170	0.0102705	0.1008227	0	1
Specialisation Contiguous Provinces	49170	0.1608655	2.527352	−5.970016	49.17066
Diversification Contiguous Provinces	49170	0.6570864	2.138994	−6.171317	6.64824
Other Manufacturing Contiguous Provinces	49170	0.0697376	0.2547069	0	1
Other Non-Mfg Contiguous Provinces	49170	0.0495424	0.2169998	0	1
Primary Global City	49170	0.0181818	0.1336099	0	1
Secondary Global City	49170	0.0181818	0.1336099	0	1
Population Density (log)	49170	5.141525	0.8102919	3.433987	7.865955

model (2) we substitute the province fixed effects with our proxies of external agglomeration economies, i.e. *Specialisation* and *Diversification*. The *Pseudo* R^2 (0.092) and the *Log-likelihood* (−1907.77), compared with the previous ones (*Log-likelihood* of −1717.919 and *Pseudo* R^2 of 0.1823, obtained in model 1), underline that our proxies capture province characteristics explaining MNEs' location choices. In line with most of the empirical studies on Marshallian and Jacobsian externalities, estimated coefficients of the variables *Specialisation* and *Diversification* are positive and significant in each specification, with a higher effect in the case of diversification (the odds ratio for the variable *Diversification* is

Table 8.3 Correlation matrix

		1	2	3	4	5	6	7	8	9	10	11	12
1	Choice	1											
2	Specialisation Economies	0.104	1										
3	Diversification Economies	0.055	0.125	1									
4	Other Manufacturing	0.091	0.053	0.073	1								
5	Other Non-Mfg	0.101	0.043	0.066	0.306	1							
6	Specialisation Contiguous Provinces	0.038	0.337	0.088	0.038	0.036	1						
7	Diversification Contiguous Provinces	0.054	0.101	0.181	0.067	0.078	0.233	1					
8	Other Mfg Contiguous Provinces	0.018	0.043	0.078	0.252	0.146	0.092	0.139	1				
9	Other Non-Mfg Contiguous Provinces	0.015	0.043	0.095	0.157	0.126	0.089	0.181	0.426	1			
10	Primary Global City	0.094	0.039	0.122	0.114	0.214	0.066	0.179	0.021	0.009	1		
11	Secondary Global City	0.069	0.068	0.134	0.072	0.044	0.029	−0.090	0.008	−0.005	−0.019	1	
12	Population Density (log)	0.078	0.103	0.274	0.110	0.132	0.109	0.240	0.055	0.080	0.324	0.090	1

Table 8.4 Location of new manufacturing greenfield investments—Conditional Logit Model

	Mod_1	Mod_2	Mod_3	Mod_4	Mod_5	Mod_6
External Agglomerations						
Specialisation Economies		1.3056***		1.2725***	1.2534***	1.2327***
		(0.0483)		(0.0419)	(0.0389)	(0.0403)
Diversification Economies		3.0865***		2.4823***	1.7075***	1.5428***
		(0.2908)		(0.2231)	(0.1354)	(0.1203)
Internal Agglomerations						
Other Manufacturing			3.9936***	6.2229***	4.6284***	4.5076***
			(1.0836)	(1.7699)	(1.3388)	(1.3030)
Other Non-Manufacturing			2.5753***	4.3943***	2.6364***	2.5269***
			(0.6678)	(1.1472)	(0.7287)	(0.6976)
Spatial Lags						
Specialisation Contiguous Provinces						1.0178
						(0.0264)
Diversification Contiguous Provinces						1.1035***
						(0.0304)
Other Mfg Contiguous Provinces						1.0299
						(0.3138)
Other Non-Mfg Contiguous Provinces						0.982
						(0.2458)
Controls						
Population Density (log)					1.5304***	1.4666***
					(0.1050)	(0.0982)

(continued)

Table 8.4 (continued)

	Mod_1	Mod_2	Mod_3	Mod_4	Mod_5	Mod_6
Primary Global City					1.5596*	1.2349
					(0.3589)	(0.3117)
Secondary Global City					3.3920***	4.4606***
					(0.5720)	(0.8441)
Fixed effects (NUTS-3)	yes	no	yes	no	no	no
No of observations	49,170	49,170	49,170	49,170	49,170	4,9170
No of MNEs	384	384	384	384	384	384
Pseudo R^2	0.1824	0.0920	0.2021	0.1331	0.1578	0.1618
Log-likelihood	−1717.919	−1907.777	−1676.473	−1821.432	−1769.491	−1761.245

Note: The dependent variable is the location decision of a new manufacturing investment *i* in Province *r*, considering all the 447 investments present in REPRINT database. Choice set: 110 provinces. Total number of observations 49,170 (= 447*110). The coefficients are reported as *odds ratio*. Standard errors are clustered by firm and reported in parentheses. Asterisks denote confidence levels: *$p < 0.10$, **$p < 0.05$ and ***$p < 0.01$

3.0865 compared to 1.3056 for the variable *Specialisation*). In model (3), the inclusion of our proxies for internal agglomeration economies (*Other Manufacturing* and *Other Non-Manufacturing*), together with province fixed effects, increase the fit of the model in comparison to model (1); indeed, the *Log-likelihood* increases to −1676.47, and the *Pseudo* R^2 to 0.2021, thus underlining the relevance of internal agglomeration factors driving location choices. Specifically, the MNEs' location choice of a new manufacturing plant in a given province is strongly driven also by the presence of other activities of the same parent company. Indeed, the variable *Other Manufacturing* presents a coefficient of 3.994, strongly significantly different from zero at $p < 0.01$. These findings confirm that MNEs tend to co-locate subsequent activities in a close proximity to existing ones in order to benefit from internal economies of scale and scope, as well as substitution mechanisms for coordination and control, for sharing and transferring knowledge and information among activities. In models (4) and (5) we jointly consider external and internal agglomeration factors, including other province characteristics. In both cases, the inclusion of variables accounting for the presence of other activities of the same parent company in the province significantly increase the model fit, confirming the role of internal agglomeration economies as a driver of MNEs' location choice; in fact, the *Log-likelihood* goes up from −1907.77 in model (2) to −1821.43 in model (4) and to −1769.49 in model (5); likewise, the *Pseudo* R^2 goes up from 0.0920 to 0.1331 and 0.1578, respectively. Moreover, controlling for internal agglomeration economies reduce the coefficients of external characteristics, suggesting the importance of looking at both internal and external factors in location decision studies.

Looking at model (5), it is also worth mentioning that a greater degree of global connectivity increases the attractiveness of the province for foreign investments. Specifically, the latter effect is stronger when the province hosts a secondary global city (the variable *Secondary Global City* shows an odds ratio of 3.39) than a primary one (the odds ratio is 1.53), potentially due to lower congestion costs and space availability particularly important for manufacturing activities, but with a certain level of connectivity compared to other locations across the country.

The significant effect of *Population Density* supports the positive role of urbanisation economies.

Finally, we analyse the effect of external and internal agglomeration economies in the contiguous provinces on the location choices of MNEs. Specifically, we introduce the spatial lags of the explanatory variables (*Specialisation Contiguous Provinces, Diversification_Contiguous Provinces, Other Manufacturing_Contiguous Provinces* and *Other Non-Manufacturing_Contiguous Provinces*), measured as discussed in Sect. 8.4.2. Results are reported in Table 8.4, model (6).

Findings show that internal agglomeration economies present a strong spatial decay effect; indeed, the presence of the focal firm in the contiguous provinces does not have any significant effect on the probability of choosing the province for a new manufacturing investment, both in the same activity and in other non-manufacturing activities. This confirms that the benefits of co-location with manufacturing activity and related activities (such as logistics, distribution, retail) arise in a close geographical proximity, within the province boundaries. Conversely, external agglomeration forces due to specialisation economies do not seem to overcome province boundaries; in fact, the estimated coefficient of the spatially lagged specialisation does not come out significant, confirming that specialisation economies operate at a smaller geographical scale, because Marshallian mechanisms require a close spatial proximity across units. However, our results also show that *Diversification_Contiguous Provinces* has a significant odds ratio of 1.104, so a focal province contiguous to provinces characterised by a higher level of industrial diversity has a greater probability of being chosen for a new investment in manufacturing activities. Indeed, Jacobsian economies require a greater and diversified area to arise, and their effects can cross the boundaries of the province, thus operating at a bigger spatial scale than specialisation economies.

8.6 Conclusions

This chapter contributes to the agglomeration literature in two ways. First, we jointly consider the role of external and internal agglomeration economies as driving factors for location decision of new greenfield investments in manufacturing activities. Specifically, our findings from a conditional logit model show that (1) both external and internal agglomeration economies have a positive role on MNEs' location decisions and (2) external forces decrease once allowing for intra-firm co-location. Thus, failing to control for internal agglomeration factors can lead to overestimating the effects of the traditional external ones. Although we are not the first to disentangle inter-firm (external) vs. intra-firm (internal) agglomeration forces (Alcácer and Delgado 2016; Woo et al. 2019; Lavoratori et al. 2019), we add some evidence on their relative weights in influencing MNEs' location choices within a foreign country. Second, we focus on the spatial decay effects of such agglomeration forces. Indeed, results from the estimation of an augmented model that includes spatial lags show a strong spatial decay effect for intra-firm co-location with firm-owned activities located in contiguous provinces, in order to benefit from economies of scale and scope, as well as to benefit from co-location as a substitute mechanism of coordination and control on geographically dispersed activities. Moreover, while Marshallian (specialisation) agglomeration economies require a stronger geographical proximity among units due to the mechanisms that generate these externalities, the benefits of diversity (Jacobsian) economies seem to cross geographical boundaries more easily.

For future research, we suggest that the study of the relationship between MNEs' location choices and agglomeration would benefit from a closer examination of heterogeneity of firms (e.g. Mariotti et al. 2019). Strengths and weaknesses of new entrants and indigenous companies might be captured along several dimensions (e.g. innovativeness, profitability, competitiveness, growth); MNEs' location choices may be influenced by experience and learning stemming both from own previous entries and from imitation of other foreign companies' location choices (e.g. Shaver et al. 1997; Belderbos et al. 2011; Koçak and Özcan 2013), thus also impacting their survival likelihood in each local context.

Moreover, this study investigates spatial decay effects of agglomeration economies using a spatial contiguity technique in a first order of contiguity. It is worth mentioning that future research could explore external and internal agglomerations including additional spatial levels. On the one hand, the investigation of agglomeration effects can be extended looking at greater spatial scales (e.g. orders of contiguity greater than the first), in order to understand whether the effects can overcome the first boundaries, especially for the diversification economies. On the other hand, the investigation can be aimed at exploring spatial effects within a narrow unit of analysis, for example moving within the province, in order to understand whether internal and external (mainly specialisation) agglomeration can operate at scales much smaller than the province or the city (Andersson et al. 2019; Lavoratori and Castellani 2020). Finally, it would be interesting to investigate the role of geographical distance and decay effects disentangling the different components behind the agglomeration economies (e.g. labour, knowledge spillovers, as well as competition) and to explore the industry heterogeneity in the micro-foundation of such agglomerations (e.g. Faggio et al. 2017).

References

Adams, J., & Jaffe, A. B. (1996). Bounding the Effects of R&D: An Investigation Using Matched Establishment-Firm Data. *RAND Journal of Economics, 27*(4), 700–721.

Alcácer, J., & Delgado, M. (2016). Spatial Organization of Firms and Location Choices Through the Value Chain. *Management Science, 62*(11), 3213–3234.

Alfaro, L., & Chen, M. X. (2014). The Global Agglomeration of Multinational Firms. *Journal of International Economics, 94*(2): 263–276.

Andersson, M., Larsson, J. P., & Wernberg, J. (2019). The Economic Micro-geography of Diversity and Specialization Externalities – Firm-Level Evidence from Swedish Cities. *Research Policy, 48*(6), 1385–1398.

Arauzo-Carod, J. M., Liviano-Solis, D., & Manjón-Antolín, M. (2010). Empirical Studies in Industrial Location: An Assessment of Their Methods and Results. *Journal of Regional Science, 50*(3), 685–711.

Barrios, S., Görg, H., & Strobl, E. (2006). Multinationals' Location Choice, Agglomeration Economies, and Public Incentives. *International Regional Science Review, 29*(1), 81–107.

Batty, M. (1976). Entropy in Spatial Aggregation. *Geographical Analysis, 8*(1), 1–21.

Beaudry, C., & Schiffauerova, A. (2009). Who's Right, Marshall or Jacobs? The Localization Versus Urbanization Debate. *Research Policy, 38*(2), 318–337.

Belderbos, R., Olffen, W. V., & Zou, J. (2011). Generic and Specific Social Learning Mechanisms in Foreign Entry Location Choice. *Strategic Management Journal, 32*(12), 1309–1330.

Belderbos, R., Sleuwaegen, L., Somers D., & De Backer, K. (2016). *Where Do Locate Innovative Activities in Global Value Chain. Does Co-Location Matter?* OECD Science, Technology and Industry Policy Papers, No. 30. Paris: OECD Publishing. https://doi.org/10.1787/5jlv8zmp86jg-en.

Berger, A. N., & DeYoung, R. (2006). Technological Progress and the Geographic Expansion of the Banking Industry. *Journal of Money, Credit and Banking Group, 38*(6), 1483–1513.

Blanc, H., & Sierra, C. (1999). The Internationalisation of R&D by Multinationals: A Trade-off between External and Internal Proximity. *Cambridge Journal of Economics, 23*(2), 187–206.

Bobonis, G. J., & Shatz, H. J. (2007). Agglomeration, Adjustment, and State Policies in the Location of Foreign Direct Investment in the United States. *Review of Economics and Statistics, 89*(1), 30–43.

Boschma, R., & Frenken, K. (2011). The Emerging Empirics of Evolutionary Economic Geography. *Journal of Economic Geography, 11*(2), 295–307.

Buciuni, G., & Finotto, V. (2016). Innovation in Global Value Chains: Co-Location of Production and Development in Italian Low-Tech Industries. *Regional Studies, 50*(12), 2010–2023. https://doi.org/10.1080/00343404.2015.1115010.

Cantwell, J., & Piscitello, L. (2005). Recent Location of Foreign-Owned Research and Development Activities by Large Multinational Corporations in the European Regions: The Role of Spillovers and Externalities. *Regional Studies, 39*(1), 1–16.

Caplin, A., & Leahy, J. (1998). Miracle on Sixth Avenue: Information Externalities and Search. *The Economic Journal, 108*(446), 60–74.

Castellani, D., & Lavoratori, K. (2019a). Location of R & D Abroad – An Analysis on Global Cities. In P. Capik & M. Dej (Eds.), *Relocation of Economic Activity* (pp. 145–162). Cham: Springer.

Castellani, D., & Lavoratori, K. (2019b). The Lab and the Plant. Offshore R&D and Co-location with Production Activities. *Journal of International Business Studies*. https://doi.org/10.1057/s41267-019-00255-3.

Chang, S. J., & Park, S. (2005). Types of Firms Generating Network Externalities and MNC's Co-Location Decisions. *Strategic Management Journal, 26*(7), 595–615.

Coase, R. (1937). The Nature of the Firm. *Economica*, New Series, *4*(4), 386–405.

Combes, P. P., & Gobillon, L. (2015). The Empirics of Agglomeration Economies. In G. Duranton, V. Henderson, & W. Strange (Eds.), *Handbook of Urban and Regional Economics* (Vol. 5, pp. 247–348). Amsterdam: Elsevier.

De Groot, H. L. F., Poot, J., & Smit, M. J. (2009). Agglomeration, Innovation and Regional Development: Theoretical Perspectives and Meta-Analysis. In R. Capello & P. Nijkamp (Eds.), *Handbook of Regional Growth and Development Theories* (pp. 256–281). Cheltenham: Edward Elgar.

Defever, F. (2012). The Spatial Organization of Multinational Firms. *Canadian Journal of Economics/Revue canadienne d'économique, 45*(2), 672–697.

Drennan, M. P. (1992). Gateway Cities: The Metropolitan Sources of US Producer Service Exports. *Urban Studies, 29*(2), 217–235.

Driffield, N., & Munday, M. (2000). Industrial Performance, Agglomeration, and Foreign Manufacturing Investment in the UK. *Journal of International Business Studies, 31*(1), 21–37.

Drucker, J. M. (2012). *The Spatial Extent of Agglomeration Economies: Evidence from Three U.S. Manufacturing Industries*. US Census Bureau Center for Economic Studies Paper No. CES–WP–12–01.

Duranton, G., & Puga, D. (2004). Micro-Foundations of Urban Agglomeration Economies. In J. V. Henderson & J. F. Thisse (Eds.), *Handbook of Regional and Urban Economics* (pp. 2063–2217). Amsterdam: North-Holland.

Ellison, G., Glaeser, E. L., & Kerr, W. (2010). What Causes Industry Agglomeration? Evidence Form Coagglomeration Patterns. *American Economic Review, 100*(3), 1195–1213.

Eurostat (2011). *Regions in the European Union. Nomenclature of Territorial Units for Statistics NUTS 2010/EU-27*. Luxembourg: Publications Office of the European Union.

Faggio, G., Silva, O., & Strange, W. (2017). Heterogenous Agglomeration. *The Review of Economics and Statistics, 99*(1), 80–94.

Giroud, X. (2013). Proximity and Investment: Evidence from Plant-Level Data. *Quarterly Journal of Economics, 128*(2), 861–915.

Glaeser, E. L., Kallal, H. D., Scheinkman, J. A., & Shleifer, A. (1992). Growth of Cities. *Journal of Political Economy, 100*(6), 1126–1152.

Gray, J. V., Siemsen, E., & Vasudeva, G. (2015). Colocation Still Matters: Conformance Quality and the Interdependence of R&D and Manufacturing in the Pharmaceutical Industry. *Management Science, 61*(11), 2760–2781.

He, C. (2002). Information Costs, Agglomeration Economies and the Location of Foreign Direct Investment in China. *Regional Studies, 36*(9), 1029–1036.

Head, K., Ries, J., & Swenson, D. (1995). Agglomeration Benefits and Location Choice: Evidence from Japanese Manufacturing Investments in the United States. *Journal of International Economics, 38*(3–4), 223–247.

Henderson, J. V., & Ono, Y. (2008). Where Do Manufacturing Firms Locate their Headquarters? *Journal of Urban Economics, 63*(2), 431–450.

Henisz, W. J., & Delios, A. (2001). Uncertainty, Imitation, and Plant Location: Japanese Multinational Corporations, 1990–1996. *Administrative Science Quarterly, 46*(3), 443–475.

Howells, J., & Bessant, J. (2012). Introduction: Innovation and Economic Geography: A Review and Analysis. *Journal of Economic Geography, 12*(5), 929–942.

Iammarino, S., & McCann, P. (2013). *Multinationals and Economic Geography. Location, Technology and Innovation*. Cheltenham: Edward Elgar.

Ivarsson, I., Alvstam, G., & Vahlne, J. E. (2016). Global Technology Development by Colocating R&D and Manufacturing: The Case of Swedish Manufacturing MNEs. *Industrial and Corporate Change, 26*(1), 149–168.

Jacobs, J. (1969). *The Economy of Cities*. London: Jonathan Cape.

Kalnins, A., & Lafontaine, F. (2004). Multi-Unit Ownership in Franchising: Evidence from the Fast-Food Industry in Texas. *RAND Journal of Economics, 35*(4), 747–761.

Kalnins, A., & Lafontaine, F. (2013). Too Far Away? The Effect of Distance to Headquarters on Business Establishment Performance. *American Economic Journal: Microeconomics, 5*(3), 157–179.

Ketokivi, M., & Ali-Yrkkö, J. (2009). Unbundling R&D and Manufacturing: Postindustrial Myth or Economic Reality? *Review of Policy Research, 26*(1–2), 35–54.

Koçak, Ö., & Özcan, S. (2013). How Does Rivals' Presence Affect Firms' Decision to Enter New Markets? Economic and Sociological Explanations. *Management Science, 59*(11), 2586–2603.

Lavoratori, K., & Castellani, D. (2020). *Too Close for Comfort? Micro-geography of Agglomeration Economies in the United Kingdom, Mimeo.*

Lavoratori, K., Mariotti, S., & Piscitello, L. (2019). *The Role of Geographical and Temporary Proximity in MNEs' Location and Co-Location Choices*. Mimeo.

Liberti, J. M., & Mian, A. R. (2009). Estimating the Effect of Hierarchies on Information Use. *Review of Financial Studies, 22*(10), 4057–4090.

Lieberman, M. B., & Asaba, S. (2006). Why Do Firms Imitate Each Other? *Academy of Management Review, 31*(2), 366–385.

Lu, S. F., & Wedig, G. J. (2013). Clustering, Agency Costs and Operating Efficiency: Evidence from Nursing Home Chains. *Management Science, 59*(3), 677–694.

Mariani, M. (2002). Next to Production or to Technological Clusters? The Economics and Management of R&D Location. *Journal of Management and Governance, 6* (2), 131–152.

Mariotti, S., & Piscitello, L. (1995). Information Costs and Location of FDIs Within the Host Country: Empirical Evidence from Italy. *Journal of International Business Studies, 26* (2), 815–841.

Mariotti, S., Piscitello, L., & Elia, S. (2010). Spatial Agglomeration of Multinational Enterprises: The Role of Information Externalities and Knowledge Spillovers. *Journal of Economic Geography, 10*(4), 519–538.

Mariotti, S., Mutinelli, M., & Sansoucy, L. (2015). *Italia multinazionale 2014. Le partecipazioni italiane all'estero ed estere in Italia*. Soveria Mannelli: Rubbettino Editore.

Mariotti, S., Mosconi, R., & Piscitello, L. (2019). Location and Survival of Foreign MNEs' Subsidiaries: Agglomeration and Heterogeneity of Firms. *Strategic Management Journal*. https://doi.org/10.1002/smj.3081.

Marshall, A. (1920). *Principles of Economics*. London: Macmillan.

McCann, P., & Acs, Z. (2011). Globalization: Countries, Cities and Multinationals. *Regional Studies, 45*(1), 17–32.

McCann, P., & Shefer, D. (2004). Location, Agglomeration and Infrastructure. *Papers in Regional Science, 83*(1), 177–196.

McFadden, D. (1974). Conditional Logit Analysis of Qualitative Choice Behaviour. In P. Zarembka (Ed.), *Frontiers in Econometrics* (*Chap*) (Vol. 4, pp. 105–142). New York: Academic Press.

Melo, P. C., Graham, D. J., & Noland, R. B. (2009). A Meta-Analysis of Estimates of Urban Agglomeration Externalities. *Regional Science and Urban Economics, 39*(3), 332–342.

Nielsen, B. B., Asmussen, C. G., & Weatherall, C. D. (2017). The Location Choice of Foreign Direct Investments: Empirical Evidence and Methodological Challenges. *Journal of World Business, 52*(1), 62–82.

Parr, J. B. (2002). Agglomeration Economies: Ambiguities and Confusions. *Environment and Planning A, 34*(4), 717–731.

Rawley, E., & Seamans, R. (2015). Intra-Firm Spillovers? The Stock and Flow Effects of Collocation. Columbia Business School Research Paper No. 15–2. Available at SSRN: http://ssrn.com/abstract=2544518.

Rodríguez-Pose, A., & Zademach, H. M. (2006). Industry Dynamics in the German Merger and Acquisitions Market. *Tijdschrift voor Economische en Sociale Geografie, 97*(3), 296–313.

Rosenthal, S. S., & Strange, W. C. (2003). Geography, Industrial Organization, and Agglomeration. *The Review of Economics and Statistics., 85*(2), 377–393.

Rosenthal, S. S., & Strange, W. C. (2004). Evidence on the Nature and Sources of Agglomeration Economies. In V. Henderson & J. F. Thisse (Eds.), *Handbook of Regional and Urban Economics* (pp. 2119–2171). Amsterdam: Elsevier.

Shaver, J. M., Mitchell, W., & Yeung, B. (1997). The Effect of Own-Firm and Other-Firm Experience on Foreign Direct Investment Survival in the United States, 1987–92. *Strategic Management Journal, 18*(10), 811–824.

Short, J. R., Breitbach, C., Buckman, S., & Essex, J. (2000). From World Cities to Gateway Cities: Extending the Boundaries of Globalization Theory. *City, 4*(3), 317–340.

Taylor, P. J. (2004). *World City Network: A Global Urban Analysis*. London: Routledge.

Taylor, P. J. (2005). Global Network Service Connectivities for 315 Cities in 2000. Data Set 12 of the Globalization and World Cities Research Network. Retrieved from http://www.lboro.ac.uk/gawc/.

Van Soest, D. P., Gerking, S., & Van Oort, F. G. (2006). Spatial Impacts of Agglomeration Externalities. *Journal of Regional Science, 46*(5), 881–899.

Veltz, P. (2000). European Cities in the World Economy. In A. Bagnasco & P. Le Galès (Eds.), *Cities in Contemporary Europe* (pp. 33–47). Cambridge: Cambridge University Press.

Vicente, J., & Suire, R. (2007). Informational Cascades Versus Network Externalities in Locational Choice: Evidence of "ICT Clusters" Formation and Stability. *Regional Studies, 41*(2), 173–184.

Woo, H., Cannella, A., & Mesquita, L. (2019). How Intra- and Inter-Firm Agglomeration Affect New-Unit Geographic Distance Decisions of Multi-Unit Firms. *Strategic Management Journal*. https://doi.org/10.1002/smj.3070.

Wood, G. A., & Parr, J. B. (2005). Transaction Costs, Agglomeration Economies, and Industrial Location. *Growth and Change, 36*(1), 1–15.

9

Unemployment and Trade in Spatial Economics

Xinmeng Li and Dao-Zhi Zeng

9.1 Introduction

It is well documented that trade policies have impacted labor markets substantially with the development of economic globalization. In recent years, President Trump has set some tough trade policies to improve the employment rate in the USA, greatly shocking the global market. During the last two decades, unemployment problems have become one of the major topics of theoretical research in spatial economics. This chapter seeks to review recent theoretical studies that link globalization to labor market outcomes, especially unemployment.

This work was supported in part by the Top Global University Project from the Ministry of Education, Culture, Sports, Science, and Technology of Japan (MEXT) and by JSPS KAKENHI Grant Number 17H02514 of Japan.

X. Li (✉) · D.-Z. Zeng
Graduate School of Information Sciences, Tohoku University, Sendai, Japan
e-mail: lixinmeng@se.is.tohoku.ac.jp; zeng@se.is.tohoku.ac.jp

S. Colombo (ed.), *Spatial Economics Volume II*,
https://doi.org/10.1007/978-3-030-40094-1_9

Our review focuses on four mechanisms of unemployment which are commonly used in trade models: labor unions, search–matching unemployment, efficiency wages or fair wages, and minimum wages. Overall, the existence of unemployment is mainly driven by the imperfection of labor markets: the equilibrium wage rate is higher than the level of the labor market clearing. Workers in labor unions always claim a higher wage rate to maximize the union preferences. In models of efficiency wages and fair wages, firms pay their employees more than the market-clearing wage in order to increase their efficiency. In the Diamond–Mortensen–Pissarides search-matching model, bargaining is also a crucial process to solve the equilibrium. Furthermore, since matches between job seekers and vacancies are frictional, unemployed workers and unfilled vacancies coexist in the labor markets.

Regarding the unemployment–trade relationship, comparative advantages remain an important issue to be addressed in this field. Davidson et al. (1999) examine the effects of differential in job-searching technology across countries on trade pattern. They illustrate that the country with the more efficient search technology has a comparative advantage in production in a high-unemployment/high-vacancy sector. Trade raises the unemployment rate in the capital-abundant large country in this model. Brecher (1974) constructs a Heckscher–Ohlin (H-O) model in which the labor market is subject to an exogenously specified floor: the minimum wage. Davis (1998) proposes a trade model between a flexible wage country and a minimum-wage-bound country. Both of them show that trade can exacerbate unemployment. In general, such papers with comparative advantages mainly compare two extreme cases of free trade and autarky, neglecting the process of trade liberalization.[1]

In contrast, new trade theory (NTT) allows us to study the details of globalization when trade costs are intermediate. For example, incorporating fair wages into an NTT model, Egger and Kreickemeier (2012) are able to illustrate that unemployment and wage inequality are hump shaped with respect to trade freeness. Helpman and Itskhoki (2010) show

[1]To review more studies about the search process in trade with comparative advantages, see Davidson and Matusz (2004). In addition, Kreickemeier (2008) surveys theoretical studies on fair wages in trade models of comparative advantages.

that a lower trade cost raises the unemployment rate if and only if the differentiated good sector has higher labor market frictions. To clarify how trade barriers and trade policies change the labor market outcomes and unemployment, we mainly review the models of NTT in this chapter.

In light of the fact that exporters have a higher productivity than nonexporters, trade liberalization leads to intraindustry resource allocation, which also greatly impacts the labor market. The seminal paper of Melitz (2003) makes it possible to examine international trade with firm heterogeneity, starting the so-called new new trade theory. In this chapter, we also review how Melitz-type heterogeneity impacts the labor market and unemployment. Unfortunately, the researchers have not yet reached consensus. These studies do not provide a unified prediction for the unemployment–trade relationship. Opposite results are derived from different frameworks. Eckel and Egger (2009) incorporate firm-union bargaining into the model of Helpman et al. (2004) with multinational firms. They show that the unemployment rate is reduced by trade liberalization, since the highly productive multinational firms offer relatively low wages, fostering employment. Developing a model with matching frictional unemployment and firm heterogeneity, Felbermayr et al. (2011) demonstrate that the average productivity increases in an open economy, and firms search for workers more intensively. As a result, the unemployment rate decreases with globalization. On the other hand, considering the fair wage preference of workers, Egger and Kreickemeier (2009) and Egger and Kreickemeier (2012) predict the opposite result, that the unemployment rate is higher under trade liberalization. The intuition is that surviving firms have a higher average productivity in open trade, which leads to higher wages and lower employment.

A number of studies have examined how trade and the labor market imperfection affect the endogenous industrial location using frameworks of new economic geography (NEG). This literature demonstrates how disparities between national labor markets evolve with endogenous industrial agglomeration in trade. Agglomeration occurs if and only if migrants (or capital owners) can benefit from a larger market. Intuitively, workers in the core region are paid higher, and unemployment is lower there in general. Moreover, it was found that the industrial agglomeration force could be amplified by various factors when labor markets are frictional, such as the bargaining power of workers (Picard and Toulemonde 2006) and fairness preferences (Egger and Seidel 2008).

The remaining parts of this chapter are organized as follows. Section 9.2 introduces the framework of labor unions and bargaining. In Sect. 9.3, we summarize theoretical studies focusing on search and matching frictions and unemployment. Section 9.4 presents the models of fair wages and efficiency wages. In Sect. 9.5, we review the studies related to minimum wages. Section 9.6 concludes.

9.2 Labor Unions

Let us start with the framework of labor unions (or collective bargaining), which is a standard way to introduce involuntary unemployment to international trade models. Due to the existence of bargaining between firms and labor unions, workers claim a wage rate that is higher than the level of labor market clearing.

In this section, we outline the basic model of a closed economy in Eckel and Egger (2009).[2] With a horizontally differentiated good x and a homogeneous good A, preferences of a consumer are given by a Cobb–Douglas utility function:

$$U = X^{\mu} A^{1-\mu}, \quad 0 < \mu < 1,$$

where

$$X = \left[\int_{v \in V} x(v)^{\frac{\sigma-1}{\sigma}} dv \right]^{\frac{\sigma}{\sigma-1}}$$

represents the composite good of the manufacturing sector, V is the set of available varieties of good x, and σ denotes the elasticity of substitution

[2]Blanchard and Giavazzi (2003) develop a one-country model with monopolistic competition in good markets and collective bargaining in labor markets. Mezzetti and Dinopoulos (1991) develop a partial equilibrium model of a domestic unionized firm and a foreign firm. They show that the way bargaining affects the labor employment depends on the form of union: wage oriented or employment oriented.

between any two varieties. Utility maximization determines the demand for variety v,

$$x(v) = \frac{\mu E}{P} p(v)^{-\sigma},$$

where $p(v)$ is the price of this variety, E denotes total consumption expenditures, and $P \equiv \int_{v \in V} p(v)^{1-\sigma} dv$ represents the price index.

Firms and unions face a three-stage game. At stage one, firms decide whether to enter the market according to their own productivity. If they decide to start production, they need to invest f units of good A to set up a plant. At stage two, there is wage bargaining at the firm level. Union activities are assumed to be restricted to a single firm. At stage three, firms choose an employment level and start production. The game is solved through backward induction.

Profit maximization yields the optimal price of a firm with productivity φ:

$$p(\varphi) = \frac{\sigma w(\varphi)}{(\sigma - 1)\varphi},$$

where $w(\varphi)$ is the wage paid by the firm. Then firm revenues and profits are derived as

$$r(\varphi) = \frac{\mu E}{P} p(\varphi)^{1-\sigma}, \quad \pi(\varphi) = \frac{\mu E}{\sigma P} p(\varphi)^{1-\sigma} - f.$$

The union preferences can be represented by a Stone–Geary utility function[3]:

$$W(\varphi) = l(\varphi) [w(\varphi) - \overline{w}],$$

where $l(\varphi)$ denotes the employment level of the firm. The average labor income is given by $\overline{w} = (1 - u) \tilde{w}$, where $\tilde{w}$ is the average wage rate outside the firm and u represents the unemployment rate. Since firms

[3]Mezzetti and Dinopoulos (1991) and Zhao (1995, 1998) choose a more general form of union preferences and allow for different weights on employment and the excess wage.

share identical productivity, $w = \widetilde{w}$ holds in the equilibrium. Given $\overline{\pi} = -f$ as the firm's profit if the bargaining breaks down, and $\pi(\varphi)$ as that if an agreement is reached, the solution to the firm–union bargaining problem is determined by maximizing the Nash product:

$$\Omega = W(\varphi)^{\gamma}[\pi(\varphi) - \overline{\pi}]^{1-\gamma},$$

where $\gamma \in [0, 1]$ is the bargaining power of the labor union. The solution of the maximizing problem is

$$w(\varphi) = \frac{\sigma - 1 + \gamma}{\sigma - 1}\overline{w}. \tag{9.1}$$

Hence, all firms pay the same wage rate in the equilibrium. Substituting $\overline{w} = (1 - u)\,w$ into (9.1), the unemployment rate is solved as

$$u = \frac{\gamma}{\sigma - 1 + \gamma}. \tag{9.2}$$

This result reveals that greater union power leads to higher wages and a higher unemployment rate in autarky. With $\gamma > 0$, unions claim a higher wage rate than the average labor income, which leads to higher labor costs from the firms' perspective.

Eckel and Egger (2009) also consider the case of an open economy with multinational entrepreneurs (MNEs) to study the interaction between union–firm bargaining and foreign direct investment.[4] Firms have two options for serving consumers in the foreign country. They can concentrate production to serve foreign consumers by bearing trade costs (exporters) or set up a second production plant abroad, i.e., become MNEs, with an extra fixed cost f_m. In equilibrium, the most productive firms invest abroad while less productive firms rely on exporting, which is consistent with the standard MNE model of Helpman et al. (2004).

However, the labor market structure changes crucially when the bargaining of multinational firms is taken into account. For an MNE, if

[4]In the case of an open economy when MNEs are not allowed, the same results can be derived in (9.1) and (9.2).

an agreement in the wage negotiations with the foreign union is not reached, it can produce in its domestic plant and serve the foreign market by exporting. Hence, compared to local firms, MNEs hold a higher outside option in the bargaining and pay lower wages than exporters. As a consequence, the wage rates are depressed by MNEs, so that the unemployment rate in the open economy with MNEs is lower for $\gamma \in (0, 1)$.

Moreover, the wage bargaining between firms and unions makes multinational activities more attractive, since MNEs have higher fallback profits. Eckel and Egger (2009) also find that a fall in trade costs could increase the share of multinational enterprises when the bargaining power is sufficiently large. By introducing collective bargaining, their model provides a possible explanation for the "apparent puzzle" that the foreign direct investment has surged at a time when trade costs declined (Lommerud et al. 2003). This phenomenon could not be explained in the traditional model of Helpman et al. (2004).

A few theoretical studies have examined how the bargaining between labor unions and firms affects the endogenous industrial location in NEG frameworks, such as Munch (2003) and Picard and Toulemonde (2006). They demonstrate the union power works as an agglomeration force by amplifying the home market effect in the core. Moreover, they show that bargaining power is a critical parameter to determine the industrial distribution in trade.

9.3 Search-Matching Model

The 2010 Nobel Prize in Economics was awarded to Peter Diamond, Dale Mortensen, and Christopher Pissarides "for their analysis of markets with search frictions."[5] In a perfectly competitive labor market, firms and workers match costlessly. Thus, any excess labor supply could be absorbed instantaneously by a decreasing wage rate. However, this is not realistic, since labor markets are imperfect in the real world and both unemployed

[5]Diamond (1982), Pissarides (1990), and Mortensen and Pissarides (1994) developed this theory.

workers and job vacancies coexist. By introducing matching frictions, many economists give an explanation of how labor market tightness and employment structure change in trade.

Following the setting in a search-matching model, firms post vacancies to find workers. The number of jobs created between job seekers (U) and vacancies (V) is determined by the matching function

$$M = m\left(U, V\right),$$

where $m(\cdot)$ is an increasing function of both arguments, concave and homogeneous of degree one.[6] Observe that $U = uL$, where u is the unemployment rate and L is the total labor force. Define the labor market tightness, $\theta \equiv U/V$, as the ratio of job seekers and vacancies. The vacancy-filling rate is $M/V = m(\theta, 1) \equiv m(\theta)$. Then the unemployed workers are hired at rate $\theta m(\theta)$. To hire l workers, firms post $v = l/m(\theta)$ vacancies, and the cost of providing one vacancy is c.[7]

In each period, firms are destroyed by idiosyncratic shocks with probability δ. Jobs are also destroyed by match-specific shocks with probability η. Assuming that these two shocks are independent, the actual rate of destroyed jobs is $s = 1 - (1 - \delta)(1 - \eta)$. In a steady state, flows into and out of the pool of unemployed workers are equal. Thus, how the unemployment rate is related to θ is solved as

$$u = \frac{s}{s+\theta m(\theta)},$$

which is a decreasing function of θ.

Define I^U and I^E as the present discounted asset values of an unemployed worker and an employed worker, respectively. Bellman equations of the unemployed and employed are given as

$$rI^U = b + \theta m\left(\theta\right)\left(I^E - I^U\right), \quad rI^E = w + \delta\left(I^U - I^E\right),$$

[6]Petrongolo and Pissarides (2001) provide some evidence for constant returns in the matching technology.

[7]Generally, vacancy-posting costs are assumed to be paid by a composite good, a homogeneous good, or labor.

where b denotes the unemployed benefit and r is the discount rate.

Similar to the labor union frameworks in Sect. 9.2, workers also engage in wage bargaining with firms. Assuming that each worker is treated as a marginal worker,[8] the outcome of bargaining over the division of the total surplus R from the match is determined by[9]

$$w = \text{argmax}\left(I^E - I^U\right)^{\beta} \cdot \left[\frac{\partial J(l)}{\partial l}\right]^{1-\beta},$$

where $\beta \in (0, 1)$ is the bargaining power of an individual worker. In the equilibrium, the optimal hiring level l (or the number of vacancies) is determined by the profit (or the firm value) maximization.

9.3.1 Searching Frictions and Average Productivity

Incorporating the searching frictions and bargaining into the Melitz model, Felbermayr et al. (2011) illustrate that trade affects labor markets by impacting the average productivity. In their framework, the present value of a firm with employment level l and productivity φ is given as

$$J(l;\varphi) = \max_{v} \tfrac{1}{1+r}\left[R(l;\varphi) - w(l;\varphi)\,l - cv - f + (1-\delta)\,J\left(l';\varphi\right)\right]$$

$$\text{s.t.(i)} \quad \frac{\partial R(l;\varphi)}{\partial l} = \frac{\sigma-1}{\sigma}\frac{R}{l}, \tag{9.3}$$

$$\text{(ii)}\; l' = (1-\chi)\,l + m(\theta)\,v,$$

where l' is the level of employment next period, $R(l;\varphi)$ represents the revenue of the firm, and r is the discount rate. The constraint (i) in (9.3) is derived from some properties of the CES utility function.

[8]This process is also called individual bargaining, which is commonly used in the framework of search and matching frictions. Considering the case of collective bargaining, Felbermayr et al. (2011) show a similar result that the vacancy–unemployment ratio increases with the average productivity.

[9]This manner is proposed by Stole and Zwiebel (1996).

Solving the problem of present value maximization and bargaining yields the wage (W) curve,[10]

$$w = \frac{\beta}{(1-\beta)(1-b)} \frac{c}{1-\delta} \left[\frac{r+s}{m(\theta)} + \theta \right].$$

This reflects how firms' behavior and labor supply interact in the presence of search costs and individual wage bargaining. Since labor market tightness is taken as given for all firms, the wage rates are identical for all heterogeneous firms in equilibrium.

According to the demand function and the bargaining solution, the labor demand (LD) curve is derived as

$$w = \left(\frac{\sigma-1}{\sigma-\beta}\right) \tilde{\varphi} - \frac{c}{m(\theta)} \left(\frac{r+s}{1-\delta}\right),$$

where $\tilde{\varphi}$ denotes the average productivity.

Felbermayr et al. (2011) show that trade liberalization influences the labor markets through the channel of average productivity shifting. Productivity heterogeneity has a great impact on the unemployment–trade relationship. In other words, if firms are homogeneous, the change in labor market tightness due to trade cannot be observed.

Figure 9.1 depicts how average productivity affects the wage rate and labor market tightness. The labor demand curve shifts upward (from the solid to the dashed line) when the average productivity rises, which leads to a larger labor market tightness and a lower unemployment rate. Using data from the USA, Felbermayr et al. (2011) predict that trade liberalization lowers unemployment and raises real wages since active firms are more productive and search for workers more intensively.

9.3.2 Wage Inequality and Workers' Ability

With search and matching frictions, wage inequality is also analyzable, as shown in Helpman et al. (2010). Unlike other works in this field

[10] More details are shown in Felbermayr et al. (2011) and Felbermayr and Prat (2011).

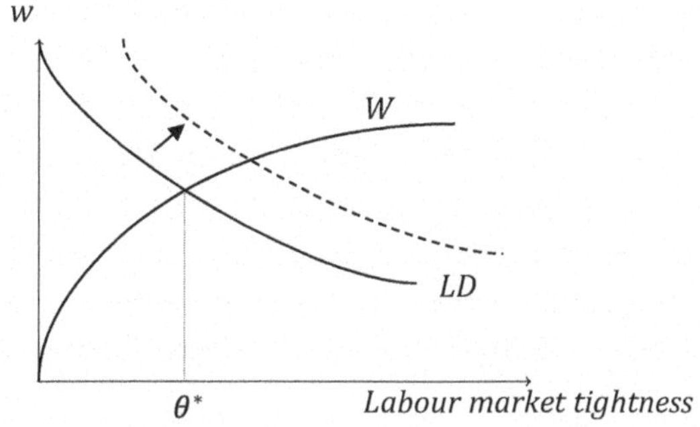

Fig. 9.1 Effect of increasing $\tilde{\varphi}$

(e.g., Helpman and Itskhoki 2010; Felbermayr et al. 2011), they propose a new framework with ex-post match-specific heterogeneity in workers' ability. In their model, the output of each variety q depends on the firm's productivity φ, the measure of hired workers l, and the average ability of hired workers $\overline{a}$:

$$q = \varphi l^{\gamma} \overline{a}, \quad 0 < \gamma < 1.$$

The workers' ability cannot be observed directly when firms and workers are matched. Firms can invest in worker screening to obtain an imprecise signal of workers' ability. Specifically, by paying a screening cost, ca_c^{δ}/δ, a firm can identify workers with ability level below a_c. Firms determine their hiring level by choosing the optimal number of sampled workers and their own screening ability threshold of profit maximization. In the equilibrium, firms with higher productivity screen more workers, hire workers with higher ability, and pay higher wages.

Their model provides an explanation of why opening trade enhances wage inequality. When the economy is open to trade, more productive firms earn higher profits through exporting, which further enhances their incentive to screen workers and hire those with higher ability. Therefore, wage inequality is amplified by trade liberalization since the dispersion of firm profits increases.

However, the overall effect of trade on unemployment is more complicated. On one hand, surviving firms are more productive in trade, so they screen workers more intensively, which has a positive effect on employment. On the other hand, firms prefer to select workers of higher ability in an open economy, since these firms have higher average productivity and offer higher wages. Hence, the ratio of succeeding contracts over screened workers is lower in an open economy. As a consequence, the overall effect of trade on unemployment is ambiguous in the model.

9.3.3 Unemployment in Asymmetric Countries

Search-matching unemployment has also been incorporated into trade models for asymmetric countries with product differentiation. Introducing search and matching frictions into competitive models of international trade, Davidson et al. (1999) show that labor market turnover (destruction rate and matching efficiency) has important implications in determining the trade pattern. More precisely, the country with the more efficient search technology has a comparative advantage in production in a high-unemployment sector. Moreover, they find that a relatively capital-abundant large country suffers a larger unemployment rate in trade. Dutt et al. (2009) incorporate search-induced unemployment into a trade model with comparative advantage. They show that unemployment and trade openness are negatively related in a Ricardian model. In an H-O model, trade openness increases unemployment in capital-abundant countries and decreases unemployment in labor-abundant countries.

Helpman and Itskhoki (2010) study a two-country two-sector model of international trade with search and matching frictions. As a result, opening to trade leads to a larger aggregate unemployment in the country with lower labor market frictions in the manufacturing sector. Moreover, only the country with lower frictions in its differentiated good sector can benefit from trade.

A few theoretical studies have examined how industrial location and frictional labor market interact with each other in NEG models. Epifani and Gancia (2005) and Francis (2009) formulate dynamic core-periphery models with mobile job seekers. They show that the unemployment rate in the core is lower than that in the periphery since firms earn high profits in the core and induce more new vacancies.[11]

9.4 Efficiency Wages

The question of why unemployed workers are unable to bid down the wages has been analyzed in published reports for a long time. The efficiency wage theory suggests that the answer is the negative incentive effects of a low wage rate. More precisely, workers' effort depends positively on their wages. On this basis, firms may find it profitable to pay wages in excess of market clearing. Efficiency wage models have also been incorporated into trade models to investigate the labor market outcome in globalization.

9.4.1 Fair Wage Preference

Akerlof (1982) and Akerlof and Yellen (1990) introduce a rent-sharing motive as a determinant of workers' fair wage preferences. In fair-wage-effort approaches, workers have a preference for fairness. If they feel that they get paid less than they ought to, they exert less effort in the work. Worker effort level, ε, is a function of the wage they are paid (w) and the wage perceived as fair ($\hat{w}$), such that

$$\varepsilon = \min\left\{\frac{w}{\hat{w}}, 1\right\}.$$

This framework postulates a positive relationship between work effort and wage so that the fairness-oriented behavior of workers may lead to involuntary unemployment.

Kreickemeier and Nelson (2006) modify the original model of Akerlof and Yellen (1990) by considering two factors: the skilled worker and the unskilled worker. They show that the competitive advantage between

[11] vom Berge (2013) and Yang (2014) also develop similar NEG models with matching frictions.

countries arises from country-specific preferences for fairness. In a country with a higher egalitarian preference, relative wages and employment levels of unskilled workers are negatively affected by the fairness preferences in its trading partner. Furthermore, the opening of trade increases unemployment rates in both countries.

Egger and Kreickemeier (2009) develop a model that incorporates fair wage preference and Melitz's firm heterogeneity into a general equilibrium framework. Compared to the matching unemployment models in Sect. 9.3, efficiency wage models allow us to analyze wage differentials among identical workers. Following Blanchard and Giavazzi (2003), the final output is assumed to be a CES aggregate of all available intermediate goods:

$$Y = \left[M^{-\frac{1}{\sigma}} \int_{v \in V} q(v)^{\frac{\sigma-1}{\sigma}} dv\right]^{\frac{\sigma}{\sigma-1}}, \sigma > 1.$$

The set of available intermediate goods V has measure M. Taking the final output as the numéraire, the price index corresponding to aggregated goods equals 1. Maximizing the profit of competitive final goods producers, the demand for variety v is

$$q(v) = \frac{Y}{M} p(v)^{-\sigma}.$$

Intermediate goods producers are monopolistically competitive and face the same fixed input, f units of final goods, before production. Following Melitz (2003), with marginal labor input l and productivity φ, the output is $q = \varphi l$. Then the profit-maximizing price of a firm with productivity φ is

$$p(\varphi) = \frac{w(\varphi)}{\rho \varphi \varepsilon}.$$

The fair wage (reference wage) is a weighted average of two factors: the market potential of an employer, which is related to the firm's productivity, and the average labor income $(1-u)\overline{w}$ ($\overline{w}$ denotes the average wage rate). Hence, the reference wage of a firm is a geometric average of the productivity and the expected labor income:

$$\hat{w}(\varphi) = \varphi^{\chi}[(1-u)\overline{w}]^{1-\chi},$$

where $\chi \in (0,1)$ is interpreted as a fairness parameter of workers.

Profit-maximizing firms have no incentive to pay less than the fair wage. This implies $\varepsilon = 1$ and $w(\varphi) = \hat{w}(\varphi)$ in equilibrium. For $\chi = 0$, the model degenerates to the perfect labor market model with full employment. For $\chi = 1$, all firms have identical marginal production costs, i.e., $w(\varphi)/\varphi = 1$.

This model captures how the rent-sharing motive of workers impacts wage inequality and unemployment in globalization. Egger and Kreickemeier (2009) find that a higher χ leads to a higher unemployment rate and greater wage inequality in a one-country model. Moreover, they predict that opening to trade raises unemployment and wage inequality, since the firms are more productive and more dispersed with globalization. They also illustrate that a decrease in trade costs has a hump-shaped effect on unemployment and wage inequality.

Egger and Kreickemeier (2012) develop another model of international trade that features intergroup inequality between managers and workers using the approach of fair wages. Their model explains the empirical fact that globalization has been accompanied by a significant increase in both inter- and intragroup inequality.

According to their model, a firm's productivity is determined by the ability of its manager. Knowing their own managerial ability, individuals can choose whether to become a manager or a worker. Workers are taken as identical marginal inputs and managers earn the operating profits. Firms run by more able managers have a higher productivity level and make higher profits. The equilibrium manager ability cutoff (φ^*) is characterized by the labor indifference condition

$$(1-u)\overline{w} = \pi(\varphi^*),$$

where $\pi(\cdot)$ represents the firm's profit. Analogously, they show that international trade leads to a higher unemployment rate by increasing the average productivity and wage. Trade also increases both the inequality within the two subgroups (workers and managers) and the intergroup inequality.

When heterogeneity is introduced into the framework of fair wages, the wage inequality exists among firms even if workers are identical. This feature is not observable in the model of frictional matching such as in Felbermayr et al. (2011) and Helpman and Itskhoki (2010).

Egger and Seidel (2008) explore an NEG model of efficiency wages. With more fairness preferences, the income differential between skilled and unskilled workers falls. However, the unemployment rate of unskilled workers increases. Moreover, they illustrate that fair wage preferences could force agglomeration.

9.4.2 Efficiency Wages and Monitoring

Shapiro and Stiglitz (1984) propose another approach of efficiency wages to determine the labor demand and wage rate, providing a technical explanation of how involuntary unemployment appears. Since shirking makes a firm's productivity decline, the firm needs to offer its workers higher wages to eliminate their shirking.

In the Shapiro–Stiglitz efficiency wage model, there are L identical workers, who dislike exerting effort but enjoy consuming goods. The instantaneous utility function of an individual is given as $U(w, e)$, where e is the cost of effort. Workers' distaste for effort tempts them to shirk. Their shirking will be discovered with probability q, which depends on the monitoring technology of firms. Utility takes the following form:

$$U(w, e) = \begin{cases} w & \text{if the worker shirks,} \\ w - e & \text{if the worker exerts effort } e > 0, \\ 0 & \text{if the worker is unemployed.} \end{cases}$$

There is a possibility, η, that jobs are destroyed, which is taken as endogenous. Define V_E^S and V_E^N as the expected lifetime utility of employed shirkers and non-shirkers, respectively, and V_u as the expected lifetime utility of an unemployed worker. The fundamental asset equation for employed non-shirkers and shirkers, respectively, are

$$rV_E^S = w + (\eta + q)\left(V_u - V_E^S\right), \quad rV_E^N = w - e + \eta\left(V_u - V_E^N\right).$$

The two equations above can be solved for V_E^S and V_E^N:

$$V_E^S = \frac{w+(\eta+q)V_u}{r+\eta+q}, \quad V_E^N = \frac{(w-e)+\eta V_u}{r+\eta}. \tag{9.4}$$

Workers choose not to shirk if and only if $V_E^N \geq V_E^S$. The firm chooses to meet this non-shirking constraint (NSC) with equality, i.e., $V_E^N = V_E^S = V_E$. Using (9.4), the NSC condition can be rewritten as

$$w = rV_u + (r + \eta + q)\, e/q. \tag{9.5}$$

The asset equation for an unemployed individual is given by

$$rV_u = a\,(V_E - V_u)\,, \tag{9.6}$$

where a is the job acquisition rate. In the steady state, the flow into the unemployment pool, ηL^w, equals the out flow, $a(L - L^w)$, so that

$$a = \eta L^w / (L - L^w)\,. \tag{9.7}$$

Plugging (9.4), (9.6), and (9.7) into (9.5), the aggregate NSC is written as

$$w = e + \frac{e}{q}\left[\frac{\eta L}{(L-L^w)} + r\right]. \tag{9.8}$$

The aggregate production function in the economy is $Q = F(L^w)$. The labor demand is determined by equating the marginal product of labor to the marginal cost of labor. Assuming that firms are identical, the aggregate demand is given as

$$F'(L^w) = w. \tag{9.9}$$

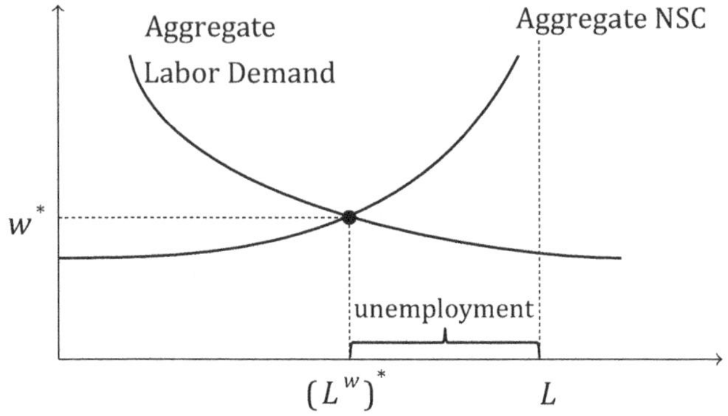

Fig. 9.2 Equilibrium unemployment

The equilibrium employed labor, $(L^w)^*$, and the equilibrium wage rate, w^*, are determined by the aggregate NSC (9.8) and the aggregate labor demand function (9.9), as shown in Fig. 9.2.

Matusz (1996) merges a model of monopolistic competition in the production of intermediate goods with the Shapiro–Stiglitz model of efficiency wages. He shows that international trade reduces the unemployment rate, since opening to trade allows for more production.

Davis and Harrigan (2011) introduce heterogeneity in productivity and monitoring technology into the Shapiro–Stiglitz efficiency wage model. Similar to Egger and Kreickemeier (2009), the intergroup inequality of workers also exists here. Heterogeneity in the monitoring ability of firms leads to different wages for identical workers in Davis and Harrigan (2011). More precisely, the firm-specific wages depend inversely on the firm-level relative monitoring abilities. They find that the national unemployment rate is little affected by liberalization with simulations. However, there is a tremendous amount of labor market churning: nearly one-fourth of all "good" jobs (jobs with above-average wages in autarky) are destroyed in trade. Workers are paid less in an open economy, since it becomes harder to survive for firms offering higher wage rates in international trade.

In NEG models with efficiency wages, firms in the more agglomerated region are able to pay higher wages, so that shirking is reduced there, which leads to a lower unemployment rate, as shown in Suedekum (2005) and Zierahn (2013).

9.5 Minimum Wage

Minimum wage is the lowest remuneration that employers can legally pay their workers. In general, supply and demand models suggest that minimum wage binding leads to losses in aggregate welfare and employment. However, if employees have greater monopsony power in labor markets, a minimum wage can increase the efficiency of the market.

Brecher (1974) first extends the H-O model of an open economy with exogenous wage constraints (minimum wages). Unemployment occurs if and only if the equilibrium wages exceed the level required for full employment. He shows that the level of employment and welfare could be less in trade. Davis (1998) develops an H-O model of trade between two countries, one of which has flexible wages (America), while the other is bound by a minimum wage for unskilled labor (Europe). International trade equalizes factor prices between the flexible-wage and the minimum-wage economies. He shows that a move from autarky to free trade doubles European unemployment.

Abstracting from Heckscher-Ohlin-type reasons for trade, Egger et al. (2012) formally incorporate minimum wages in an NTT model with heterogeneous firms. They find that a rise in the minimum wage in a country will force inefficient intermediate good suppliers to exit the market, leading to a decline in exports. They show that trade increases the unemployment rate in all countries.

9.6 Conclusion

In this chapter, we reviewed recent theoretical studies on the relationship between trade and unemployment. Four frameworks are commonly used to collaborate frictional unemployment into international trade: labor unions, search-matching frictions, efficiency wages and fair wages, and minimum wages. There are two core intuitions for the mechanism of unemployment. First, the wage rate claimed by workers (or unions) is higher than the level of labor market clearing. The high wage rate claim can be generated by bargaining power, fairness preferences, shirking prevention, or the binding of minimum wages determined by the government. Second, the match between job seekers and vacancies is imperfect. Due to the existence of matching frictions, job seekers and vacancies always coexist in the economy.

In trade models of competitive advantages, trade could be driven by the disparity of labor markets, such as labor market turnover (Davidson et al. 1999), the binding of minimum wages (Brecher 1974; Davis 1998), and fairness preferences (Kreickemeier and Nelson 2006). In contrast to the traditional model of competitive advantages, new trade theory allows us to study the impact of variable trade costs. For example, in Helpman and Itskhoki (2010), a lower trade cost raises the rate of unemployment when the differentiated sector has higher labor market frictions. Egger and Kreickemeier (2012) illustrate that trade freeness has a hump-shaped effect on unemployment.

Furthermore, we illustrate how Melitz-type heterogeneity impacts the labor markets in different frameworks. In the paradigm of fair wages, the unemployment rate increases in trade, since the firms are more productive and the equilibrium wage is higher. Considering search and matching unemployment, the result is opposite. Firms earn higher revenues and search for workers more intensively in trade, which leads to a lower unemployment rate. In contrast, the predictions of wage inequality are consistent: they illustrate that globalization amplifies the inequality of labor incomes in a country.

References

Akerlof, G. A. (1982). Labor Contracts as Partial Gift Exchange. *The Quarterly Journal of Economics, 97*(4), 543–569.

Akerlof, G. A., & Yellen, J. L. (1990). The Fair Wage-Effort Hypothesis and Unemployment. *The Quarterly Journal of Economics, 105*(2), 255–283.

Blanchard, O., & Giavazzi, F. (2003). Macroeconomic Effects of Regulation and Deregulation in Goods and Labor Markets. *The Quarterly Journal of Economics, 118*(3), 879–907.

Brecher, R. A. (1974). Minimum Wage Rates and the Pure Theory of International Trade. *The Quarterly Journal of Economics, 88*, 98–116.

Davidson, C., & Matusz, S. J. (2004). *International Trade and Labor Markets: Theory, Evidence, and Policy Implications*. WE Upjohn Institute.

Davidson, C., Martin, L., & Matusz, S. (1999). Trade and Search Generated Unemployment. *Journal of International Economics, 48*(2), 271–299.

Davis, D. R. (1998). Does European Unemployment Prop Up American Wages? National Labor Markets and Global Trade. *American Economic Review, 88*, 478–494.

Davis, D. R., & Harrigan, J. (2011). Good Jobs, Bad Jobs, and Trade Liberalization. *Journal of International Economics, 84*(1), 26–36.

Diamond, P. A. (1982). Aggregate Demand Management in Search Equilibrium. *Journal of Political Economy, 90*(5), 881–894.

Dutt, P., Mitra, D., & Ranjan, P. (2009). International Trade and Unemployment: Theory and Cross-national Evidence. *Journal of International Economics, 78*(1), 32–44.

Eckel, C., & Egger, H. (2009). Wage Bargaining and Multinational Firms. *Journal of International Economics, 77*(2), 206–214.

Egger, H., & Kreickemeier, U. (2009). Firm Heterogeneity and the Labor Market Effects of Trade Liberalization. *International Economic Review, 50*(1), 187–216.

Egger, H., & Kreickemeier, U. (2012). Fairness, Trade, and Inequality. *Journal of International Economics, 86*(2), 184–196.

Egger, P., & Seidel, T. (2008). Agglomeration and Fair Wages. *Canadian Journal of Economics, 41*(1), 271–291.

Egger, H., Egger, P., & Markusen, J. R. (2012). International Welfare and Employment Linkages Arising from Minimum Wages. *International Economic Review, 53*(3), 771–790.

Epifani, P., & Gancia, G. A. (2005). Trade, Migration and Regional Unemployment. *Regional Science and Urban Economics, 35*(6), 625–644.

Felbermayr, G., & Prat, J. (2011). Product Market Regulation, Firm Selection, and Unemployment. *Journal of the European Economic Association, 9*(2), 278–317.

Felbermayr, G., Prat, J., & Schmerer, H. J. (2011). Globalization and Labor Market Outcomes: Wage Bargaining, Search Frictions, and Firm Heterogeneity. *Journal of Economic Theory, 146*(1), 39–73.
Francis, J. (2009). Agglomeration, Job Flows and Unemployment. *The Annals of Regional Science, 43*(1), 181–198.
Helpman, E., & Itskhoki, O. (2010). Labour Market Rigidities, Trade and Unemployment. *The Review of Economic Studies, 77*(3), 1100–1137.
Helpman, E., Melitz, M. J., & Yeaple, S. R. (2004). Export Versus FDI with Heterogeneous Firms. *American Economic Review, 94*(1), 300–316.
Helpman, E., Itskhoki, O., & Redding, S. (2010). Inequality and Unemployment in a Global Economy. *Econometrica, 78*(4), 1239–1283.
Kreickemeier, U. (2008). Unemployment in Models of International Trade. In *Globalisation and Labour Market Adjustment* (pp. 73–96). London: Palgrave Macmillan.
Kreickemeier, U., & Nelson, D. (2006). Fair Wages, Unemployment and Technological Change in a Global Economy. *Journal of International Economics, 70*(2), 451–469.
Lommerud, K. E., Meland, F., & Sørgard, L. (2003). Unionised Oligopoly, Trade Liberalisation and Location Choice. *The Economic Journal, 113*(490), 782–800.
Matusz, S. J. (1996). International Trade, the Division of Labor, and Unemployment. *International Economic Review, 37*, 71–84.
Melitz, M. J. (2003). The Impact of Trade on Intra-industry Reallocations and Aggregate Industry Productivity. *Econometrica, 71*(6), 1695–1725.
Mezzetti, C., & Dinopoulos, E. (1991). Domestic Unionization and Import Competition. *Journal of International Economics, 31*(1–2), 79–100.
Mortensen, D. T., & Pissarides, C. A. (1994). Job Creation and Job Destruction in the Theory of Unemployment. *The Review of Economic Studies, 61*(3), 397–415.
Munch, J. R. (2003). The Location of Firms in Unionized Countries. *Scandinavian Journal of Economics, 105*(1), 49–72.
Petrongolo, B., & Pissarides, C. A. (2001). Looking into the Black Box: A Survey of the Matching Function. *Journal of Economic Literature, 39*(2), 390–431.
Picard, P. M., & Toulemonde, E. (2006). Firms Agglomeration and Unions. *European Economic Review, 50*(3), 669–694.
Pissarides, C. A. (1990). *Equilibrium Unemployment Theory*. Oxford: Basil Blackwell.

Shapiro, C., & Stiglitz, J. E. (1984). Equilibrium Unemployment as a Worker Discipline Device. *The American Economic Review, 74*(3), 433–444.
Stole, L. A., & Zwiebel, J. (1996). Intra-firm Bargaining Under Non-binding Contracts. *The Review of Economic Studies, 63*(3), 375–410.
Suedekum, J. (2005). Increasing Returns and Spatial Unemployment Disparities. *Papers in Regional Science, 84*(2), 159–181.
vom Berge, P. (2013). Search Unemployment and New Economic Geography. *The Annals of Regional Science, 50*(3), 731–751.
Yang, X. (2014). Labor Market Frictions, Agglomeration, and Regional Unemployment Disparities. *The Annals of Regional Science, 52*(2), 489–512.
Zhao, L. (1995). Cross-Hauling Direct Foreign Investment and Unionized Oligopoly. *European Economic Review, 39*(6), 1237–1253.
Zhao, L. (1998). The Impact of Foreign Direct Investment on Wages and Employment. *Oxford Economic Papers, 50*(2), 284–301.
Zierahn, U. T. (2013). Agglomeration, Congestion, and Regional Unemployment Disparities. *The Annals of Regional Science, 51*(2), 435–457.

Part VI

Marketing

10

From Geomarketing to Spatial Marketing

Gérard Cliquet

10.1 Introduction

Geomarketing has been developed from geographic information system (GIS) techniques, which enable both researchers and practitioners to map in a rather quick way markets they are working on. However, even though easy mapping constitutes a real progress toward a better understanding of markets, the true aim is now to introduce more or less systematically space into marketing research and marketing decisions (Cliquet 2006). Such a purpose imposes to link several disciplines. Geomarketing relates already marketing, geography, and information systems, but now it cannot go without considering sociopsychology, economics, and, once again, information systems through mobile technologies. That is the reason why geomarketing should move toward spatial marketing in a more global and local vision of markets called "glocal" (Bartlett and Ghoshal 1989).

G. Cliquet (✉)
Université Rennes 1, Rennes, France
e-mail: gerard.cliquet@univ-rennes1.fr

S. Colombo (ed.), *Spatial Economics Volume II*,
https://doi.org/10.1007/978-3-030-40094-1_10

This chapter is divided into five sections according to the marketing themes likely to be changed by a spatial vision. After a definition of geomarketing and spatial marketing, it deals with spatial consumer behavior, then a new conception of a geomarketing mix, before a complete approach of what we can call geo-retailing, and, finally, some issues about mobile marketing in its spatial conception (Cliquet 2020).

10.2 What Is Geomarketing?

"Geomarketing" is an English word invented by European marketing practitioners to refer to a discipline mixing marketing, geography, and computer science resulting in the determination of "geographic information systems" (GIS). But this term is totally unknown in the US as the acronym GIS is predominantly used. The problem is that GIS points out very technical tools and masks the true question: How can we integrate space in marketing decision (Cliquet 2006)? This is the reason why we do prefer talking about spatial marketing rather than "geomarketing" even though this latter term should be used whenever technical tools (GIS) are used. Hence, we first strive to distinguish geomarketing and spatial marketing before describing applications and technical tools like software, specific statistics, and models.

10.2.1 Why Geomarketing and Spatial Marketing?

Geomarketing applications involve GIS and specific mapping software to get a better understanding of markets through their geographical aspects. Spatial marketing means, more generally speaking, introducing space in marketing decisions without entailing the systematic use of these techniques. The purpose of spatial marketing is first of all strategic, and defining strategic marketing implies that marketers should localize market features, a real revolution (Rigby and Vishwanath 2006), by taking into account local characteristics of customers, suppliers, outlets, and logistics, with and/or without GIS. It concerns what is now called "location business intelligence." New mobile technologies with devices like smartphones and touch pads enforce to consider spatial dimensions as these devices are equipped with GPS.

It is strange to see that, since a very long time, many economists (Hotelling 1929; Von Thünen 1826; Weber 1909) have been aware of the necessity to take into account spatial considerations, whereas marketers have often neglected these aspects by favoring more global approaches. GIS have been used for several decades almost exclusively for retail purposes like store location. But now interactive maps are available to help marketers in their decision process and mobile devices enforce space as a determinant marketing variable.

Spatial marketing can be then defined as everything dealing with the introduction of space in marketing at the conceptual, methodological, and strategic levels (Cliquet 2006). This means not only everything concerning local and regional environment at the micro-economic level (Grether 1983), but also with territorial coverage in its geographical sense. And this does not imply necessarily to consider political boarders as cultures often go over the edge (Hofstede et al. 2002; Ohlin 1931). Geomarketing can be defined as a set of techniques enabling to enter spatial data in order to build maps related to markets because "About 80% of all business-relevant information within a company has a relation to spatial data" (Menne 2009, citing Wagner 2006).

Spatial marketing affects consumer behavior, and hence we should talk about spatial consumer behavior, marketing research which should take into account spatial data, and, finally, strategic marketing and marketing management. Then the critical strategic question now is: Adaptation or standardization (Cliquet 2020)? As today consumers want customized products possible through technology, and politicians around the world ready to "deglobalize" economy, predicting the future of standardization seems to be very difficult.

10.2.2 Applications of Spatial Marketing

As applications in retailing have been developed for decades, concerning essentially store location problems (Ghosh and McLafferty 1987), it is necessary to gather and synthetize all the spatial applications concerning other marketing activities. Retailers or bankers should work predominantly with customers located close to their units (stores, branches, etc.) creating then a stock of clientele, whereas hotel managers deal with people coming sometimes from very far, in other terms a flow of clientele. Banks have develop since decades many geomarketing applications to extend their branch network and now to reduce it, but this problem is identical to the retail question of store location. Concerning restaurants and hotels, the problem is more complex as customers are not necessarily located close to the unit.

The public sector (public communities, regions, states, etc.) has also developed many geomarketing applications to better understand citizens' needs and to respond to them through public services. Real territorial information systems have then been built like, for instance, in Italy (Amaduzzi 2011). Another example deals with health policy showing how maternities could be better located to serve the population, avoid problems for maternities with low rate of activity, and reduce costs (Baray and Cliquet 2013; Kong et al. 2010).

Internet and the possibility to display maps facilitate the diffusion of geomarketing techniques in tourism (Bourliataux-Lajoinie and Rivière 2013; Parker 2007).

10.2.3 Techniques and Software of Geomarketing

Developing geomarketing involves the use of specific techniques and, first, the adjustment of a relevant GIS, which means: a geocoding system, a spatial database, a database on studied actors (consumers, companies, stores, etc.), and a mapping system to display maps on a computer screen and to print them. However, nothing is possible without a geographical division of the studied territory. This division can concern zip codes in the US or Iris in France, where it is against the law to work on set of less than 2000 individuals. Interactive mapping software are now more and more commonly used by marketing decision-makers.

Statistical tools can also be employed like I of Moran (Moran 1950), C of Geary (Geary 1954), or the Gini coefficient (Gini 1914, 1921). Geomarketing software packages are based on GIS, and many of them offer these statistical tools. One usually distinguishes software, websites, and platforms. Software are generally expensive and devoted to companies able to use them on a regular basis, whereas software on websites or on platforms are available for others. Some of these software give the opportunity to use attraction models (see Sects. 10.2 and 10.4), and simulation systems like agent-based model (ABM) already used in logistics for retail companies (He et al. 2013).

10.3 Spatial Consumer Behavior

A marketing approach starts by studying consumer behavior. As space is treated here as an essential variable, we talk about spatial consumer behavior. Surprisingly, this topic has not been much tackled by marketing researchers. Geographers and more recently sociologists have developed a consistent literature on spatial consumer behavior. Geographers have found very interesting results stemming from observations and models but without any business orientation (Golledge and Stimson 1997). In sociology, recent publications deal with mobility which is considered a major change in behaviors (Centola 2018). Two main spatial consumer behavior types appear: one consists in understanding and predicting outdoor spatial consumer behavior, whereas another deals with in-store spatial consumer behavior.

10.3.1 Outdoor Spatial Consumer Behavior

Many concepts are useful in understanding outdoor spatial consumer behavior and concern mainly the following: attraction, gravitation and spatial interaction, several approaches of distance, shopping trips, mobility, ubiquity, clientele stock and clientele flow, market area, trade area, spatial indifference, market saturation, and retail leakage.

Attraction, gravitation, and spatial interaction are the three major concepts to be considered in spatial marketing. Attraction is a very global concept which can be treated as spatial or a-spatial. Psychologist are used to consider interpersonal attraction in an a-spatial approach defining it as "a product of the initial evaluations we make about others": this evaluation is realized through two dimensions: "capacity to facilitate the perceiver's goals/needs and potential willingness to facilitate those goals/needs and willingness" (Montoya and Horton 2014). In its spatial meaning, attraction is a true strategic element in retailing in a sense that consumers are more and more mobile. As far as consumers are considered living in a permanent dwelling, we talk about gravitation as this concept implies a mass and a geographic (or temporal) distance. But concerning various cases like a threshold effect (Malhotra 1983), when distance is not a key choice element within a given area, or through the use of Internet, we talk about spatial interaction because many other variables can enter into account (Cliquet 1995).

Distance is a polysemous concept. The most-often-used distance is the geographical or temporal distance according to the measurement method: kilometric (or mileage) or time that is the most often used (Brunner and Mason 1968) as transportation means play a critical role in outdoor spatial consumer behavior. Probabilistic models like Huff (1964) model or multiplicative competitive interaction (MCI) (Nakanishi and Cooper 1974) model use the temporal distance. This last fact becomes now questionable as an increasing number of consumers come back to closer and smaller retail stores for time, convenience (Gahinet and Cliquet 2018), or environmental reasons.

Psychological distance (Mulder 1960) related to power relationships can also influence this behavior. The social or socio-spatial distance, defined as proxemy (Hall 1968), has been used to measure distances in communication between individuals, theses distances being different according to cultures. These differences are present not only in consumer behavior but also in organizational management, and this implies that space should be considered in both market analysis and managerial practices, and learning about these practices can be of great interest in commercial negotiations at the international level. Hence, distance is not only a quantitative variable to include in geomarketing software but also a complex notion of spatial international marketing.

Shopping trips are central in outdoor spatial consumer behavior. Several distinctions should be considered: single purpose shopping trips and multipurpose shopping trips, and with Internet, research online, buying offline (ROBO) (Kalyanam and Tsay 2013), which can be developed in several omni-channel shopping trips insofar as consumers tend to use any channel of communication and test any marketing channel when purchasing (Fulgoni 2014). Recent techniques based on GPS or any other technology enable a follow-up of consumers during their trips even though regulation tends to protect them against privacy violation.

Mobility and ubiquity have been recently introduced to understand outdoor spatial consumer behavior as smartphone usages have considerably changed the way shopping trips are envisaged by consumers. Consumers adopt increasingly a browsing behavior developing thus more complex mobility where distance can play a role in value assessment (Brooks et al. 2004). With their mobile devices, they can stay connected anytime, anywhere, and with any device (ATAWAD) and about any content (ATAWADAC). This phenomenon is defined as ubiquity which is the capability to be everywhere at any time.

Clientele should be split into clientele stock and clientele flow. Given the increasing mobility of consumers, markets cannot be only analyzed from the retailer's point of view and from the store perspective. Now marketers talk about consumer trade area which means that retailers should be located along possible shopping trips. "Big boxes" like hypermarkets located in peripheral zones which were accustomed to draw a clientele stock dwelling in the surroundings are now facing great difficulties not only due to transactional websites but also to convenience stores which can supply consumers anywhere at almost any time. Anywhere at any time means here that consumers can choose the way they go shopping, favoring then opportune frequentation instead of time saving: Kairos versus Chronos (Gahinet and Cliquet 2018). But most of spatial consumer behavior models deal with clientele stock as modeling clientele flows is much more difficult because of the number of possible shopping trip categories and the ignorance of spatial origins of these mobile consumers.

The principle of spatial indifference relies on the notion of "just noticeable distance." Applied to consumer behavior, it means that consumers do not choose inevitably the closest store, but a store located in a spatial area of indifference given that the marginal cost is minimal (Nystuen 1967). This has been confirmed by a study using a threshold model of store choice (Malhotra 1983): beyond a given distance, consumers do not visit the stores as it is the case in the furniture market (Cliquet 1995). Geomarketing software can be of great interest to delineate this threshold and determine market areas within a given territory.

Market area and trade area should not be confounded. A market area is a local market which should be considered when studying competition among retailers. Examining this competition at the national level is often meaningless. For instance, in France, a specific study using a giant geomarketing software at the level of this country (Brafman 2008) revealed that 60% of the 629 French local markets were actually in a local monopoly situation, whereas 25% had only two competitors and 15% several. Each competitor in such a market area has a trade area which is supposed to include the potential population living around. Actually these trade areas do not look like three circles any more. These circles represent a primary trade area with between 60 and 70% of consumers, a secondary trade area between 15 and 25% and a tertiary trade area with the residual portion (Applebaum 1966). But they have probably never existed. Using geomarketing software researchers have shown that a trade area looks like an archipelago composed of a series of spots of various sizes sometimes located far from the studied store, each spot, within the market area, corresponding to specific categories of consumers sharing the same store patronage (Baray and Cliquet 2007).

Market saturation and retail leakage are two related concepts. Retail leakage may happen in a local market for at least two reasons: either the retail offer is not sufficient and consumers should drive to another market area for shopping or, on the contrary, retail offer is totally saturated, consumers should wait for a long time before being served, and they do prefer shopping outside. In the first case, retail activity must be reinforced, whereas in the second case new stores have to be opened. Geomarketing software may display these retail leakage and market saturation through purchase flows (Douard et al. 2015).

10.3.2 Models of Outdoor Spatial Consumer Behavior

Researchers and consultants have proposed models in spatial consumer behavior: the law of retail gravitation (Reilly 1931), Huff model (1964), and MCI model, either objective (Nakanishi and Cooper 1974) or subjective (Cliquet 1995). These models are also useful to determine store locations (see Sect. 10.4).

Reilly (1931) proposed the first model to determine the relative attraction between two cities, and hence the breaking point (Converse 1949) where the attraction is equal between the two cities given their relative importance in terms of population or purchase power. Two variables area involved in the model: a geographic distance and a mass represented by a population or its purchase power. This model is deterministic, which means that when a consumer is living in a given area, she/he should shop in a given city or in a given store: this model does not consider that a consumer has a choice, and it is its main drawback with the fact that only two variables can be introduced in the model.

Huff (1964) suggested to replace the deterministic approach of the Reilly's law by defining a probabilistic model which is more adapted to urban contexts. It is a probabilistic model as it enables to give a probability for a consumer to choose one store or another. But once again, only two variables are involved: a geographic or temporal distance and a mass here representing the size of the store. Many geomarketing software have integrated the Huff model.

Nakanishi and Cooper (1974) have generalized the Huff model to a theoretical infinity of variables even though actually only a few variables are usually utilized in these models: this is notably due to the difficulty to measure qualitative variables, which implies to use questionnaires. This is the reason why a subjective MCI model has been proposed to measure every variable by consumers' judgments as human decisions are made from the perception of the reality rather than from the reality itself (Cliquet 1995).

As far as spatial consumer behavior is concerned, these former models (see formulas in Sect. 10.4) are only useful when dealing with clientele stock and not at all concerning clientele flows. Building a model for clientele flows is difficult as many situations of mobility can be met in the real life and the smartphone usage extension generates more hinders (see in Sect. 10.5). However these models are still useful and used for store location (see Sect. 10.4).

10.3.3 In-store Spatial Consumer Behavior

If we consider now in-store spatial consumer behavior, we should notice that the literature is rather poor concerning that topic. However, the stake is critical for most retail companies because Internet is changing in-store spatial consumer behavior and most hypermarkets, supermarkets, and supercenters should adapt quickly to this new deal and many of them are facing strong difficulties. The implementation of click and collect systems allow customers to stay out of the store. To make them coming back into the store, retailers should improve welcome and accompaniment of customers in their shopping trips within stores: this is called now indoor location-based applications.

The stake of understanding in-store shopping trips consists clearly to increase the number of visits, to transform these visits into shopping and then shopping into purchases. But indoor shopping trips are not easy to capture. Technologies can help to follow customers with their agreement in order to avoid privacy violation. Beyond usual observations, researchers, marketing companies, or even retailers are developing systems based on technologies like Near field communication (NFC) (Kahn 2012), radio frequency identification (RFID) (Larson et al. 2005), WIFI and mobile devices (Yaeli et al. 2014), and a mecatronic intelligent system called sCREEN (Paolanti et al. 2017). Another technology is based on magnetic fields in order to get round the difficulty to use GPS inside building as this technology is related to satellites which cannot cross concrete ceilings.

10.4 Geomarketing Mix

Marketing strategies are mostly defined at a global level without taking into account of local aspects. In an economic world where "glocalization" (Svensson 2001) already applied at McDonald's (Crawford et al. 2015) seems to be more important than the traditional "globalization" (Levitt 1983) so much criticized (Douglas and Wind 1987). Such an evolution cannot but point out the importance of spatial marketing development and the use of geomarketing software among other things.

Despite some very severe critics, a marketing strategy is usually defined by the famous four Ps (McCarthy 1960) of the marketing mix: Product, Price, Place, and Promotion (Van Watershoot and Van der Bulte 1992). But these four elements can be spatialized. If this is obvious for Place (see Sect. 10.4), this is not the case for the three other Ps. However, several research works can be attached to each of them.

10.4.1 Geomarketing and Products

As far as products are concerned, two important research topics have been tackled: innovation diffusion, and merchandising.

Innovation diffusion is based on five categories of behaviors vis-à-vis innovation (Rogers 1962): innovators, early adopters, early majority, late majority, and laggards. A model (Bass 1969) based on word-of-mouth gives the opportunity to distinguish these five categories (Mahajan et al. 1990). Many other models have been built from this basis but this is an a-spatial approach. Very few research exist in marketing about spatial diffusion of innovation. Actually there are two approaches of spatial diffusion of innovation (De Palma et al. 1991): a geographic diffusion or neighborhood diffusion on the one hand, and a hierarchical diffusion on the other hand based on the theory of central places (Christaller 1933). However, these two logics do exist in Hägerstrand (1967) model: this model considers innovation a spatial process and the author could show how innovations are diffused in agriculture, as others explain the diffusion of tractors in a similar environment (Cliff and Ord 1975). Steyer (2005) proposed an interesting theory of avalanches to explain the diffusion of ideas, products, and technologies based on a random diffusion like in the Bass model and a geographic distance.

Merchandising is another type of product management likely to be spatialized. Its contents are: assortment management, product display and commercial animation within store departments, and sales promotions. Passing from merchandising to geo-merchandising means adapting the merchandising to the local context of the store. Geomarketing can help by designing maps displaying data to better match product assortment and trade area (Kalyanam and Putler 1997) and that could need to adapt also the structure of the retail organization (Vyt 2008): it is obviously easier within a franchise or a cooperative system where stores are managed by their owners. The stake is clear and consists in adapting the sales surface to the trade area (Volle 2006). And another managerial stake is at work: a precise knowledge of trade areas enables retailers to better assess the work of store managers or franchisees as a benchmarking implemented with a data envelopment analysis (DEA) including spatial data could show this (Vyt and Cliquet 2017).

10.4.2 Geo-pricing

When considering spatial aspects in pricing, we can talk about a true geo-pricing. Analyzing pricing strategies at the global level is often a vain simplification: too many local factors are involved to really understand pricing policies. A first reason concerns the local competitive situation. According to the local number of competitors, pricing policies change, and this is true at the very local level as it is also at the level of countries: when a competitor is leader in a given country and challenger in another, it cannot implement the same policy in both countries. A second reason stands in the retailers' power: many of them apply their own pricing policy, which is not always compatible with manufacturers' pricing policies. A third reason is given by consumers' imperfect information (Miller 1996). A fourth reason depends on transportation costs and logistics means according to factories' locations (Weber 1909): this problem sometimes questions outsourcings (Lampóna et al. 2015). Many other reasons can play a role like the country of origin (COO) (Peterson and Jolibert 1995), local regulation, or local consumer's taste.

At the theoretical level, the minimal differentiation principle (Hotelling 1929) gives an excellent example of relationship between pricing and location. As far as products can be differentiated, stores delivering these products have great interest in locating close to one another, pricing being fixed according to various criteria like assumed quality or positioning. Too many pricing theories rely on product homogeneity, which is far from being true in the real world (Anderson and de Palma 1988). When comparing three pricing policies applied by manufacturers, uniform pricing, mill pricing, and spatial discrimination pricing, the most favorable to consumers is uniform pricing, whereas mill pricing is the most unfavorable (Anderson et al. 1989). At the retail level, two main pricing policies can be met: everyday low price (EDLP) as implemented by Walmart, and HILO pricing, which consists in attracting consumers with very low prices, whereas other products are priced with much higher margins, even though this last policy is now questionable as consumers use more and more their mobile devices to compare prices. Actually, some retail chains price their products the same way in every store like Lidl, whereas others develop a geo-pricing strategy (Khan and Jain 2005), which means a local autonomy for store managers. It has been shown that implementing a geo-pricing strategy within an adapted micromarketing could bring a higher margin (Montgomery 1997).

10.4.3 Geo-promotion

Every promotional technique can also be spatialized, and we can talk about geo-advertising whatever media is used, spatial direct marketing, geo-promotion concerning specifically sales promotions, or geo-management of salesforce.

As far as advertising is concerned, the marketing literature is rather poor (Gallopel 2006), whereas practitioners have been using geomarketing since a long time. Geomarketing software can help in locating billboards: for example, there are about 600,000 billboards in France and over one million with 6700 digital displays in the US, then choosing a site can be both of interest and difficult for the advertising company and its client. Knowing where movie theaters are located can be important as well. GIS gives a good idea of where newspapers and magazines readers are dwelling not only to better know readers but also to help client firms to choose the right media vehicle. The interest is the same for radio and television audience. However, we can wonder whether GIS can be a real support when advertising on Internet: actually there is a web geography even though the technique to control it is somewhat different from usual mapping.

Spatial direct marketing cannot be implemented without geomarketing anymore. Some decades ago, flyers and prospectus were delivered in letter boxes or within the newspapers. Every store manager had a map in his/her office displaying assumed trade areas. Now with GIS it is much easier, more accurate, and more efficient.

Dealing with sales promotion, the approach is similar geo-merchandising. These techniques are also related to direct marketing. But the true stake is now to advertise sales promotions on mobile devices according to potential customers' location. It can be costly and that is why many small retail companies gather together to reduce costs (Carlbäck 2012).

Most of companies strive to better control their salesforce, and geo-marketing brings real advantages. And it is also today an essential tool for salespeople to better organize their rounds and better know their clients even though they sometimes complain that they are tracked the all day long. For that purpose, *Google* and Salesforce.com are now associated to develop *Google geospatial technology* (Arnold 2009).

10.5 Geo-retailing and Spatial Strategies

Economic activity location has been tackled in literature for a very long time (Von Thünen 1826). Marketing researchers have been more specifically attracted by store location problems, which is of interest for retailers almost exclusively. Several methods and models have been designed, and some of these models can be found in geomarketing software.

10.5.1 Store Location Methods

First of all and before developing store location methods, it is important we understand the store location decision process. This process is indeed different according to the size of the retail company: a new retailer who is looking for a good location for his/her first store develops a simpler process than the chain which is seeking to locate a new store. The complete process concerning a chain should start by an analysis of the company strategy before making three decisions concerning the market, the market area within this market, and the site in this market area. Then the company should assess the sales potential of the future store located in this site. If it concerns a chain, this new site corresponds to the desire of reticulation of this chain: Should it be franchised or company-owned? Answering this question consists in wondering whether this reticulation process fits into the continuing development of a strictly franchised network or of a wholly owned chain, or into the development of a plural form network (Bradach 1998). Once this last decision made, financial simulations can assess the potential profitability of this project. Hence, this process implies several studies.

An opportunity study should respond to the question: Is it the right moment to set a new unit (can be a store, a branch, a hotel, or a restaurant)? A market study, a market area study, and a site study can answer the question: Where is it worth to make it? Finally, a feasibility study on marketing and financial issues deals with the profitability of the project.

The PESTEL model (Evans and Richardson 2007) can help in analyzing targeted markets by explaining political, economic, sociological, technological, ecological, and legal issues before selecting a market. Studying a market area also requires secondary data to understand an eventual market leakage or a market saturation (Ghosh and McLafferty 1987). Analyzing purchase flows with a geomarketing software can help to better understand how consumers shop on a spatial basis (Douard et al. 2015). A GIS may be used to draw a much more precise potential trade area than the traditional primary, secondary, and tertiary circles (Applebaum 1966).

Other methods like the proximal area (Thiessen and Alter 1911) or the spline functions (Huff and Batsell 1977) have been proposed by researchers. The site evaluation is usually based on five principles (Lewison and DeLozier 1986): interception (can the unit catch passing consumers?), cumulative attraction (are similar units present around?), compatibility (are other units running compatible activities present?), accessibility (is the site accessible?), and store congestion (is the drawing power too strong generating then disadvantages for customers?). This analysis can be a good basis for a check list. A more recent method suggests to use filtering and convolution techniques (Baray and Cliquet 2007) and has been applied to locate a shopping center.

10.5.2 Store Location Models

Many location models can be found in the literature but three of them are still used by practitioners: the law of retail gravitation, the Huff model, and the MCI model, the two latter under various form being present in most of geomarketing software. These models are able to either predict consumer behaviors (see Sect. 10.2) or design future store locations.

The law of retail gravitation (Reilly 1931) suffers critics because of its deterministic conception and its limited number of variables (a mass—population or buying power—and a distance). However, it has been used for locating supermarkets in a rural context where consumer's choice is often reduced as it was done in Italy (Guido 1971) or shopping centers in the US (McKenzie 1989). Here is the Reilly's law formula:

$$A_X / A_Y = \left(P_X / P_Y\right) * \left(D_Y / D_X\right)^{\beta}$$

where:

- A_X, A_Y = activities drawn, respectively, by cities X and Y, in other terms the attraction of each of these two cities;
- P_X, P_Y = respective populations (or buying powers) of cities X and Y;

- D_X, D_Y = respective distances from the breaking point vis-à-vis the two cities X and Y;
- β = a coefficient specific to the distance but generally considered equal to 2 according to many experiences because determining β is a complex operation.

But urban environments demand a probabilistic methodology. The Huff model (1964) offers this opportunity, but like in the Reilly's law, only two variables can be introduced: a mass (here a store sales surface) and a distance (here measured by the driving time). Here is the Huff model's formula:

$$P_{ij} = \frac{S_j (T_{ij})^{\beta}}{\sum_{j=1}^{q} S_j (T_{ij})^{\beta}}$$

where:

- P_{ij} = probability for a consumer i to patron store j;
- S_j = sales surface of store j;
- T_{ij} = distance in time from home of consumer i to store j;
- β = coefficient related to the distance generally equal to 2 (cf. Reilly's law).

In order to compensate the very weak number of variables to be introduced in the Huff model, a generalization of this model was proposed called multiplicative competitive interaction (MCI) model (Nakanishi and Cooper 1974) with the following formula:

$$\pi_{ij} = \frac{\prod_{k=1}^{q} \left(X_{ijk}^{\beta_k} \right)}{\sum_{i=1}^{m} \left[\prod_{k=1}^{q} \left(X_{ijk}^{\beta_k} \right) \right]}$$

where:

- π_{ij} = probability that a consumer living in area i chooses the store j;
- X_{ijk} = value of the kth variable describing store j in area i;

- β_k = parameter for sensitivity of π_{ij} with respect to variable X_k;
- m = number of choice possibilities (here stores);
- q = number of variables X_{ijk}.

The MCI model can theoretically accept as many variables despite some limits. Its formula can be simplified through geometric means and a logarithm transformation, and so the resolution procedure has been demonstrated through a regression analysis (Nakanishi and Cooper 1974) which demands only ratio scale variables. But unlike the Huff model, the MCI model is based on both gravity models and market share models: if the distance does not appear as a determinant variable, this model becomes an attraction model able to supply market shares.

However, the MCI model presents a certain number of flaws. It needs a sufficient number of objects (here stores) to determine regression coefficients, otherwise a composite model is better adapted (Cooper and Finkbeiner 1983). There is a real difficulty to delineate the market area and to define an adequate geographical division like the Huff model and to measure determinant variables likely to explain store attraction: to do so, Cliquet (1995) suggests a subjective MCI model where every variable is measured with a questionnaire in a market survey. But in that last case, two conditions should be considered: (1) a survey collects ordinal data treated often as interval scale data, which should be transformed into ratio scale data by the zeta squared transformation (Cooper and Nakanishi 1983); (2) Bayesian statistics is needed as consumers do not know every store, and there are too many nonresponses in the final matrix. Finally, as every market share model, the MCI model comes up against the problem of independence of irrelevant alternatives (IIA) (McFadden 1974).

The MCI model has been used for multiple store location associated to a location-allocation model, defining thus the MULTILOC model (Achabal et al. 1982), which has been applied by American retailers sometimes to open several stores in the same time. This model is also useful when downsizing a chain by reducing the number of units. A recent research developed a method based on an analytic hierarchy process (AHP) and on the center of gravity method using a GIS to locate franchisees within a franchise network (García-Castro and Mula 2019).

Even though these models are still used and are integrated in geomarketing software, they remain incomplete as they do not consider clientele flows of mobile consumers.

10.5.3 Spatial Strategies

Store location methods and models concern the opening of one or several units to choose the best site in a given market area. But most of retail and service chains should now develop spatial strategies to improve their territory coverage as quickly as possible and to be able to struggle against competitors. It should be noticed that most of unit sets are plural form (Bradach 1998) organized, which means that franchise and company-owned units coexist in the same set: this set is rather called a network as every unit can be in relationship with the others as there is legally no hierarchical power between the franchisor and the franchisees.

The first decision should strive to select the right spatial strategy. Three main spatial strategies can be distinguished (Davidson et al. 1988):

- A contiguous or contagious strategy consists in opening units in the same market area or in the same region;
- A beachhead strategy invites to locate units in other more or less remote market areas;
- An acquisition or merger strategy can be a good option if the targeted network may improve the territory coverage, but also expensive and difficult to "swallow up."

Other strategies have been implemented by retail firms:

- An infilling strategy: like *McDonald's* opening as many units as possible to prevent contenders to enter the market;
- A secondary market strategy: like *Walmart* in the US or *Groupe Beaumanoir* in France when they select first small and medium towns where there are few competitors;
- Recycled locations: for example, gas station transformed into bakeries.

Then in order to structure both organizational and spatial sides, a choice process concerning the unit status and a measurement process can be implemented. As far as the organizational side is concerned, a plural form network has to define which status (franchise or company-owned) a unit should get: this depends on the global strategy of the chain but also on the local situation and on the presence of potential franchisees. This location should also be able to complete the territory coverage of the network to diffuse the brand, to reduce logistics costs and to get access to national media. This coverage can be measured with the relative entropy; then it becomes possible to know whether the new unit adds something to the territory coverage or not and to compare with competitors' coverage (Cliquet 1998).

Location speed is also of great interest as a contender can occupy a very good site if the firm is too slow to decide. Whenever a retail or service firm decides to invade a new region, improving this speed needs to choose the best locations in order once again to diffuse the brand and to reduce logistics costs. The percolation theory is of great help to display the best way from one point to another (Cliquet and Guillo 2013).

Spatial strategies concern also plural form networks and it should be of great interest to model a store network location taken into account the choice process between franchise and company-owned units (Pirkul et al. 1987). But this last research suffers from little knowledge about plural form networks. Several publications have exposed since the advantages of this organizational form regarding the location of units (Bradach 1998; Cliquet 2000).

10.6 Geo-positioning and Smartphone Usages

The apparition of the smartphone in the market in 2007 is a real revolution in human behavior, and it justifies the concept of spatial marketing. Geomarketing is too restrictive and limited to GIS usage on computers. Even though some geomarketing software are GPS connected, every smartphone is GPS related, and it is today the favorite device with the touch pad. Consumers can be tracked when using their smartphone or their touch pad (we will further use only the term "smartphone" but it includes also touch pad). And this is why firms strive to offer the best services enabling consumers to reach a store, a restaurant, or a hotel. The creation of a true mobile marketing or m-marketing in manufacturing companies is under way to complete the e-marketing for consumers' usage of informational and transactional websites and m-commerce for retail firms to respond to consumers' m-shopping.

Some authors has wondered whether distance is still alive with Internet (Cairncross 1997). The answer is obviously yes: distance is still of great interest and stores are far from being devoted to disappear. Among many other examples, *Amazon* decided to buy *Whole Foods* stores to be concretely in the market and diffuse a better image.

Implementing spatial m-marketing demands to well understand some specific concepts like proximity, mobility, omni-channel, and spatial databases. We already met proximity and mobility when talking about spatial consumer behavior in Sect. 10.2. Omni-channel (Fulgoni 2014) means that consumers tend to use any marketing channel at anytime and anywhere, and firms, whatever activity they run (retailing or manufacturing), should be able to manage cross-channel strategies in order to respond at anytime and anywhere to this behavior. Spatial databases, or spatial big data, are built with data stemming from loyalty cards, browsing data on websites, or data about shopping trips recovered from smartphones. All these data can then be used by GIS. But we see at this point how much legal limits could be overpassed: this is the problem of privacy violation insofar as consumers refuse more and more often to be tracked by location-aware marketing techniques even though they like to get relevant promotions whenever they are on mobility (Xu et al. 2011).

The relationship between Internet and franchising can be difficult to manage in its spatial dimension in retail and service networks. The problem of encroachment is well known when a franchisee advertises for sale and really sells products or services to consumers located in a trade area of another franchisee of the same network (Vincent 1998). With Internet it is easier for either the franchisor or other franchisees to advertise everywhere and then to attract customers located outside of one's own trade area; then encroachment can be more frequent and more difficult to deal with. Retailers have implemented several solutions to cope with that because franchisors have never interest in seeing their franchisees suffering from these bad practices (Cliquet and Voropanova 2016). "Click and collect" systems help to stay in touch with customers through Internet and to better know their favorite products to propose relevant promotions. But these customers often do not enter the store anymore. Hence, retailers should know more about the place they live and the time they come in order to suggest visits and geo-positioning can play a role for that purpose: sending promotions through smartphones can change the way consumers shop. M-marketing is then partially spatial even though GIS should use new devices which are much smaller than usual computers. Practitioners talk about location marketing and location-aware marketing when using geo-positioning is accepted by consumers. Retailers then use location-based advertising when a potential customer walks or drives within the geofencing limits of a given store and offer location-based services and even context-aware services (Schilit and Theimer 1994).

However, smartphones come up against the problem of accurate geo-positioning. First of all, GPS is unable to position somebody or something within a building as it works from satellites: technology based on magnetic fields has been proposed to cope with that flaw, and it could help to better understand in-store consumers' shopping trips. Two other errors have been found in Danish justice system. An error was found in the conversion by an I.T. system phone companies' raw data entailing a wrong position of a person at the scene of a crime. And finally, "some cellphone tracking data linked phones to the wrong cellphone towers, potentially connecting innocent people to crime scenes" (Selsoe Sorensen 2019). Beyond the fact that it calls into question the Danish justice system which should now review more than 10,000 verdicts, retailers or any other firms are now also able to consider consumers' geo-positioning questionable: Who can trust such a system? A European geo-positioning system, Galileo, which is supposed to be more accurate, is still in progress.

10.7 Conclusion

Spatial marketing can be defined as a set of domains as follows:

- A geomarketing relying on GIS techniques;
- A localized marketing to adapt commercial offers to various market areas;
- A spatial strategic marketing reinforcing marketing mix elements (geo-merchandising, geo-pricing, geo-advertising, etc.) and devoted to better manage local markets with a "glocal" strategy;
- A geo-retailing to deal with store location problems, in-store management, and spatial strategies within retail and service networks;
- A location-based marketing concerned by spatial behavior of consumers connected with mobile devices involved in omni-channel strategies.

Geomarketing has been the main pillar for spatial marketing for years, useful to locate commercial units or factories and to adapt marketing strategies to local markets with maps and models. Now location-based marketing enables to also develop a better knowledge of spatial consumer behavior and an efficient mobile marketing. But this evolution based on both technology and consumers' desire of customized offers should take care of privacy concerns.

References

Achabal, D., Gorr, W. L., & Vijay, M. (1982). MULTILOC: A Multiple Store Location Decision Model. *Journal of Retailing, 58*, 5–25.

Amaduzzi, S. (2011). *Geomarketing. I sistemi informativi territoriali (SIT-GIS) a supporto delle aziende e della pubblica amministrazione*. EPC Editore.

Anderson, S. P., & de Palma, A. (1988). Spatial Price Discrimination with Heterogeneous Products. *Review of Economic Studies, 55*(4), 573–592.

Anderson, S. P., de Palma, A., & Thisse, J.-F. (1989). Spatial Price Policies Reconsidered. *Journal of Industrial Economics, 38*(1), 1–18.

Applebaum, W. (1966). Methods for Determining Store Trade Areas and Market Equilibrium. *Journal of Marketing Research, 3*(2), 127–141.

Arnold, S. E. (2009, July–August). Google and Salesforce: Composite Applications for Better Enterprise Lift. *KM World*, pp. 18–20.

Baray, J., & Cliquet, G. (2007). Delineating and Analyzing Trade Areas Through Morphological Analysis. *European Journal of Operational Research, 182*(2), 886–898.

Baray, J., & Cliquet, G. (2013). Optimizing the Maternity Locations in France: A Dual Maximum Covering / p-median Hierarchical Model. *Journal of Business Research, 66*(1), 127–132.

Bartlett, C. A., & Ghoshal, S. (1989). *Managing Across Borders*. Boston, MA: Harvard Business School Press.

Bass, F. (1969). A New Product Growth for Model Consumer Durables. *Management Science, 15*(5), 215–227.

Bourliataux-Lajoinie, S., & Rivière, A. (2013). L'enjeu des m-services en marketing touristique territorial: proposition d'un cadre d'analyse. *Recherches en Sciences de Gestion, 95*(2), 65–82.

Bradach, J. L. (1998). *Franchise Organizations*. Boston, MA: Harvard Business School Press.

Brafman, N. (2008). Prix alimentaires: législation rigide et forte concentration gonflent la facture. *Le Monde*, 9 et 10 mars.

Brooks, C. M., Kaufmann, P. J., & Lichtenstein, D. R. (2004). Travel Configuration on Consumer Trip-Chained Store Choice. *Journal of Consumer Research, 31*, 241–248.

Brunner, J. A., & Mason, J. L. (1968). The Influence of Driving Time Upon Shopping Center Preference. *Journal of Marketing, 32*(2), 57–61.

Cairncross, F. (1997). *The Death of Distance*. Boston, MA: Harvard Business School Press.

Carlbäck, M. (2012). Strategic Entrepreneurship in the Hotel Industry: The Role of Chain Affiliation. *Scandinavian Journal of Hospitality & Tourism, 12*(4), 349–372.

Centola, D. (2018). *How Behavior Spreads. The Science of Complex Contagions*. Princeton: Princeton University Press.

Christaller, W. (1933). *Die Zentralen Orte in Süddeutchland*. Iena (translation Baskin C. W., as *Central Places in southern Germany*. Englewood Cliffs, NJ: Prentice Hall, 1966).

Cliff, A. D., & Ord, J. K. (1975). Space-time modelling with an application to regional forecasting. *Institute of British Geographers, 64*, 119–128.

Cliquet, G. (1995). Implementing a Subjective MCI Model: An Application to the Furniture Market. *European Journal of Operational Research, 84*, 279–291.

Cliquet, G. (1998). Integration and Territory Coverage of the Hypermarket Industry in France: A Relative Entropy Measure. *The International Review of Retail, Distribution and Consumer Research, 8*(2), 205–224.

Cliquet, G. (2000). Plural Forms in Store Networks: A Proposition of a Model for Store Network Evolution. *International Review of Retail, Distribution and Consumer Research, 10*(4), 369–387.

Cliquet, G. (2006). *Geomarketing: Methods and Strategies in Spatial Marketing*. London: ISTE.

Cliquet, G. (2020). *Location-based Marketing: Geomarketing and Geolocation*. London: ISTE & Hoboken (NJ): Wiley, Inc.

Cliquet, G., & Guillo, P.-A. (2013). Retail Network Spatial Expansion: An Application of the Percolation Theory to Hard Discounters. *Journal of Retailing and Consumer Services, 20*, 173–181.

Cliquet, G., & Voropanova, E. (2016). E-commerce and Encroachment: Evidence from French Franchise Networks. *Journal of Marketing Channels, 23*(3), 114–128.

Converse, P. D. (1949). New Laws on Retail Gravitation. *Journal of Marketing, 14*(4), 339–384.

Cooper, L. G., & Finkbeiner, C. T. (1983). A Composite MCI Model for Integrating Attribute and Importance Information. *Advances in Consumer Research, 11*(1), 109–113.

Cooper, L. G., & Nakanishi, M. (1983). Standardizing Variables in Multiplicative Choice Models. *Journal of Consumer Research, 10*, 96–108.

Crawford, A., Humphries, S., & Geddy, M. (2015). McDonald's: A Case Study in Glocalization. *Journal of Global Business Issues, 9*(1), 11–18.

Davidson, W. R., Sweeney, D. J., & Stampfl, R. W. (1988). *Retailing Management* (6th ed.). New York: Wiley.

De Palma, A., Droesbeke, J.-J., & Lefèvre, C. (1991). *Modèles de diffusion en marketing*. Paris: PUF.

Douard, J.-P., Heitz, M., & Cliquet, G. (2015). Retail Attraction Revisited: From Gravitation to Purchase Flows, a Geomarketing Application. *Recherche et Applications en Marketing, 30*(1), 110–129.

Douglas, S., & Wind, Y. (1987). The Myth of Globalization. *Columbia Journal of World Business, 22*(4), 19–29. (the reference 1986 is in French language)

Evans, C., & Richardson, M. (2007). Strategy in Action: Assessing the Environment. *British Journal of Administrative Management, 60*, 1–3.

Fulgoni, G. M. (2014). "Omni-Channel" Retail Insights and the Consumer's Path-to-Purchase. *Journal of Advertising Research, 54*(4), 377–380.

Gahinet, M-C., & Cliquet, G. (2018). Proximity and time in convenience store patronage: Kaïros more than chronos. *Journal of Retailing and Consumer Services, 43*, 1–9.

Gallopel, K. (2006). Advertising Policy and Geographic Information. In G. Cliquet (Ed.), *Geomarketing: Methods and Strategies in Spatial Marketing* (pp. 241–266). London: ISTE.

García-Castro, J. D., & Mula, J. (2019). Decision Model to Locate a Franchisee Applied to a Fast Food Restaurant. In J. Windsperger, G. Cliquet, G. Hendrikse, & M. Srećković (Eds.), *Design and Management of Interfirm Networks: Franchise Networks, Cooperatives and Alliances*. Heidelberg: Springer.

Geary, R. C. (1954). The Contiguity Ratio and Statistical Mapping. *The Incorporated Statistician, 5*(3), 115–145.

Ghosh, A., & McLafferty, S. (1987). *Location Strategies for Retail and Service Firms*. Lexington, MA: Lexington books.

Gini, C. (1914). Sulla misura della concentrazione e della variabilit'a dei caratteri. Atti del Reale Istituto Veneto di Scienze. *Lettere ed Arti, 62*, 1203–1248. English Translation in Metron (2005) 63, 3–38.

Gini, C. (1921). Measurement of Inequality of Income. *Economic Journal, 31*, 22–43.

Golledge, R. G., & Stimson, R. J. (1997). *Spatial Behavior: A Geographic Perspective*. New York: The Guilford Press.

Grether, E. T. (1983). Regional-Spatial Analysis in Marketing. *Journal of Marketing, 47*(4), 36–43.

Guido, P. (1971). Vérification expérimentale de la formule de Reilly en tant que loi d'attraction des supermarchés. *Revue Française de Marketing, 39*, 101–107.

Hägerstrand, T. (1967). *Innovation Diffusion as a Spatial Process* (Translated from Swedish by A. Pred). Chicago: University of Chicago Press.

Hall, E. T. (1968). Proxemics. *Current Anthropology, 9*(2–3), 83–95.

He, Z., Wang, S., & Cheng, T. C. E. (2013). Competition and Evolution in Multi-product Supply Chains: An Agent Based Retailer Model. *International Journal of Production Economics, 146*(1), 325–336.

Hofstede, F. T., Wedel, M., & Steenkamp, J.-B. E. M. (2002). Identifying Spatial Segments in International Markets. *Marketing Science, 21*(2), 160–177.

Hotelling, H. (1929). Stability in Competition. *The Economic Journal, 39*, 41–57.

Huff, D. L. (1964). Defining and Estimating a Trading Area. *Journal of Marketing, 28*(3), 34–38.

Huff, D. L., & Batsell, R. R. (1977). Delimiting the Areal Extent of a Market Area. *Journal of Marketing Research, 14*(4), 581–585.

Kahn, W. (2012). Mobile Payments Strategy. *Journal of Payments Strategy & Systems, 6*(3), 210–218.

Kalyanam, K., & Putler, D. S. (1997). Incorporating Demographic Variables in Brand Choice Models. *Marketing Science, 16*(2), 166–181.

Kalyanam, K., & Tsay, A. A. (2013). Free Riding and Conflict in Hybrid Shopping Environments: Implications for Retailers, Manufacturers, and Regulators. *The Antitrust Bulletin, 58*(1), 19–68.

Khan, R. J., & Jain, D. C. (2005). An Empirical Analysis of Price Discrimination Mechanisms and Retailer Profitability. *Journal of Marketing Research, 42*(4), 316–524.

Kong, N., Schaefer, A. J., Hunsaker, B., & Roberts, M. S. (2010). Maximizing the Efficiency of the U.S. Liver Allocation System Through Region Design. *Management Science, 56*(12), 2111–2122.

Lampóna, J. F., Lago-Peñas, S., & González-Benito, J. (2015). International Relocation and Production Geography in the European Automobile Components Sector: The Case of Spain. *International Journal of Production Research, 53*(5), 1409–1424.

Larson, J. S., Bradlow, E. T., & Fader, P. S. (2005). An Exploratory Look at Supermarket Shopping Paths. *International Journal of Research in Marketing, 22*(4), 395–414.

Levitt, T. (1983). *The Globalization of Markets. Harvard Business Review, 61*(3), 92–101.

Lewison, D. M., & DeLozier, M. W. (1986). *Retailing.* Merril Publishing Company.

Mahajan, V., Muller, E., & Srivastava, R. K. (1990). Determination of Adopter Categories by Using Innovation Diffusion Models. *Journal of Marketing Research, 27*(1), 37–50.

Malhotra, N. K. (1983). A Threshold Model of Store Choice. *Journal of Retailing, 59*(2), 3–21.

McCarthy, E. J. (1960). *Basic Marketing: A Managerial Approach.* Homewood, IL: Richard D. Irwin Inc.

McFadden, D. (1974). Conditional Logit Analysis of Qualitative Choice Behavior. In P. Zarembka (Ed.), *Frontier of Econometrics* (pp. 105–142). New York: Academic Press.

McKenzie, S. B. (1989). Retail Gravity Model. *The Appraisal Journal, 57*(2), 166–172.

Menne, P. (2009). *Potential of Geo-Marketing-Tools for the Development of Advanced Online-Marketing Business Models.* Norderstedt, Germany: Grin Verlag GmbH.

Miller, H. J. (1996). Pricing Policy Reactions to Agglomeration in a Market with Spatial Search. *Journal of Regional Science, 36*(3), 393–415.

Montgomery, A. L. (1997). Creating Micro-Marketing Pricing Strategies Using Supermarket Scanner Data. *Marketing Science, 16*(4), 315–337.

Montoya, R. M., & Horton, R. S. (2014). A Two-dimensional Model for the Study of Interpersonal Attraction. *Personality and Social Psychology Review, 18*(1), 59–86.

Moran, P. A. P. (1950). Notes on Continuous Stochastic Phenomena. *Biometrika, 37*, 17–33.

Mulder, M. (1960). The power variable in communication experiments. *Human Relations, 13*(3), 241–257. (the reference 1958 is a text in Dutch language)

Nakanishi, M., & Cooper, L. G. (1974). Parameter Estimation for a Multiplicative Competitive Interaction Model: Least Squares Approach. *Journal of Marketing Research, 11*(3), 303–311.

Nystuen, J. D. (1967). A Theory and Simulation of Intraurban Travel. In W. L. Garrison & D. F. Marble (Eds.), *Quantitative Geography, Part I: Economic and Cultural Topics* (pp. 54–83). Evanston, IL: Northwestern University Press.

Ohlin, B. (1931). *Interregional and International Trade.* Boston, MA: Harvard University Press.

Paolanti, M., Liciotti, D., Pietrini, R., Mancini, A., & Frontoni, E. (2017). Modelling and Forecasting Customer Navigation in Intelligent Retail Environments. *Journal of Intelligent & Robotic Systems, 91*(2), 1–16.

Parker, R. D. (2007). Provincial and Territorial On-line Tourism: How Canadian Provinces and Territories Are Using the Internet for Travel Marketing and Promotion. *Academy of Marketing Studies Journal, 11*(2), 39–55.

Peterson, R. A., & Jolibert, A. (1995). A Meta-analysis of Country-of-origin Effects. *Journal of International Business Studies, 26*(4), 883–899.

Pirkul, H., Narasimham, S., & De, P. (1987). Firm Expansion Through Franchising: A Model and Solution Programming. *Decision Sciences, 18*, 631–645.

Reilly, W. J. (1931). *The Law of Retail Gravitation.* New York: Knickerbrocker Press. Et William J. Reilly ed., 285 Madison Ave., NY.

Rigby, D. K., & Vishwanath, V. (2006). Localization: The Revolution in Consumer Markets. *Harvard Business Review, 84*(4), 82–92.

Rogers, E. M. (1962). *The Diffusion of Innovation.* New York: Free Press.

Schilit, B. N., & Theimer, M. M. (1994). Disseminating Active Map Information to Mobile Hosts. *IEEE Network, 8*(5), 22–32.
Selsoe Sorensen, M. (2019). Legal System in Denmark Cites Errors in Cell Data. *The New York Times*, Aug. 20, Section A, Page 6.
Steyer, A. (2005). Géométrie de l'interaction sociale: le modèle de diffusion en avalanches spatiales. *Recherche et Applications en Marketing, 20*(3), 3–20.
Svensson, G. (2001). "Glocalization" of Business Activities: A "Glocal Strategy" Approach. *Management Decision, 39*(1), 6–18.
Thiessen, A. H., & Alter, J. C. (1911). Precipitation Averages for Large Areas. *Monthly Weather Review, 39*, 1082–1084.
Van Watershoot, W., & Van der Bulte, C. (1992). The 4P Classification of the Marketing Mix Revisited. *Journal of Marketing, 56*(4), 83–93.
Vincent, W. S. (1998). Encroachment: Legal Restrictions on Retail Franchise Expansion. *Journal of Business Venturing, 13*, 29–41.
Volle, P. (2006). Products and Geographic Information: Geo-merchandising. In G. Cliquet (Ed.), *Geomarketing: Methods and Strategies in Spatial Marketing*. London: ISTE.
Von Thünen, J. H. (1826). *Der isolierte Staat in Beziehung auf Landwirtschaft und Nationalökonomie*. Hamburg: Friedrich Perthes.
Vyt, D. (2008). Retail Network Performance Evaluation: A DEA Approach Considering Retailers' Geomarketing. *The International Review of Retail, Distribution and Consumer Research, 18*(2), 235–253.
Vyt, D., & Cliquet, G. (2017). Towards a Fairer Manager Performance Measure: A DEA Application in the Retail Industry. *The International Review of Retail, Distribution and Consumer Research, 27*(5), 450–467.
Weber, A. (1909). *Über den Standort der Industrie*. Tübingen: Mohr. Translated by Freidrich C.J. (1929) *The Theory of the Location of Industry*. University of Chicago Press.
Xu, H., Luo, X. R., Carroll, J. M., & Rosson, M. B. (2011). The Personalization Privacy Paradox: An Exploratory Study of Decision Making Process for Location-Aware Marketing. *Decision Support Systems, 51*, 42–52.
Yaeli, A., Bak, P., Feigenblat, G., Nadler, S., Roitman, H., Saadoun, G., Ship, H., Cohen, D., Fuchs, O., Ofek-Koifman, S., & Sandbank, T. (2014). Understanding Customer Behavior Using Indoor Location Analysis and Visualization. *IBM Journal of Research and Development, 58*(5/6, 3), 1–12.

Index

Note: Page numbers followed by 'n' refer to notes.

S. Colombo (ed.), *Spatial Economics Volume II*,
https://doi.org/10.1007/978-3-030-40094-1

The manufacturer's authorised representative in the EU is Springer Nature Customer Service Centre GmbH, Europaplatz 3, 69115 Heidelberg, Germany. If you have any concerns regarding our products, please contact ProductSafety@springernature.com

Printed and bound by CPI Group (UK) Ltd, Croydon, CR0 4YY

30/09/2026

02225644-0012